Clustered injustice
and the level green

Luke Clements is the Cerebra Professor of Law and Social Justice at the School of Law, Leeds University and a solicitor.

The Legal Action Group is a national, independent charity which campaigns for equal access to justice for all members of society. Legal Action Group:

- provides support to the practice of lawyers and advisers
- inspires developments in that practice
- campaigns for improvements in the law and the administration of justice
- stimulates debate on how services should be delivered.

Clustered injustice and the level green

Luke Clements

Legal Action Group
2020

This edition published in Great Britain 2020
by LAG Education and Service Trust Limited
c/o Oliver Fisher Solicitors, Royalty Studios
105–109 Lancaster Road
London W11 1QF
www.lag.org.uk

British Library Cataloguing in Publication Data
a CIP catalogue record for this book is available from the British Library.

Crown copyright material is produced with the permission of the Controller of HMSO and the Queen's Printer for Scotland.

This book has been produced using Forest Stewardship Council (FSC) certified paper. The wood used to produce FSC certified products with a 'Mixed Sources' label comes from FSC certified well-managed forests, controlled sources and/or recycled material.

print ISBN 978 1 913648 07 7
ebook ISBN 978 1 913648 08 4
print / ebook bundle ISBN 978 1 913648 09 1

Typeset by Refinecatch Limited, Bungay, Suffolk
Printed in Great Britain by Hobbs the Printers, Totton, Hampshire

for Mo

Preface

The central focus of this book concerns the extent to which our legal system generates and exacerbates disadvantage – even when there is no conscious resolve so to do. It seeks to describe what a better system would look like – from the perspective of those who live with disadvantage – but ultimately a system that is better for us all.

I am not someone who can claim to have personal experience of disadvantage – and so the insights in this book are vicarious. For 40 years I have worked as a lawyer for people who live with disadvantage. People who are homeless, Roma, Gypsies and Travelling people, people working on God-awful chicken processing lines, disabled people, carers, young people in the care system, people with addiction problems, people within the criminal justice system, people who have been abused, chronically poor people – but mostly with people who fall into many of the above (or other) categories. Pretty well everything of any value that I have learned about the law and of the meaning of injustice has come from the insights of these extraordinary people.

When I started writing this book, in pre COVID-19 times, the world was a different place. It was one where successive governments had been hell-bent on running down the state – to liberate the free market: to 'encourage' independence, user choice and personal responsibility. It was one where we had been told there was no such thing as 'society' or 'magic money trees'. It was (like all systems) one where the laws were created by (and for) those who enjoyed 'advantage', and one that cared little if those laws made life hard for those who lived with disadvantage – in fact, for many in power, it was all the better if they did.

In many respects, the world has since been turned upside-down. We realise today that the underfunding of the health and social care services was the single greatest cause, not only of the COVID-19 related deaths of tens of thousands of people, but also of the catastrophic economic harm the UK has experienced. We can also see that those most at risk from the epidemic have been those failed by a dysfunctional social welfare system and those at the sharp end of the inequalities spectrum – BAME communities and those in low-paid, undervalued work and poor housing.

We have also come to realise that what appears to be politically impossible can change in an instant: that a government of a mean persuasion can miraculously decide to pay the wages of millions of workers to prevent layoffs; to accommodate homeless people in hotels; release prisoners from overfull prisons; pump money into domestic violence refuges; and put on hold benefit sanctions and residential evictions.

At an incredibly bleak time – we must therefore 'hope'.

Luke Clements
September 2020

Acknowledgments

This book could not have been written without the generosity and the support of two inspirational institutions: the School of Law at the University of Leeds and the disabled children's charity, Cerebra.

Almost every idea contained in this book has been sparked by comments and suggestions made by friends, colleagues, authors and those I have encountered who have been struggling with their clustered injustices. It is an enormous debt that I owe to so many people and must be acknowledged.

In addition, a number of colleagues and organisations have played a vital part in shaping, critiquing and getting this book to press – and for this special thanks are due to: Adrian Rhead, Ana Laura Aiello, Ann James, Elizabeth Steel, Janet Read, Lucy Series, Maggie Steel, Mitchell Woolf, Peter Baines, Phil Fennell and Suzanne Morrison – as well as to colleagues at the Access Committee for Leeds, Full of Life and the Legal Action Group. Grateful thanks due to Jen Cowan for her careful and thoughtful editing of the book.

Particular thanks are due, as ever, to my publisher, Esther Pilger, for her patience, expertise and constant good (and wicked) humour.

I have almost certainly omitted from this list many who have also assisted me and to them I apologise sincerely.

What is wrong in this text is entirely of my own doing.

Contents

Introduction

Poor people get hit by cars too; they get evicted; they have their furniture repossessed; they can't pay their utility bills. But they do not have personal legal problems in the law school way. Nothing that happens to them breaks up or threatens to break up a settled and harmonious life. Poor people do not lead settled lives into which the law seldom intrudes; they are constantly involved with the law in its most intrusive forms ... Poverty creates an abrasive interface with society; poor people are always bumping into sharp legal things. The law school model of personal legal problems, of solving them and returning the client to the smooth and orderly world in television advertisements, doesn't apply to poor people.

Stephen Wexler, 'Practicing Law for Poor People',
The Yale Law Journal (1969–1970) 79, pp1049–1967 at 1049–1050

Introduction – the meaning of clustered in justice

This book is concerned with the legal problems encountered by people who live with disadvantage: disabled people, carers, people at risk of homelessness, people in significant debt, people falling foul of immigration laws, people fleeing domestic abuse ... it is a long list. People in this position often experience multiple and synchronous legal problems (clusters of problems) for which the traditional 'single issue' lawyering approach is ill-equipped. Such people – to quote Stephen Wexler above – 'do not lead settled lives into which the law seldom intrudes; they are constantly involved with the law in its most intrusive forms'. Their legal challenges don't come in single discrete packages (eg a personal injury claim; a consumer dispute; a divorce) but are multiple, interlinked and both concurrent and successional. No sooner has one problem been addressed than another is encountered.

The research findings which underpin many of the examples used in this book derive from a project concerning the 'legal problems' that confront disabled children and their families, funded by the research charity Cerebra. Cerebra is the national charity helping children with brain conditions and their families. Working with the charity's in-house 'entitlements' service[1] it identifies commonly occurring problems that families encounter and then undertakes research into these problems with the aim of (among other things) developing strategic action that can bring about systemic change to reduce or remove the causes of the problem. In doing this, we are particularly concerned about the adverse effects that these problems have on families who experience 'disadvantage': families who are, for example, not wealthy or who are poorly networked.[2] We often summarise the focus of our work as helping those 'who don't have a sister who is a barrister'.[3]

Early on in the research project we discussed the issue of 'outcomes' and how difficult it was proving to be to obtain feedback from families we had advised and supported. 'Impact feedback' and 'measurable outcomes' is something that almost all funding bodies require as part of their grant conditions.[4]

The strong impression of the research team was that families were pleased with the support we had provided and the action we had helped them take – however, getting them to put this in writing was proving to be a challenge. We had tried a variety of techniques – sending families simple feedback forms with stamped return addressed envelopes; sending follow-up emails; and so on – but these were largely unsuccessful.

'Feedback' remained a regular item on meeting agendas and each time we came to it, there was a general sigh and a feeling of failure.

At one meeting, towards the end of the first year of the project, a colleague told the following story. She had been approached for help by a parent – let's call her Maria. She was someone we had in fact advised (on a different matter) many months earlier. During the discussion, my colleague asked Maria whether the earlier advice had resolved that particular problem, and Maria confirmed that it had. Apologising for not letting us know of this, Maria explained that a new problem had arisen at about that time and she simply didn't have the time or 'headspace' to contact us: all her thoughts had been fixed on this new issue.

Maria's story is a useful point of departure for this book. She was disadvantaged because she was a parent of disabled child. In consequence, she faced a cluster of problems: no sooner had one been resolved, than another (a benefits problem, a social care problem, a special educational needs problem, a healthcare problem etc) arose to fill the vacant 'problem slot'. Our earlier advice had been useful, but it had not resulted in her living the 'ordinary life' lived by those who are not disadvantaged.

The point about Maria's story is that the polycentric ripple-effects of clustered problems also wash up on other shores. Because the 'single issue legal problem' paradigm is so deeply entrenched in our collective legal psyche, because we consider it to be abnormal to have lives dominated by clusters of problems (if we consider it at all), we create systems and expectations based on this perception. The fact that many grant bodies have become obsessed with measurable impact (the 'theology of outcomes'[5]) and because people with clustered problems are poor at playing this game, it creates additional difficulties for advice agencies and researchers working in this field. Potentially that reduces the grant funding available for this sector, and that in turn exacerbates people like Maria's disadvantage.

Vicious circles of this kind and problems caused by a lack of 'cognitive space' are reoccurring themes that inform the analysis that follows. Trying to make sense of Maria's self-perpetuating cluster of entangled legal problems requires us to see it for what is: a complex system with many perverse 'feedback loops' – best analysed from a 'systems thinking' perspective.[6] Any strategy that is developed to help disadvantaged people cope must take into account, at a fundamental level, their depleted reserves of 'mental effort'.[7]

For Maria, the 'trigger'[8] cause of the multiple problems that she experienced was her daughter's disability. For some it will be (for example) a relationship breakdown; an illness; a loss of employment; a bankruptcy – and for many others it may not be possible to identify a single root cause. What they all have in common is that they live with disadvantage, and for one reason or another this disadvantage results in the accumulation of clusters of associated legal problems. This state of affairs is referred to in this book as the experience of 'clustered injustice'.

Disadvantage and legal problems

Disadvantage, in the context of this book, is a more general concept than 'social exclusion' or indeed, poverty. People who experience social exclusion are generally considered to be those who have 'low material means' and who are unable 'to participate effectively in economic social political and cultural life', as well as those who may be alienated or otherwise distanced from the mainstream society.[9] Although most people who are disadvantaged will have 'low material means', that is not a 'universal'.

For the purposes of the analysis that follows, people are considered to live with disadvantage if they (and others for whom they may care) have need for a level of support from the state (support that a 'responsive state' should legitimately provide[10]) and the state has failed to meet this need; and the consequence of this failure being that they then accumulate multiple synchronous legal problems.

Much of the research concerning the development of such clusters has characterised these as 'justiciable problems'[11] – ie problems that are capable of being argued in a court and on which a court can make a judgment. In this book, a 'legal problem' has a wider meaning –

encompassing cases of maladministration and other objective 'wrongs' committed by public bodies – even if, for 'queer technical'[12] legal reasons, they may not be justiciable.

The primary focus of much of the research that underpins the analysis that follows has been directed at problems generated by our system of public laws – laws that regulate public bodies such as local councils, government bodies, the NHS etc – and for this reason, examples of legal problems of this kind predominate in this study. However, these problems then often trigger private law problems – tumbling the dominos of debt, divorce, dismissal and many more.

Before moving on, it is important to acknowledge that the use of the phrase a 'legal problem' is itself contested:[13] contested, not only because it assumes (incorrectly) that its meaning is self-evident, but also because it suggests 'that once a problem is identified as legal, then only a lawyer . . . can sensibly be expected to take care of it.'[14] This is a fault I hope this book avoids.

Clusters of legal problems

A significant literature exists that identifies the phenomenon of 'clustered legal problems'.[15] It describes how commonly experienced legal problems can coalesce into clusters: how the experience of one problem can lead to another, in a 'cascade'[16] or a 'compounding' effect, and how this can then 'set in motion a process in which the cluster of problems creates out of the series of individual problems, lives of trouble'.[17]

Individuals identified as likely to experience multiple problems include those 'vulnerable to disadvantage, such as lone parents, social renters, adults with a long-standing illness or disability, and adults on means-tested benefits'.[18] A 2017 Ministry of Justice Survey concerning 'justiciable' legal problems found, for example, that:[19]

- Those aged between 25 and 44 were more likely to experience four or more problems (28 per cent), than those aged 45 or over (11–17 per cent for the different age groups over 45).
- Adults with a limiting illness or disability were more likely to experience four or more problems (32 per cent) than those with no disability/illness (19 per cent) or non-limiting disability/illness (18 per cent).
- Lone parents were more likely to experience four or more problems (42 per cent) than adults living as a couple with dependent children (22 per cent) or those living in adult-only households (20 per cent).

- Adults who were unemployed were more likely to experience four or more problems (39 per cent) than their counterparts who were economically inactive or in employment (21 and 20 per cent respectively).
- Adults with a household income of under £15,000 per year were more likely to experience four or more problems (31 per cent) than those in higher household income bands (12–23 per cent).
- Adults receiving means-tested state benefits were twice as likely to experience four or more problems (39 per cent) than those not receiving state benefits (19 per cent).
- Social renters (37 per cent) and private renters (29 per cent) were more likely to experience four or more problems than adults who owned their house outright (12 per cent) or with a mortgage (18 per cent).

The 2017 survey found no significant difference by gender, ethnicity or educational qualifications in reporting multiple problems – and in this respect it differs from a 2007 Canadian survey that found that members of a visible minority group were more likely to experience multiple problems.[20]

As with the English research, the Canadian survey found that certain groups were far more likely to have multiple problems: thus, of those respondents reporting more than six problems, over 35 per cent were disabled people and over 33 per cent were in receipt of social assistance.[21] The survey evidence suggested that single parents; people who were unemployed; those in the lowest income groups; and people with housing and debt problems all had an increased risk of experiencing multiple legal problems.[22] It also identified a 'snowballing' effect – that the risk of experiencing additional legal problems increased as the number of problems already experienced increased.[23]

Vulnerability, disadvantage and undue privilege

When this book was first conceived and when the first chapters were sketched out, coronavirus was an unknown word as far as 99.9 per cent of the UK's population was concerned. Disadvantage was (as now) rife – but for those in power it was a matter of indifference, if not denial. The United Nations (UN) Special Rapporteur on extreme poverty and human rights had just made a statement in 2018 on his visit to the UK,[24] noting that:

14 million people, a fifth of the population, live in poverty. Four million of these are more than 50% below the poverty line, and 1.5 million are destitute, unable to afford basic essentials. The widely respected Institute for Fiscal Studies predicts a 7% rise in child poverty between 2015 and 2022, and various sources predict child poverty rates of as high as 40%. For almost one in every two children to be poor in twenty-first century Britain is not just a disgrace, but a social calamity and an economic disaster, all rolled into one.

The Rapporteur concluded his final report[25] with the following comments:[26]

> The philosophy underpinning the British welfare system has changed radically since 2010. The initial rationales for reform were to reduce overall expenditures and to promote employment as the principal 'cure' for poverty. But when large-scale poverty persisted despite a booming economy and very high levels of employment, the Government chose not to adjust course. Instead, it doubled down on a parallel agenda to reduce benefits by every means available, including constant reductions in benefit levels, ever-more-demanding conditions, harsher penalties, depersonalization, stigmatization, and virtually eliminating the option of using the legal system to vindicate rights. The basic message, delivered in the language of managerial efficiency and automation, is that almost any alternative will be more tolerable than seeking to obtain government benefits. This is a very far cry from any notion of a social contract, Beveridge model or otherwise, let alone of social human rights. As Thomas Hobbes observed long ago, such an approach condemns the least well off to lives that are 'solitary, poor, nasty, brutish, and short'. As the British social contract slowly evaporates, Hobbes' prediction risks becoming the new reality.

The UK government rejected the Rapporteur's findings as 'completely inaccurate' and lodged a formal complaint with the UN.[27]

Re-reading the UN report today, it is impossible not to be struck by the repeated references to the word 'vulnerable' – as in (for example) the 'loss of institutions that previously protected vulnerable people'; 'leaving vulnerable people and those facing emergencies without anywhere to turn'; treating 'vulnerable people like guinea pigs'; 'vulnerable children'; 'vulnerable claimants'; 'vulnerable groups'; and 'leaving vulnerable people facing a "cliff edge" scenario'.

Since the coronavirus outbreak in early 2020, many things have changed, not least that we have all had to confront the fact that we are vulnerable. Epidemic diseases are, as Frank Snowdon explains, 'not random events that afflict societies capriciously and without warning. On the contrary, every society produces its own specific vulnerabilities'.[28] We are all at risk of being harmed by the virus – but it is one that has killed far more people living with disadvantage than those more privileged.[29] Epidemics are amplifiers, not levellers.[30] They are the antithesis of Old Testament avenging angels: they point to societies' shames (in this case 'persistent poverty and widening social inequalities'[31]) and then murder those least culpable.

Although as a word 'vulnerability' has 'an air of victimhood, deprivation, dependency, or pathology attached to it'[32] this is something that needs to change.

'Vulnerability theory', and the writings of Martha Fineman in particular, informs much of the analysis in this book. It starts with a recognition that vulnerability is an essential characteristic of the human condition: of living with an ever-present risk of harm – from the 'mildly annoying' to the catastrophic – be it through injury, disease, aging or misfortune.[33] Although we can 'attempt to lessen risk or act to mitigate possible manifestations of our vulnerability, the possibility of harm cannot be eliminated'.[34] The harms we face are broadly internal (our own physical and mental state of well-being) and external. As Fineman observed a decade ago, we may:

> ... suffer or succumb to diseases that are random or the result of pandemics or other biologically based catastrophes. In addition to viruses and bacteria, our bodies are also vulnerable to environmental forces, such as weather systems that produce floods or droughts accompanied by famine or fire. [35]

Fineman speaks of the compounding of disadvantage caused by the accumulation of economic and institutional harms – both for individuals and their families: disadvantage that 'can be transferred from one generation to another' and can 'cluster around members of a socially or culturally determined' group.[36]

Given that none of us are 'invulnerable', all we can hope for is to be as resilient as is possible – and for Fineman the state has central responsibility for building that resilience – be it through education, health care, social care and the whole panoply of social welfare, environmental and security measures at its disposal. Fineman's reoccurring question, when analysing the many harms that confront us, is: 'What should a responsive state do to build resilience against this particular harm?'

Just as individuals are vulnerable, so too are the vital state institutions that exist to build our resilience. 'Powerful entrenched interests can hijack even the most egalitarian' regimes which are ever vulnerable to 'capture and corruption'.[37] As we have seen in the recent emergency, the ability of the state to respond was severely impaired by the previous decades of decimation of the civil service and its underfunding of public health[38] and social care services.[39]

One of the defining insights Fineman provides, concerns her focus on 'privilege'. Privilege enables individuals to bolster their resilience – for example, through private education; better healthcare; inheritance; membership of well-connected networks; living in environmentally benign neighbourhoods; and so on. Fineman's analysis is particularly concerned with what she refers to as 'undue privilege'[40] and the importance of recognising 'the ways in which power and privilege are conferred through the operation of societal institutions, relationships and the creation of social identities'.[41] As she points out, 'our individual experience of vulnerability varies according to the quality and quantity of resources we possess or can command'[42] and the state's role therefore is to take action to address:

> . . . existing inequalities of circumstances that result from undue privilege or institutional advantage. State mechanisms that ensure a more equitable access to institutional assets by adjusting unjust distribution of privilege and opportunity across society would also contribute to a more robust democracy and greater public participation.

States shape their legal systems: systems that protect and suppress, privilege and punish. If states choose, laws can help to build the resilience of disabled people, carers and people whose childhoods were less than ideal. Alternatively, they can choose to privilege others – for example, the wealthy, the second homeowners and multinational corporations. In the UK, it is reasonably clear where the privilege lies. We continue to be surrounded by examples of 'undue privilege' – where disadvantaged children are poorly shod[43] so that rich people's children can live idle lives; where rentiers 'reap where they never sowed';[44] where obscene wealth comes from plunder,[45] from playing the markets, offshoring and debt-leveraging, by stealing employees pensions, by asset-stripping decent businesses, and by acquiring public assets for pitiful sums. And we are simultaneously immersed in systems awash with disadvantage – of Disraeli's two nations which today remain as divided as they did two centuries ago when, as now they were 'not governed by the same laws'.[46] If this was in doubt, we only have to look to the backgrounds of those who have been affected the coronavirus – people living with socio-economic disadvantage were twice as likely to catch the virus, twice as likely to have severe side-effects from the illness and twice as likely to die as those who did not live with disadvantage of this kind.[47]

End note: the book's structure

The succeeding chapters of this book explore the causes and the effects of clustered injustice. They describe the many and varied adverse consequences that people like Maria experience, and explain why core responsibility for this harm rests squarely with the state. The analysis draws heavily on vulnerability and systems thinking theories, as well using gaming analogies to illustrate the invidious position of people who experience clustered injustice – ie people compelled to play legal and administrative 'games' in which the odds are heavily stacked against them.

The chapter that follows ('The grain of law') is concerned with the 'loaded' nature of the law: a system that privileges the already 'advantaged'. It is a scene-setting chapter which establishes that, as a tool, the law (including its basic legal principles and maxims) has difficulties in addressing the needs of disadvantaged people – because it has not been designed for this purpose. The chapter is not a diatribe against the law – but simply makes explicit the problems that a property-based legal system has, in delivering social justice for people who live with disadvantage.

Chapter 3 tilts at a number of windmills – although its principal target is the notion that legal problems can only be resolved through a process of reductionism: reducing clusters of problems to singular issues. It argues that such a process fails when confronted by the complex entangled legal problems experienced by so many people living with disadvantage. The chapter develops an alternative 'systems thinking' approach for dealing with the challenges of clustered problems. In such cases, it advocates 'going up a level of abstraction' rather than seeking to fragment, distill and compartmentalise the cluster into individual isolated claims before addressing each one separately. In doing so, it challenges the arguments of a number of influential commentators that in an internet society people will neither want nor need personalised problem-solving services: that artificial intelligence (AI), chatbots, apps and the like will render them redundant.

Chapter 4 considers the growing complexity of the legal system and challenges the notion that there is no situation that cannot benefit from more law. It argues that even if complexity is inevitable (ie that laws become complex in complex societies), this must be underpinned by a recognition that this is a state-generated phenomenon – and accordingly, that the state has responsibility for addressing the adverse consequences it creates – particularly for those whose problems have coalesced into messy clusters. The chapter considers two examples of spiralling law-making, namely: (1) juridification and (2) identity-based rights. For Maria, many of her family's entitlements will depend upon how they are legally identi- fied – eg as a woman; as a black woman; as a disabled child; as a parent carer; as a young carer; as a child in need; as a British citizen; as a child with special educational needs; and so on. Using non- discrimination and 'carers' recognition' laws as an example, this chapter argues that laws of this kind (although brought in with the best of intentions) create complexity, fragment entitlements and are generally ineffective in terms of addressing the disadvantage experi- enced by people with clustered legal problems.[48]

Chapter 5 is concerned with bureaucracy – in particular, mana- gerialist administrative systems; and dysfunctional organisational cultures. It considers how every public body develops systems to facilitate their administrative processes and how individuals must learn and conform to these: systems designed for the benefit of the public body, and not the individual. Just as at the micro level the system requires a cluster of problems to be broken down into indi- vidual isolated claims, bureaucratic systems require fragmentation at the macro level – different departments, authorities and agencies dealing with different rights, and each with its own operating system. People with clustered problems often fit, as in a Venn diagram, into margins of several such entities and find themselves shunted from one public budget to another. As the chapter explains, the fact that this approach makes no macro economic sense seems to hold no sway: everything has to be sacrificed to maintain the purity of the public body's accounting process.

Chapter 6 considers the harm caused by the state's failure to address the disadvantage that blights the lives of those who experi- ence clustered injustice. The exhaustion, the frustration, the stress, the mental harms and the economic impact that results from the relentless experience of having to start again – it is Sisyphus endlessly pushing the stone up the hill; it is Snakes and Ladders without the ladders. The traumatic stress resulting from living on a cliff-edge: of trying to avoid crises but knowing that until there is a crisis there is often little chance of accessing support. The fear of reprisals: of the withdrawal of support; of accusations (so easily made) of fabrication; of prosecution; and so on. The chapter includes an analysis of the phenomenon of 'warrior' mothers and fathers – people who battle on many fronts to challenge the multiple synchronous injustices that they and their families experience. People who may then get labelled as 'difficult': thus locating the cause of the problem with them, and not the institution.

The final chapter draws heavily on 'vulnerability' and 'systems thinking' theories and outlines how a responsive state would and should address the disadvantage experienced by people whose lives are disfigured by clustered legal problems. The analysis builds on the premise that it is the state that has created this disadvantage, and accordingly it is the state's responsibility to remedy it. An approach that is, in many respects, analogous to the principle that the 'polluter pays'. It examines the importance of support for those who live with disadvantage; it then explores both proactive and reactive measures that could lead the way to increased justice for those currently experiencing clustered injustice.

An appendix forms the final section and contains brief descriptions of various groups who experience clustered injustice. This section illustrates the extent of the problem and the range of people who find themselves in this intractable situation. The examples are by no means exhaustive, but include: people with irregular immigration status; people with disabilities; carers; Gypsies and Travelling people; people enmeshed in the criminal justice system; people who are homeless or at risk of homelessness or living in precarious tenancies; and people who experience poverty and problem debt.

The grain of the law

Lawn Bowls Rules

The green must be level . . .

Every bowl has a bias – it is so constructed that when rolled along a level ground it traces a curving path. The amount of the curve increases as the speed of the bowl decreases. With the average speed of delivery of a bowl the effect of the bias is negligible until the bowls has travelled about three-fifths of its distance. From that moment until it comes to rest it curves more and more in response to the bias.

Extract from 'Lawn Bowling – A Complete Beginners' Guide'[1]

Introduction: the level playing field

To the distant observer, a bowl so carefully rolled along the green may seem round and true, but the more its course runs, the clearer it becomes – that it is anything but. To a bowls player, this bias is an inherent part of the game and unremarkable – it is a fact of life. To an outside observer – it is mesmerising.

Thus, to a clerk in a magistrates' court, it is utterly normal that she has every day paraded before her people who live with disadvantage, people with severe mental health problems, people with alcohol and drug addictions, people dependent upon pitifully small sums of social security and at the whim of loan sharks; and yet also utterly normal that behind her sit three magistrates with none of these characteristics and little or no comprehension of what it is like to live such a life. To an outside observer, it is mesmerising – a glimpse of our two nations, of *Sybil* and *The road to Wigan Pier*.[2] Before these decent onlookers, justice rolls its predestined course – and the longer the process rolls on, the more inevitable is its outcome weighted against those who live with disadvantage.

These are degradation ceremonies[3] – not because there is any malice in those operating the system – magistrates are volunteers and frequently deeply humane and public-spirited people, as are the prosecutors and defence lawyers, the probation officers, tribunal chairs and ushers – so are they all honourable people, bending over backwards to act fairly, scrupulously adhering to the creed of impartiality. So too, those judges who actively seek to compensate for these biases, who chose to work against the grain of the law – often with the consequence that their judgments display a rough and uneven texture, lacking the polished refinement of those who instinctively 'go with the flow'.

These judges, magistrates and tribunal chairs who strive to make their courts level playing fields are in reality the self-same bowling green keepers whose lives have been devoted to perfecting the evenness of their greens: keepers who have rolled, mown and smoothed out generations of imperfections to make the perfect games court – perfectly true and perfectly fair. By focusing on the evenness of the playing field, we are distracted from the loaded nature of the contest – and yet without the perfection of the green, the predictability of the outcome would be in doubt. We overlook the plain fact that the only way to compensate for the bias of the bowl would be to create a *compensatory bias* in the green. The analogy does not hold entirely true – but it serves its purpose: to strive for the proverbially level playing field in the administration of justice is not a sufficient end – indeed, it may accentuate the inherent bias of the law, when, as Bankowski and Mungham[4] have observed: 'although the system might administer justice impartially, "justice"[5] itself is partial'.

Overview – the law's role in creating injustice

This chapter is concerned with the reach of the law and its impact on the lives of those that live with disadvantage: the law's role in creating clusters of problems, and its potential to address this phenomenon. It is a scene-setting chapter – more concerned with identifying the nature and the extent of this bias than divining the no doubt esoteric sociological reasons that gave rise to it.

A basic, and certainly naïve, premise underlying this approach is that these inequalities are generally unwilled; generally unintended; and that for many of today's key players in the justice system, there is no obvious benefit to be gained from perpetuating these biases. It is merely that this is the way the game is, and has always been, played and for a variety of reasons (not least the law's attachment to precedent) many practioners have not sought to critically analyse why the law and its institutional apparatus is predisposed to produce outcomes unfavourable to people who live with disadvantage.

The 'law' (including its basic 'legal principles') is of course 'loaded': it was engineered by the 'advantaged', and it is therefore inevitable that it has some difficulty in understanding and addressing the needs of the disadvantaged. This is, however, a well-trodden field – for it is a truth universally acknowledged that states 'divided into a small number of rich and a large number of poor will always develop a government manipulated by the rich to protect the amenities represented by their property'[6] – or as Adam Smith put it:

Civil government, so far as it is instituted for the security of property, is in reality instituted for the defence of the rich against the poor, or of those who have some property against those who have none at all.[7]

In the context of this book, the analysis that follows is important for several reasons – primarily and most obviously, because these biases create unfairness and undermine confidence in the law, and if 'we desire respect for the law, we must first make the law respectable'.[8] However, two other associated reasons are of particular relevance.

The first reason goes to the heart of this book's critique of the traditional legal approach to clustered problems: namely, that it requires that legal problems be considered in isolation. Clusters must therefore be broken down into their elemental parts before being addressed. Fragmenting – or perhaps more accurately, 'fractionating' – such problems tends to distill and to concentrate their inherent biases, and accordingly suggests (at the very least) the need for caution in pursing this approach. Although these inherent biases can be counteracted by cross-cutting principles (such as the concept of 'justice') it is these very mechanisms of interconnectedness that are lost during the severing process: the process of subdivision that renders the disconnected legal problems capable of being analysed and understood by traditional legal methods.[9]

The second reason that this analysis is important is that, if these biases are acknowledged, then the law can be modified so that in its inestimable daily exchanges, it generates a myriad of micro resistances to inequality – and thereby helps to create a more equitable society: a society with less need for macro rebalancing interventions. For example, there was no inevitability to the content of the rules that have come to shape contract law. As a number of commentators have observed, small changes could have a dramatic impact in terms of redistributive justice.[10] The current rules are merely testimony to the influence of wealth: an influence that has levered the law into its service – like Darwin's hundred thousand wedges[11] thrusting aside the weaker forces of justice and humanitarian considerations. On each occasion, the rules could have taken a different tack: but they didn't – they went with the grain – the unruffled 'stream of justice'[12] along which legal arguments seem destined to flow.

The law's biases need to be constantly and consciously acknowledged – that the law privileges and that the law excludes: that the law is political and so too is lawyering. In the words of Allan Hutchinson, 'lawyers have nowhere to stand or serve that does not implicate them in the existing allocation of economic and social power – they are either working to maintain the status quo (or even worsen it) or they are part of the struggle to change and improve it'.[13]

The section that follows is an illustrative (and unmethodical) scene-setting review of various legal biases that have particular relevance for this book's analysis. These legal principles are not infrequently cited in public law proceedings. They are, however, principles that should only be applied after a public health warning has been given – accompanied by an acknowledgement that they have a disproportionate and adverse impact on those who live with disadvantage.

Legal maxims and clustered injustice

Warnings about the dangers of legal maxims are not new. In the mid-1600s Thomas Hobbes complained that lawyers 'had infected most of the gentry of England with their maxims and cases prejudged, which they call precedents'[14] and 250 years later Smith warned of the danger of relying on 'brevity' and phrases 'clothed in the words of a dead language'.[15] Sir Henry Sumner Maine put it more bluntly – phrases that 'pretended to have had their origin in the New Testament, but which were really derived from indelible recollections of the Cæsarian despotism'.[16] He cautioned, however, that they were 'part of the law which is the last to alter'[17] – and time has certainly vindicated this observation.

Maxims are still part of legal education and are still trotted out by advocates and judges: uncritical litanies – as religious creeds, or at the very least, self-evident truths. Maxims have survived because they go with the grain of the law. The 'common sense' grain of the mahogany benches polished by silk gowns – but not of the splintered timbers of the docks that discomfort the law's disadvantaged objects.

We will examine two legal maxims – remoteness and 'ex turpi causa' – and how they contribute to clustered injustice for the disadvantaged.

The maxim of remoteness

The first of Sir Francis Bacon's 25 'maxims of the common law' concerned 'remoteness': 'in jure non remota causa, sed proxima spectatur', which translates as 'in law it is the immediate, not the remote, cause which is regarded'.[18] This remains a much-cited principle – not infrequently used in order to justify the courts' tendency to limit the damages for a wrongful act to the 'proximate' impacts of that act, and not to more remote causes.[19]

Remoteness is of course a relative term. At what point does the law consider that a 'cause' is 'outside the scope of its selection'?[20] Many of the clustered problems experienced by those who live with disadvantage will have several causes and consequences – some more proximate than others. Many Gypsies and Travelling people, for example, live with considerable disadvantage[21] and are often juggling multiple legal problems: problems relating to their children's education; planning problems; healthcare problems; discrimination problems and so on. Not infrequently, each one of these problems will have several 'causes', some of which may well result from what has been referred to as 'cross-generational dynamic clustering' – namely where 'parents' disadvantage . . . appears among their offspring'.[22]

Buckley v UK (1996),[23] for example, concerned the inability of a Gypsy to obtain planning permission to site her caravan on land that she owned. In his dissenting opinion, Judge Pettiti sought to explain why courts found it so difficult to address the injustice Mrs Buckley encountered. He referred to 'the deliberate superimposition and accumulation of administrative rules (each of which would be acceptable taken singly)' but which cumulatively made it 'totally impossible for a Gypsy family to make suitable arrangements for its accommodation, social life and the integration of its children at school'.[24] These 'rules' were imposed by government departments and included 'measures relating to town planning, nature conservation, the viability of access roads, planning permission requirements, road safety and public health' with the consequence that 'the Buckley family are caught in a vicious circle'.

The courts were, in his analysis, unwilling to consider these 'measures' and so decided that they were 'too remote' – as was the fact that she had lived in the area all her life and that hundreds of houses had been granted permission, and built on the surrounding land during that time (and many with holiday caravans parked on their forecourts). The proximate cause of Mrs Buckley's problem was that she tried, but failed, to get planning permission. The planning process had been scrupulously fair: a proverbial 'level playing field'.

Many of the clustered legal problems that people living with disadvantage experience, are exacerbated by their poverty.[25] However, in the 1933 *Liesbosch* case,[26] the House of Lords held that in proceedings for compensation, 'impecuniosity' was too remote to be considered:[27] that in effect 'poverty is a misfortune for which the law cannot take responsibility'.[28] The court accepted that an unlawful act may result in poor people suffering greater losses than the wealthy – but their 'actual loss in so far as it was due to their impecuniosity arose from that impecuniosity . . . extraneous to and distinct in character from the tort'.[29] As Lord Wright explained:[30]

> The law cannot take account of everything that follows a wrongful act; it regards some subsequent matters as outside the scope of its selection, because 'it were infinite for the law to judge the cause of causes'.

But of course, the 'law' decides what it will take into account and what it will not. 'Impecuniosity' may be too remote to be considered, but wealth – it seems – is not. The Local Government and Social Care Ombudsman in England, for example, takes the view that compensation is payable where a council's maladministration results in the loss of a support service. The compensation is calculated on the basis of the complainant's out-of-pocket costs: costs incurred by purchasing alternative support pending the outcome of their complaint. It follows that an impecunious complainant who has been unable to afford the cost of purchasing alternative support will, therefore, have no expenses to claim.[31] Of course, the compensation could be calculated on the basis of the cost of the lost services – but that is not the way the system operates: 'poverty is a misfortune for which the law cannot take responsibility'.

King has described problems of this kind as 'polycentric':[32] problems that comprise 'a large and complicated web of interdependent relationships, such that a change to one factor produces an incalculable series of changes to other factors'.[33] Disputes of this kind have the potential to spawn clusters of problems (as they did for Mrs Buckley), and classically courts have actively avoided them, by praying in aid 'remoteness' and their unwillingness to 'judge the cause of causes'. King argues that this is particularly so, where there is a strong component of public policy / public interest – where decisions can have 'significant ramifications for public revenue'; where public policy may be 'highly complex and interdependent with other social goals'; where the courts may be a 'less competent institution for understanding the nature of such goals and the best means for accomplishing them'.[34]

His analysis demonstrates that this holds true for social welfare decisions (for example, those concerning the provision of accommodation for homeless people) but demonstrably not so, when the issue at stake concerns taxation – for example, tax avoidance – that:[35]

> . . . where certain values are at stake, courts will apply stricter standards of review than they ordinarily do where such values are not at stake, come what may for the Treasury. These reasons may be instruct-

ive in cases involving discretionary allocative decision-making, where people's fundamental human rights, rather than corporate tax liability, are often at stake. . . . [That there] is little reason to think that those seeking to deflect tax liability through the courts (typically corporations and wealthy individuals) have a more important interest at stake than do the beneficiaries of government revenue.

The maxim of 'ex turpi causa' and the accumulation of handicaps

'Ex turpi causa non oritur actio' is a common law maxim or 'brocard'[36] that is mirrored in a number of respects by the equitable maxim 'he who comes to equity must come with clean hands'. It is generally interpreted as 'a deliberate wrongdoing cannot found a cause of action'.[37] 'Turpi' has a range of yet wider meanings – 'shapeless, unsightly, foul, deformed, ugly, base, nauseous'. The maxim renders void actions arising out of 'base or shameful causes': it precludes, for example, highwaymen suing for their share of a Hounslow Heath robbery.[38] Its relevance appears undiminished by the passing of the time, although today (perhaps unsurprisingly) many of the base and shameful causes to which it is attached, are alleged to have taken place within the City of London rather than on Hounslow Heath.[39]

It is, however, a principle applied in other contexts – because it 'goes with the legal grain' and where (to cite Lord Mance) it encourages 'fast thinking' that produces 'easy' (but potentially fallacious) answers.[40]

The state has the power to decide what is lawful, what is wrongful and what is 'base'. The 'dirty hands' phrase is of course unfortunate – but there it is – and there before the law stand many of the 'unwashed'.

Gypsies and Travellers

Tommy Smith and his family[41] and countless generations of Smiths before them, lived in Herefordshire, moving between traditional stopping places. This way of life became increasingly difficult as legislation was enacted that criminalised camping on land without planning permission. This resulted in Gypsies, throughout the land, spending more time camping on the greensward of lanes and as these were rendered inaccessible by ditching, moving to the lay-bys of busier and more dangers roads. In response to this, councils and the Department of Transport systematically closed off these lay-bys – filling them with large piles of stone. It was a pincer movement –

with Gypsies additionally being threatened with prosecution since, at law, the greensward adjoining roads as well as their lay-bys form part of the highway, and so camping on either is a criminal offence – 'an obstruction of the highway'.[42] It was less brutal than General Custer's way of dealing with Native Americans 'off reservation', but the shared aim was undeniable.

With support, Mr Smith compiled an exhaustive list of all the traditional stopping places that the council and Department of Transport had rendered inaccessible, and then applied to the High Court for a declaration that this action was itself an unlawful obstruction of the highway.

Gypsies are not traditionally cast as plaintiffs, and in such unusual occasions the government is not supposed to 'retire from the courts defeated'[43] – but the Department of Transport conceded the point and agreed to remove the obstructions it had created. The rule of law cuts both ways – imposing, in this case, 'effective inhibitions upon power and the defence of the citizen from power's all-intrusive claims'.[44]

Sadly for the Smiths, the council was not prepared to settle on similar terms and the case proceeded. The Court of Appeal invoked 'ex turpi' and refused to rule on the impugned local authority action. Mann LJ holding:

> I find it unnecessary to resolve my doubt [about the legality of the local authority's actions] because in my judgment this is a case where in discretion, relief must be refused. The appellant's plain object is to camp, as he hitherto has, on lay-bys and roadside waste. That camping is an unlawful obstruction and possibly a criminal offence under section 137 of the Highways Act. The appellant's purpose in this appeal and in his original application is to facilitate an unlawful activity by himself and others.[45]

A common law maxim trumped the 'rule of law': in the eyes of the law, Mr Smith's claim was base and no doubt shameful. The court could have taken a different tack, but it didn't – it went with the grain, and there was therefore no reason to ask itself *why* the family was camping on dangerous roadside verges. That was, of course, 'too remote' – as was the fact that the local council had been in breach of its duty to provide them with a site for 25 years.[46] The combined effect of the state's action (through 'an accumulation of handicaps' on Gypsies) was to 'transform nomadism into vagrancy':[47] the state, after all, has the power to decide what is lawful and what isn't.

Chapman v UK[48] concerned a not dissimilar complaint by an English Gypsy. She had nowhere lawful to camp and so camped on her own land despite being refused planning permission to do so. As with Mr Smith, her local authority had – in breach of its legal duties[49] – failed to provide adequate sites for Gypsies. Judge Bonello (in his dissenting opinion) observed that:

> 5. I believe that a public authority which is in breach of its legal obligations should not be allowed to plead that it is acting 'in accordance with the law'. The classic constitutional doctrine of 'clean hands' precludes those who are in prior contravention of the law from claiming the law's protection.
>
> 6. A public authority owes as great an obligation to comply with the law as any individual. Its responsibility is eminently more than that of individuals belonging to vulnerable classes who are virtually forced to disregard the law in order to be able to exercise their fundamental right to a private and family life – individuals who have to contravene the law due to the operation of the prior failures of the public authorities.
>
> 7. In the present case, both the public authorities and the individual had undoubtedly trespassed the boundaries of legality. But it was the public authority's default in observing the law that precipitated and induced the subsequent default by the individual. That failure of the authorities has brought about a situation which almost justifies the defence of necessity. Why a human rights court should look with more sympathy at the far reaching breach of law committed by the powerful, than at that forced on the weak, has not yet been properly explained.

Homelessness and begging

One further example suffices – as to the state's power to decide what is lawful, and what is not: to criminalise an activity, which is itself precipitated by the state's failure to meet its basic humanitarian obligations.

It was estimated that in 2019 in England almost 300,000 people were homeless, over 200,000 were threatened with homelessness[50] and that on any one night somewhere between 4,500[51] and 22,500[52] people were sleeping rough (more than double the number estimated in 2010).[53] Levels of homelessness are 'strongly associated' with reductions in spending on social welfare by councils and central government.[54]

People who are homeless or at risk of homelessness often have clusters of legal problems arising out of a complex mix of 'multiple (often interrelated and multi-directional)'[55] causes – causes that can include: poverty; the breakdown of family and other 'anchor' social relationships; traumatic experiences during childhood; domestic violence; substance misuse; mental health problems; physical health problems; leaving care; anti-social behaviour or crime; overcrowded housing; debt; and financial problems caused by benefits reduction.[56] The appendix at the end of this book provides a brief review of the literature concerning the causes of homelessness and the clustered legal problems that arise in consequence.

A 2019 House of Commons Library briefing paper[57] noted that 'rough sleeping is often associated with nuisance activities such as begging'. Putting to one side for the moment the question of why begging is considered to be a 'nuisance' – it is certainly the case that begging is a criminal offence.[58] Once convicted, individuals then become liable to be prosecuted as 'rogues and vagabonds' for behaviour such as 'wandering abroad', 'lodging . . . under a tent' or indeed 'not giving a good account' of themselves.[59] In 2015, 2,365 people were charged with the offence of begging in England and Wales, and 558 for being a rogue/vagabond.[60] Rough sleeping can also be a criminal offence. Anti-social Behaviour, Crime and Policing Act 2014 s59 enables councils to make public space protection orders (PSPOs) which can be used to prohibit rough sleeping in public places – and it is a criminal offence to fail to comply with such an order.[61] It appears that in 2019 at least 60 councils used PSPOs to prohibit 'people putting up tents, seeking charity and other behaviour associated with rough sleeping'.[62]

There were (from the perspective of the 'advantaged') sound economic reasons for criminalising vagrancy in 1330 (which is what the Statute of Labourers[63] did): reasons concerned with the feudal lords' labour shortages caused by the Black Death.[64] Over the next 500 years, similar justifications existed: the shoring up the Poor Law, the control of those disposed by enclosures and those demobbed at the end of the Napoleonic Wars. By the time of the Vagrancy Act 1824, the belief that the homeless and 'those without a consistent means of support were a dangerous class'[65] went with the grain of the law – as indeed it continues to do, to this day.

Possibly because of their colonial provenance, some of the most objective (and withering) critiques of laws criminalising vagrancy and begging have come from US courts. The US Supreme Court judgment in *Papachristou v City of Jacksonville*[66] found Douglas J in full throttle, crushing mode. The Jacksonville Ordinance criminalised (among much else) begging, night walkers, persons wandering or strolling around from place to place without any lawful purpose or object, and habitual loafers. Holding the provision to be unconstitutional, Douglas J observed that that the Elizabethan poor law conditions[67] 'which spawned these laws may be gone, but the archaic classifications remain'. Citing Walt Whitman, Vachel Lindsay and Henry D Thoreau, he extolled the value of night walking, strolling around and loafing as 'amenities' that 'encouraged lives of high spirits rather than hushed, suffocating silence'. Laws that undermined these rights tipped the scales of justice and made 'the even-handed administration of the law' impossible. For Douglas J, in holding the ordinance to be 'void', the rule of law that applies with equal force 'to minorities as well as majorities, to the poor as well as the rich, is the great mucilage that holds society together'.

Academic condemnation of such laws has been equally fierce, with many critics reasoning that begging is a form of free speech. Hershkoff,[68] for example, argues that 'by alerting listeners to the conditions and existence of poverty and deprivation' it provides vital information for 'society's decision makers'.[69] She also highlights the contradiction in forbidding begging but not other 'communications among strangers' – for example 'the tourist's request for directions, the newspaper seller's exhortation to "read all about it," the politician's pitch to "vote Democratic," and the Christmas Santa's plea to give to the needy' – suggesting that these laws permit free speech *provided* 'it is a topic the government prefers'.[70]

Moon compares begging to commercial advertising[71] (in that they both involve a request for money) and notes that in public spaces we are bombarded with advertising messages, whether we like it or not. Begging, on his analysis, is however deemed to be invasive because it 'takes place at the margins of public discourse' – and is in stark contrast to the iconography of capitalism – advertising and marketing.[72]

For all these powerful condemnations, camping on greensward, begging and rough sleeping all remain 'base and shameful' causes for which the law has chosen to criminalise the Gypsy, the beggar and the rough sleeper. Though some might consider that the legislature and the executive share some of the shame for the prevalence of poverty and homelessness – the law-makers (the legislature and the executive) have decided otherwise.

Natural justice

The common law has always been conveniently vague as to what is encompassed within the concept of 'natural justice', but it is undoubtedly a cross-cutting principle concerned with the evenness of the playing field. It requires that judges be even-handed, and that each party to a dispute be given a fair opportunity to state their case.

Natural justice is about procedural fairness, and a hearing is fair if there is, between the parties, 'equality of arms': that they each have the same opportunities to adduce evidence, to call and to cross-examine witnesses and so on. It is a conception of justice as *process* – not of *substance*: justice measured in terms of *equality of opportunity* rather than *equality of outcome*. The McDonald's libel case serves as a useful case study.

The McDonald's libel case

In the late 1980s, a number of members of an organisation called London Greenpeace distributed leaflets alleging that McDonald's – among other things – was a bad employer, was responsible for cruelty to animals and that its food was harmful. McDonald's issued proceedings seeking damages and injunctions against five of the protesters. Three of these apologised and the High Court considered it 'immaterial' whether they did this 'because they had no answer to McDonald's claims . . . or because they could not face a long and costly court case'. The remaining two protesters (a bar-worker and an unwaged single parent) did not apologise, and McDonald's then spent an estimated £ 10 million suing them. The protesters were unrepresented, as there is no legal aid for libel actions in the UK. The domestic proceedings[73] took over nine years – including 313 hearing days in the High Court. The Court of Appeal held that the defendants had not refuted all McDonald's claims and ordered that they pay £76,000 in compensation.

In so finding, the court specifically rejected the defendants' claim that the action by McDonald's amounted to an 'abuse of process' by using its 'great resources to bring a complicated case against unrepresented defendants of slender means'. Although to many lay observers this may appear to be an astonishing finding, in terms of natural justice the process was 'fair': the judges were unbiased, and the parties had the same rights to call and to cross-examine witnesses. The point being that natural justice doesn't actually produce 'real justice' – it is indeed the 'level green' that can accentuate the biases in the law and work against the rights of those who live with disadvantage.

Of course, in substantive terms, the proceedings were not fair and in due course the European Court of Human Rights came to this blindingly obvious (and unanimous) conclusion.[74] For sure there had been level playing field – fair-minded judges had administered justice impartially – but 'justice itself was partial':[75] the law (libel law) was loaded, and the outcome predetermined. Justice was a game: a charade – or more aptly, Monopoly, where McDonald's owned all the property as well as being the banker.

The (so-called) 'McLibel' proceedings stand as a paradigm example of the way that the biases within the law and the unequal distribution of wealth combine to produce outcomes weighted against those who live with disadvantage.

Paradoxically, the case also highlights a similarity between entities such as McDonald's and people who live with disadvantage – namely that they both spend much of their time 'bumping into the law'. The difference, however, is that for major corporations and high net-worth individuals (HNWIs), this constitutes an inherent part of their business model. These are entities that can exploit the law's potential to 'problem cause' and use their financial clout to intimidate[76] and neutralise those that get in their way. They not only have the resources to litigate – as and when they choose – but they also have the benefit of the law's biases.

Wealth, privilege and the justice game

A vulnerability analysis would interrogate the reasons why wealth enjoys such a privileged position when playing the justice game. For the corporations and HNWIs, it is difficult to envisage how a rational argument can be advanced to counter the view that this is undue privilege.[77] What benefit does wider society gain from their ability to buy privileged access to the legal system; to impose non-disclosure agreements on those that they have harmed; and to injunct – at will – those who question their bona fides?[78]

Removing the privileging biases that favour corporations and HNWIs calls for a radical recasting (or repealing) of unfair legal provisions as well as a reprofiling of the playing field – for example, to amend the 'standing rights' (discussed below) of corporations. Reflecting on these issues, before the enactment of the Human Rights Act 1998, Sir Stephen Sedley expressed his concern that society's losers and winners would merely become the same losers and winners after the Act's enactment.[79] He suggested that one mechanism for addressing this problem would be to develop a 'more sophisticated concept of "locus standi"'.[80] In this respect he had in mind the disproportionate power wielded by multi-nationals and the need to develop mechanisms to 'shut out corporations . . . to try to ensure that it's not those with the sharpest elbows and lawyers who get to drink at the well'.

The point being, that if our legal system has developed procedures to exclude busybodies and those bent on 'base and shameful causes' (see below) then it should be capable of limiting the power of the 'privileged'. Two decades on from Sir Stephen's paper, it is clear that the grain of the law is still aligned with the interests of the traditional 'winners' – wealthy individuals and corporations.

In cases such as the McLibel proceedings, further amending (or abolishing) libel law could address the law's bias, as could Sir Stephen's suggestion. However, making legal aid more freely available would not. Libel law (even in its amended post Defamation Act 2013 form) remains a fertile field for bullying oligarchs and overly sensitive corporations – replete as it is with subjective criteria: for example, the meaning of 'public interest'; of 'serious harm'; of 'substantially true'; and of 'honest opinion'. Criteria to be contested within a civil justice system that has sustained laws of this kind since time immemorial. Although legal aid could provide economic protection for some (but certainly not all), it could not provide protection from the trauma of finding oneself at the wrong end of an injunction or for the years of disrupted lives as the unwanted case 'drags its dreary length'[81] through the Chancery Court. To quote Tawney – 'if the rules of a game give a permanent advantage to some of the players, it does not become fair merely because they are scrupulously observed by all who take part in it'.[82]

Fairness, privilege and public bodies

The state also enjoys a privileged position when playing the justice game.[83] The state creates the rules and dictates the processes to be followed: processes that fragment, silo and compartmentalise, and in so doing, generate the complexity that is the root-cause of clustered injustice. The state also has deep pockets when it comes to funding litigation, as well as enjoying specific protections from legal challenge.

However, unlike corporations and HNWIs, there are clear and rational reasons why the state should enjoy a degree of 'privilege' in this process. Public bodies are subject to a myriad of legal obligations, and daily must make countless difficult decisions about how they exercise these functions. If aggrieved individuals had an unrestricted right to litigate unfavourable decisions, then judges would end up administering public bodies (and of course the court system would then be overwhelmed).

In consequence, there are a number of provisions that restrict the right to 'judicially review' a public body. Applicants must (among other things) demonstrate that there is no alternative remedy before they are given 'permission' to proceed with a claim[84] and that they have a 'sufficient interest': in legal parlance – that they have 'locus standi' ('sufficient standing'). Historically 'standing' meant 'social standing' in the sense of having a proprietary interest in the decision being challenged (even if only being a 'ratepayer'[85]), but in recent years the courts have, it appears, adopted a more liberal approach. Today the rule is, ostensibly, only used to weed out meddlesome busybodies who have 'no interest whatsoever' in challenging the public body's decision[86] – and 'no interest whatsoever' is no longer the same as having no pecuniary or special personal interest'.[87]

It might be thought that these procedural restrictions have proved to be highly effective. Given the fact that public bodies must make tens or hundreds of millions of decisions every year – the volume of judicial review challenges is small. In 2018, for instance, there were only 3,600 applications,[88] of which only a small proportion made any progress. For example, of the 1,200 claims against the Home Office, only 20 per cent were granted permission to proceed, and only 12 succeeded at a final hearing. The figures for claims against local authorities were not markedly different: of the 652 applications, only 23 succeeded at a final hearing.[89]

Objectively, the reason why there are so few judicial reviews of public bodies has little to do with these restrictions – and everything to do with the cost of legal action and the penalties faced by applicants (and their lawyers) if they fail. In practice, therefore the privilege afforded to public bodies is primarily the privilege of wealth – little different, in fact, to that at the heart of the McLibel proceedings.

The severe reduction to the legal aid budget over the last decade[90] has meant that those who live with disadvantage have little or no prospect of challenging bad behaviour by public bodies – not least children, disabled people and people who are from ethnic minorities.[91]

Although judicial review is an incredibly important mechanism for holding 'power' to account (and for creating precedents that can have wider benefits) on an individual level it is seldom transformative for those who live with disadvantage and who have multiple synchronous legal difficulties. I learned this in a small but Damascene moment, many years ago (when legal aid was more accessible). I had by that time spent a decade or so judicially reviewing council decisions to evict Gypsies and other Travelling people. On one particular day I found myself on a lay-by speaking to a Gypsy I had come to know well. He gave me an 'obstruction of the highway' notice that he had received, and I asked him to sign a legal aid application form so that this could be challenged. He paused, evidently reluctant to sign, and the gist of his explanation said it all – that he had been signing such forms for many years – that he was still stuck on the side of the road and I had a new car. And of course, he was absolutely right.

There are forms of oppression that legal proceedings can't 'push back' – wider trends like social security poor law attacks, racism and clustered problems that point to social justice systems' failures. Instituting judicial review proceedings can be a useful lever to be pulled in the struggle to highlight such problems and ameliorate some of their impacts, but proceedings of this kind cannot get to the heart of these wrongs. As a legal process, it also has a poor track record in effecting organisational change. When courts find illegality in the way a particular decision was reached, the remedy is generally that the public body is required to reconsider the facts and retake the decision. In response, public bodies tend to do just that: they re-run the process, careful to avoid their previous errors, and come to the same decision.[92]

The legal privilege to which public bodies are justifiably entitled, concern the exercise their judgment in discharging their myriad statutory obligations. It is clearly reasonable for courts not to over-scrutinise the way public bodies exercise their legal powers. The privilege derives from their responsibilities and not their relative wealth. Where, however, their behaviour can be characterised as oppressive or unlawful, then it is unpalatable to suggest that this privilege should remain, when the behaviour harms those who live with disadvantage but not when it disturbs the wealthy. Sadly, this is not the way the system works, and the injustice that results severely undermines trust in public institutions. Public bodies (like private corporations) can – and do:

- employ deceit, denial and neutralisation to protect, even exonerate, the interests of the 'powerful – they can and do undermine the credibility, subordinate and disqualify the accounts of the marginalised';[93]
- become culturally insensitive to the experience of minorities;[94]
- create deliberately 'hostile' policies towards specific disadvantaged groups and then fail to keep track of the impact of these policies 'to make sure that, where members of the public are affected, particularly where they are at risk, it supports them appropriately';[95]
- develop a culture that includes: 'A lack of openness to criticism; A lack of consideration for patients; Defensiveness; Looking inwards not outwards; Secrecy; Misplaced assumptions about the judge-

ments and actions of others; An acceptance of poor standards; A failure to put the patient first in everything that is done.'[96]

These few extracts, from what could be a very long list, are all from findings that emerged from (or anticipated the findings of) public inquiries and not from judicial review proceedings. The reason for this, is that complex messy problems – often arising from systems failures – are not capable of being addressed by standard single issue legal problem hearings. The millions who live with clustered injustice are unable to have their own personally tailored public inquiries, and so in the search for mechanisms that will help address their problems, we must look elsewhere.

The preceding section has focused on public law – including laws that criminalise – since in the context of this study, people who live with disadvantage do so because they (and others for whom they may care) have a legitimate need for a level of support from the state, which has not been forthcoming.[97] The state has created legal barriers to protect public bodies from being challenged for this failure and has sought to deflect criticism through a number of mechanisms, including characterising those in such need as 'undeserving', 'dirty' and (on occasions) as criminals.

These prejudices are not simply genies escaping from the dark ages that set the grain for our property-based legal system – they are in the air we breathe and in our every thought and perception. They are in the defendant's dirty fingernails and their crumpled court papers; in the layout of the benches; in the deference of the ushers; in the abruptness of the lawyers; and in a thousand, unconsciously but instantly 'clocked', ways. These rituals are a vital backdrop to this book's analysis: of the disadvantaged in the presence of the advantaged; of the disadvantaged as an irritant to the smooth running of the legal process: as complainants and as litigants in person – as out of place as Joe at Pip's party,[98] and lepers in Harley Street.

Private law

This book is primarily concerned with the shortcomings of *public law* (the law that regulates public bodies): the failure of state institutions to provide those who live with disadvantage with the support to which they are legally entitled; the inadequacy of the remedies available to those who experience clustered injustice; and the state's failure to address the biases within this system of laws.

These failings are of course, no less blatant when the focus shifts to a consideration of *private law*:[99] the laws regulating such things as personal injury claims, property rights, employment rights and the rights of corporations. The clusters of legal problems that blight the lives of many people who live with disadvantage also contain many private law problems: for example, problems of debt, poor pay and one-sided tenancy agreements.

Private law and the indignant student

Many years ago, one of my students expressed his general displeasure at having to study jurisprudence, and his particular irritation at having seminars which discussed the sociology of law. He complained that this was tantamount to political indoctrination: he had come to university to study company law – 'traditional law' – and not 'left wing' critiques of this kind. He was voicing the 'standard model of lawyering' which 'enables lawyers to obscure and finesse the blatantly political nature of law'.[100]

The student – like so many lawyers – genuinely believed that company law was the epitome of the *apolitical*. A law which allows companies to enjoy the privileged status of being a legal 'person'; privileged by being accorded human rights when several are far larger than many nation states; entities given the right to create independent and highly transferable property (shares) – property that can move across frontiers – property afforded all manner of taxation privileges; company directors who can hide behind a veil of secrecy – who can multiply their corporate iterations, offshore its assets and then dissolve the whole edifice without incurring liability.

As unpolitical as land law, which protects the rights of one per cent of the population to own half of all land in Britain; the rights of the aristocracy to own a third and corporations and oligarchs / bankers to own a further third of the land. To use the law of trespass to exclude not just people who are homeless, but all of the 'public' from 92 per cent of the land.

As unpolitical as revenue law, which – for example – allows the land registered to offshore companies (the size of Greater London) to avoid stamp duty and inheritance tax.[101]

And on and on – with almost every turn of the pages of Halsbury's Laws of England.

If there is one central role for university law schools, it is to disabuse law students of the notion that 'lawyering is a neutral exercise that does not implicate lawyers in any political process or demand a commitment to any particular ideology'.[102]

Case example – contract law

'Vulnerability theory' fundamentally critiques key premises that underpin much of our legal system – not least the notion that individuals are independent, autonomous and self-sufficient. It is an ideal that Fineman suggests is best captured in our approach to contract law – which assumes that individuals 'have the ability to negotiate contract terms, their options and make rational choices'.[103] Contract law is based upon the fiction of equality where commonly and self-evidently many parties start from materially unequal bargaining positions.[104] Contract law is the dominant legal force in shaping many of the problems experienced by those who live with disadvantage: not least employment contracts, tenancy and credit agreements.

Although there are many ways that a contract can be held to be invalid[105] – the fact that there is a profound inequality in bargaining position between the parties is not one. In general, 'advantage-taking' by the wealthy over the poor is fair game – despite the fact that 'the more money an individual has, the better he is likely to do in his transactions with other persons'.[106]

It doesn't, of course, have to be that way. There is no reason in principle why advantage-taking of this kind should not be deemed unlawful. Indeed, a number of states in the US have provisions prohibiting advantage-taking (referred to as 'price-gouging') in times of emergency.[107]

In the UK, however, the 'advantaged' are free (subject to statutory restrictions) to impose punitive credit terms; to impose poor pay and poor employment conditions; to impose one-sided tenancy agreements – and then to call on the state, in the form of its courts, its bailiffs and its bankruptcy laws, to enforce these harsh terms.

Historically, the courts were prepared to take a more interventionist approach. For example, to declare advantage-taking unlawful in cases where 'expectant heirs' had taken loans subject to severe conditions.[108] In similar terms, Dawson cites[109] a number of cases from the 18th and 19th centuries where the courts were willing to intervene to similarly constrain advantage-taking in contract. These included, for example, holding contracts to be unconscionable where they involved a man 'in humble life . . . and unable to judge of himself the precautions to be taken in selling';[110] an illiterate man in

desperate poverty;[111] vendors in a state of 'most abject and impor-
tunate distress';[112] an elderly woman 'in humble life, of slender
education';[113] 'poor, ignorant men';[114] and a 'poor solicitor's clerk'
who whose 'position of poverty and necessity . . . put him practically
at the mercy of the lenders'.[115]

Today, however, in this brave new world where individuals are
held to be independent, autonomous and self-sufficient, cases of this
kind no longer win the day. Contract law has hardened, and the bar
to finding contracts unconscionable has been raised to unreachable
heights.[116] As the above examples demonstrate – it doesn't have to be
this way. Contract could be a bulwark against unfair 'advantage-
taking' and a powerful instrument of redistributive justice[117] – but it
isn't: and this is because the grain of the law is not predisposed to run
in that direction. And that is something we must not forget when we
try to discover what a socially just outcome should be for a person
who lives with disadvantage and experiences multiple, synchronous
legal problems.

CHAPTER 3

What's your problem?
Personal legal problems
as singular

Pinball rules

The main components of the game are the flippers and the pinball. The flippers are usually located at the bottom of the playfield, directly above the drain. One purpose of the flippers is to keep the pinball out of the drain. The other purpose is to propel the ball up the table toward the bumpers and ramps in order to score points . . . The flippers are controlled with two buttons, one on either side of the machine, about an inch below the table's top glass. The left button controls any and all flippers on the left side of the table, and the right button controls the ones on the right side.

'How Pinball Machines Work'[1]

In pinball, nudging (which involves shaking the pinball machine to influence the motion of the ball) is tolerated – but excessive nudging is not: it is considered to be 'tilting' which activates the machine's 'tilt bob' (a trip switch) and finishes the game.

Introduction: discrete, random and inscrutable processes

You have just contacted your doctor to ask how one of your daughter's disability-related healthcare needs can be addressed. In doing this, you have just pulled the plunger and started playing pinball. This may be the first time you have played, or you may be familiar with the process. Your daughter's healthcare support depends upon how well you can play the game: how long you can keep the pinball in play. If you lack the expertise, if you are exhausted or distracted, or simply unlucky, and the ball falls down the drain – then all is lost: your only option is to start again. Each machine is different: having different flippers, different bumpers and different ramps. Acquiring expertise on the healthcare machine will not stand you in good stead when you need to play the social care machine, or the education, or the social security, or the housing machine. And of course, the inevitable effect of experiencing clustered problems is that you will be playing several pinball machines simultaneously – machines that randomly nudge and sometimes tilt the adjoining machines and sometimes flip to 'multi-ball' mode – with more than one ball in play.

You have not chosen to play pinball – this is not pinball for fun – it is nightmare pinball. You are playing these different, absurd and sometimes impossible games because the state dictates that this is how you must endeavour to resolve your problem and access support: it has to be done by activating discrete, random, often inscrutable processes where the chances are heavily stacked in favour of the drain.

Playing multiple games of pinball simultaneously simplifies nothing for you – on the contrary, it adds enormous strain and complexity. From the state's perspective, however, it appears to make sense: simple, single-issue processes, which it has designed and over which it thinks it has control. In reality – as this chapter seeks to explain – this approach to resolving clustered legal problems makes no more sense for the state than it does for the individual.

Overview – personal legal problems as 'singular'

This chapter critiques the conceptualisation of personal legal problems as 'singular': that such problems (unlike buses) come along at regular, well-spaced intervals – 'clean', single and discrete. It is an approach that *can* accommodate compound legal problems – but only by breaking them down, and then addressing them separately: a claim and a counterclaim; a personal injury schedule with distinct 'heads of damages'; a probate and a conveyance; and so on. Unfortunately for many people living with disadvantage, their problems arrive in clusters – multiple, interconnected and messy.

The analysis in this chapter draws heavily on 'systems thinking' theory which provides an alternative approach to problem-solving through reductionism (ie the process of subdividing problems until they are simple enough to be analysed and understood).[2] Systems thinking theory suggests that in appropriate contexts, complexity can be simplified by 'going up a level of abstraction' – that 'higher levels of abstraction lose detail, and it is the loss of detail that provides the simplification'.[3]

'Normal' legal problems

Law students are taught a legal version of the periodic table. Dozens and dozens of distinct elements – rights, wrongs and processes – all separately labelled in neat boxes and stacked in adjoining columns (a separate column for torts, for crimes, for trusts and so on). Whereas chemistry students move on to consider compounds – combinations of elements – lawyers stop at the elements. When a question confronts them with a cluster of different legal problems, they are trained to fractionate and distil – until the problem is rendered into its elemental parts. It may be self-evident to a chemist that a compound is more than the sum of its parts – that sugar and vinegar contain the same elements – but this is an idea that has obtained precious little traction within the legal profession. Most lawyers can only recognise a legal problem in its disentangled form – and until that revelatory moment, all that can be said of the cluster is that it is a 'mess'. The fact that 'systems thinking' has developed a process for dealing with 'messes' is something only grasped by an increasingly rare species of practitioner – the experienced generalist. Someone who knows enough about social justice – housing, social security, social care, debt and other branches of social welfare law: enough to provide practical advice and support to those whose legal problems are messy – multiple, synchronous and unending. In medicine we revere our general practitioners – in law, the state is hell-bent on their extermination.

This is a policy that has led to the closure of half of all law centres and not-for-profit legal advice services (between 2013 and 2019) in England and Wales – and the severe contraction of many of those that remain.[4] In tandem, the legal aid budget has been decimated,[5] resulting in the almost complete disappearance of practices undertaking 'general' legal aid work. The loss of legal aid funding for 'non-specialist' practices (ie firms that can advise and support individuals who have a range of different legal problems) has been mirrored by (and contributed to) the increasing specialisation of law firms and law services.[6]

The consensus today, among contemporary legal professional commentators, appears to be that personal legal problems are 'singular' and that each one calls for a distinct treatment.[7] That when a compound problem is encountered, the only tenable legal approach is to break it down into its elemental parts, and then to compartmentalise their adjudication. The Susskinds,[8] for example, state that 'for any piece of professional work, it is possible to decompose the work into constituent tasks and allocate each task to the most appropriate of the boxes';[9] that problems of this kind should be '*decomposed*, that is, broken down into its constituent "tasks" – identifiable, distinct, and separable modules of work that make it up. Once decomposed the challenge then is to identify the most efficient way of executing each type of task'.[10]

This is an approach first pioneered by Procrustes in Greek mythology, and is the process promoted by 'command and control' theorists. Procrustes was a reasonably unpleasant giant. He ran a remote inn where he offered solitary travellers a rest in his perfect bed: a bed that would fit everyone who used it. Unfortunately, he achieved this by either stretching or 'top and tailing' all those who slept on it. From this we get the word 'Procrustean': an obsession with compartment-alising or putting into separate boxes; a one-size-fits-all approach; the forcing of people to conform to one's own biases; the antithesis of a person-centred problem-solving approach.[11] Procrustes was a frus-trated bureaucrat with a binary approach to what was normal and what was not. If you were too tall or too short, you were 'abnormal' because you didn't fit – but he had a way of making you 'normal'.

'Normal people' may have a legal problem now and then. Once it is resolved, however, they no longer have a legal problem. That is the Procrustean view shared by most public bodies (and probably by most people who do not live with disadvantage). People with clustered problems, however, don't have a single problem, and when one of their problems is resolved they still have problems – and in fact will continue to have problems, so long as they live with disadvantage.

Systems thinking – the importance of recognising interconnectedness

The understandable purpose of breaking down clusters of legal prob-lems into constituent parts is to simplify them, as the 'legal system' is generally incapable of grappling with complex, messy, compound problems. However, if one considers any of the 'pen sketches' of disad-vantage in the appendix at the end of this book, it is difficult to see how a reductionist approach of this kind can actually provide a meaningful resolution for the individuals concerned (even assuming that an array of dedicated legal expert support is on hand to help them).

When describing the basics of 'systems thinking',[12] Anderson and Johnson note that it is human nature, when struggling with an over-whelming problem to 'want to simplify things, create order, and work with one problem at a time'. Although systems thinking doesn't reject this approach, it 'reminds us that simplification, structure, and linear thinking have their limits' – and that this approach can indeed generate as many problems as it resolves.[13]

A systems thinking critique of traditional legal problem solving is fundamental to this book's theoretical analysis. The essence of this critique is captured by Chapman in the following terms:[14]

> The essential aspect of the reductionist approach is that complexity is simplified by dividing a problem into sub-problems or lesser compon-ents. The process of sub-division is continued until the resulting bits are simple enough to be analysed and understood. The operation of

the original complex entity is then reconstructed from the operation of the components. But herein lies a potential problem. What if essential features of that entity are embedded not in the components but in their interconnectedness? What if its complexity arises from the ways in which its components actually relate to and interact with one another? The very act of simplifying by sub-division loses the interconnections and therefore cannot tackle this aspect of complexity.

Systems thinking takes a different approach in cases of complexity. Rather than trying to simplify by breaking down the problem, it advocates 'going up a level of abstraction'[15] or 'zooming out' as the current jargon would have it, and seeing the 'big picture'. As Chapman explains: 'Higher levels of abstraction lose detail, and it is the loss of detail that provides the simplification . . . But the interconnection of the components is largely maintained in the process of abstraction.'[16]

Systems thinking is an approach that is as interested in the cross-cutting interconnections within a cluster of legal problems as it is in the individual legal problems. As noted in the preceding chapter, a reductionist approach that only considers the individual legal 'components' within the cluster, brings with it the danger of distilling or concentrating their inherent biases: legal biases that are generally inimical to the interests of people who live with disadvantage. The compensatory element to these biases is of course the diffuse, cross-cutting notion of 'justice' – and it is this that risks being lost in the reductionist process.

The loss of a 'just' resolution may be an unintended consequence – but it is not an inevitable one. Hard cases do not have to make bad law: hard cases simply pressure-test the resilience of the legal system and its ability to deliver just outcomes. Justice requires that a cluster containing a mass of entangled 'loaded laws' is seen for what it is: a complex mess that requires abstraction – and if needs be, the unlevelling of the green and the unwarping of constitutional space.

Systems thinking requires that we consider factors outside a programme's traditional boundaries. Chapter 4 below, in its consideration of the proliferation of law (juridification) draws on the example (curious as it may seem) of using insecticides to eradicate mosquitos. Faced with the problems caused by mosquitos, spraying them with insecticide makes sense – but only if you consider this to be a 'single discrete' problem and adopt a linear – cause and effect – approach (ie you define the problem simply – as 'How do I get rid of the mosquitoes?'). In practice, such a policy will have unintended consequences 'outside the boundaries' of the programme – environmental problems, for example, such as an explosion of other pests that were previously controlled by the mosquitos; impacts on other species that fed on the mosquitos; the emergence of insecticide-resistant mosquitoes, and so on. Adopting a linear-thinking, reductionist 'simple solution' to a complex, messy problem can be calamitous. Legal change (no matter how well-intentioned) invariably has impacts well outside the 'boundary' of the problem that prompted the change. Changing the law to increase the protection of abused children can result in greater harm[17] and policies designed to reduce the number of snakes can – as the 'cobra effect'[18] suggests – lead to their proliferation.

Where legal change has the potential to impact on those who live with disadvantage, then paradoxically, even if its impetus is (ostensibly) to simplify processes, the result will be an increase in their clustered problems, unless accompanied by significant additional support to manage that change. For example, one need look no further than the implementation of universal credit (which 'simplified' the benefit system by replacing six previous benefits) and the legal aid reforms. As Harris notes,[19] both complexity and simplicity can serve 'justice demands' but one has to be 'suspicious about the effect that simple rules have on complex lives . . . the main effect of imposing basic, common rules will be to help some at the expense of creating hardship for others'.[20]

The reductionism and compartmentalisation that characterises current political approaches to issues such as social welfare and social justice, simplifies by moving the complexity outside the narrow boundary drawn by the policy-maker – and dumping it (together with its attendant unforeseen adverse consequences) in the wasteland inhabited by those who live with disadvantage. In so doing, the state transfers risk to those with the least resilience to cope with it: those with the least cognitive space to manage the complexity and those in most need of the state accepting responsibility for the complex mess it has created.

The decomposition of legal problems described and advocated by legal reductionists is, in many respects, a response to the growing complexity of the law (discussed in the chapter that follows) and the perception that addressing the problems experienced by those who live with disadvantage is not the proper concern of the legal profession.

The end of the decomposition process described by the Susskinds is that the disaggregated problem is then able to be allocated 'to identify the most efficient way of executing each type of task'.[21] The expectation is that this will be digital where possible – routed via an electronic app, or directed to a chatbot; or failing this, to a paralegal[22] factory. In the process, the traditional professional intermediaries will become redundant – or as the Susskinds put it, they will 'be disintermediated'.[23]

This is the mass production approach to legal problem solving – the fragmentation of process: of sweated labour and machines. That said, it may well be an effective way of dealing with divorces, conveyances, contracts and wills. If, however, the problem that arrives at this satanic law mill is an entangled cluster of complex difficulties caused by multiple failures of several social welfare agencies then it will fail: it will fail dramatically and in so doing it will (for the reasons given in the section that follows) almost certainly generate many additional problems to be added to the cluster.

The call centre: reductionism and compartmentalism in action

Many call centres epitomise the reductionist approach to legal problem 'solving'. The process requires that the caller is able to identify and categorise their problem in a way that fits 'the internal departmental requirements':[24] to press '1', or '2' or '3' and so on. A failure to do this results in disconnection, and the need to make a fresh call. In the jargon of systems thinking, this phenomenon is referred to as 'failure demand'. Because the caller did not give (or get) the required answer, they had to make a new call. For those running a call centre, getting more calls is interpreted as evidence of success (of 'demand') – but in objective terms it is evidence of the system's failure. Once the caller makes it through to a call handler, they may then be transferred to another handler as they may have miscategorised their problem: handlers have generally only been trained to use one specific script concerning one specific problem. Each call (even if rejected or redirected) has a target time for being answered, and provided this target is met – it matters not if the caller's problem is resolved. Once the caller has made contact with the correct handler, they are then taken through the set script – and so the process progresses. For each stage there is a service level agreement that stipulates:

> . . . how long it takes to pick up phone or respond to a letter, how many things are done in three, five or however many days. At the same time, they audit the worker's work, assuming this to be 'quality-control'. It is not hard to see that this is a factory view of service work in which managers share the assumptions of their progenitors, that

people need to be commanded and controlled. Scripts, procedures, targets, standards and compliance govern the way the organisation works.[25]

Not infrequently, before a person makes contact with a centre, they have been pressured to use a chatbot and/or to consider a set of 'frequently asked questions' (FAQs), and increasingly, a requirement to download an app. All these systems operate to a standardised reductionist linear model and require the caller to be able to categorise their problem.

John Seddon has written extensively about the reasons why call centres and IT processes consistently fail when confronted by the complex, messy problems of the clustered variety that blight the lives of those who live with disadvantage. In relation to people who are in need of social care support, he describes[26] how when a call or a referral arrives at the call centre, the first question is always 'Is this for us?', and if it is (ie if it is not rejected) the worker then follows a prescribed script – for example, a 'Department of Health – approved assessment tool'. The call handler's purpose is not to try to understand or to help with the person's problem – but rather to get the information necessary to then refer the case to the designated department and then to complete the relevant forms. If the caller manages to cross this hurdle, they are then told that someone will be in touch within a specified period – and 'when this fails there is failure demand – calls asking what is happening'.[27] As noted above, more calls means more demand, which is then interpreted as success. As Seddon demonstrates, this approach makes no practical or economic sense: the 'fragmentation of the work to fit the internal departmental requirements mean that needy people experienced any number of assessments, each requiring answers to much the same questions'.[28]

The systems thinking approach to addressing these problems is to reject simplification by fragmentation and instead 'to go up a level of abstraction'. By analysing the nature of the problems people are experiencing, it is not difficult to conclude that what they want, is to be listened to by someone who can then quickly help them with their need. The crucial importance of this insight is considered in the concluding chapter.

The whole ethos of call centres (like Henry Ford's production line) is to severely curtail (or dispense with) the use of those with a *broad range* of key skills – professionals and others who have acquired expertise through experience. Reductionist approaches can, of course, work well for the relatively simple and the routine – such as making pins, telling you the state of your bank balance, and even filling out probate forms. They are, however, generally disastrous when confronted with 'messes': for example, clusters of interconnected problems 'unbounded in scope, time and resources, and [which] enjoy no clear agreement about what a solution would even look like, let alone how it could be achieved'.[29] In cases of this kind, it makes no sense (practical or economic) for public bodies or other institutions concerned with the delivery of social welfare support to barricade their experts in a backroom – accessible only to 'warrior' mothers, fathers and others with the determination and stamina to break down these barriers.

Silos of control

Making contact with skilled and experienced advisors – important as it is – is not in itself sufficient. People who provide support of this kind must be able to work across institutional boundaries – the boundaries of discrete and competing command and control systems.

Systems boundaries

One way an institution can draw tight programme boundaries is to define (ie restrict) its role in terms of the individual's identity (an issue also considered in the next chapter). In his analysis of the multiple crosscutting and 'common' problems experienced by people living with disadvantage, Corner observes[30] the strong tendency of institutions (public and charitable) to:

> . . . categorise people in separate boxes defined by single issues. So a person who takes drugs to deal with childhood trauma, who falls into offending as a consequence, and loses their home when entering prison acquires three quite distinct labels. Each of these labels triggers a different response from statutory and voluntary systems, different attitudes from the public and media, different theoretical approaches from universities, different prescriptions from policy makers.

At a macro level, it is difficult to see how labelling of this kind can be avoided. The point Corner makes, however, is that even if labelling is inevitable, it is something we need to be aware of, as it has many consequences – not least in the way data is collected, kept separately and not 'joined up'.

For example, someone who contacts a housing department of a local council for help is going to be labelled as 'a person with a housing need'. The extent to which such a label is problematic is determined by the extent to which the department constrains its inter-agency engagement (including its problem-solving responsibilities) – from coal-face to boardroom, but particularly at the coal-face. The more the institution seeks to control the way its frontline staff work, then – from a systems perspective – the more tightly it draws its 'systems boundary'. If staff cannot cross that boundary (even where it makes economic sense for the institution), the greater likelihood there is, that additional problems will be generated and added to that person's cluster. If every department in the local authority adopts similarly constrained systems boundaries, then they can all attempt to locate the person in need's 'problem' on the far side of their responsibility wall.

Systems boundaries can hamper or prevent the resolution of problems, which then adds to a disadvantaged person's cluster of problems. The person made homeless because of his addiction will not be accommodated until he has quit his addiction – but his 'rehab' will be not commence until he is accommodated: feedback loops that generate ever more problems and ever more failure demand. The fact that he is also enmeshed with the criminal justice system and trying to come to terms with an abusive childhood are yet more reasons to place him the in the wastelands beyond the institution's self-defined boundary. Vicious circles of this kind arise where the problem is not a simple linear one of cause and effect, but one where there are potentially 'hundreds of nested feedback loops, which result in significantly non-linear behaviour.'[31]

False economy and blighted lives

In 2016/17 the Cerebra Legal Entitlements and Problem-solving (LEaP)[32] Project undertook research concerning the 'costs/benefits' that result from the award of a disabled facilities grant (DFG):[33] a grant covering the cost of adaptations designed to make a home accessible and safe for a disabled person and the home's other occupants. The research focused on children with autism whose sensory difficulties and attendant behavioural challenges, meant that they needed (among many other things) dedicated quiet space. Without this additional space, many families are unable to cope and in consequence the child is at risk of becoming a 'looked after child' (ie a child in the care of their local authority). The cost to a local authority of accommodating a looked after child with such significant needs is generally considerable – running to £1,000s a week. The research findings were in many respects predictable. DFGs are highly cost-effective: in the study sample, DFG expenditure of £300,000 had led to a saving for the authority of (at the very least) £1.5 million.

Other studies have come up with even more dramatic evidence concerning the cost effectiveness of DFGs.[34] And yet, it is open to question as to whether research of this kind has any impact in terms of increasing the availability of DFGs. Meeting the needs of disabled children and their families is a complex 'messy' problem – that calls for a systems thinking approach – but in practice each and every social welfare need that families have is addressed in reductionist terms. In consequence, families with disabled children are classic examples of people who experience disadvantage and live with clusters of legal problems.

DFGs are paid by a housing department of a local council, and the housing manager's modus operandi are highly controlled – including (among much else) a fixed budget from which these grants can be paid; the use of complex application forms; waiting lists; strict assessment procedures; target times for the processing of applications; and prescribed lists of people who can project manage adaptations (even if the works are straightforward). Awarding a grant from the DFG budget is straightforward 'net expenditure' for the housing department – it makes no savings and derives no financial benefit from the making of such a grant. For the housing department, the process is simple and linear: it has an annual budget and it makes payments to the value of the budget over a 12-month period – after which it will have another budget to spend, and so on. If it gets more applications than it can fund from its budget, it operates a waiting list (even though this is legally impermissible[35]) – deferring awards until the next financial year. The fact that the making of a grant is likely to save another department (eg the children's services department) at least five times the value of the grant, is of no benefit to the housing manager, whose job depends on 'staying within budget' – as an officer in research by O'Flynn et al put it: 'Who got promoted for putting their own Agency's future second?'[36] This saving is a 'loop-back' in the systems programme: a saving that would be recorded in the accounts, if the systems boundary encircled the *whole authority* – but in general the boundaries are not drawn that way. Even if the systems boundary enveloped the whole authority – it would still fail to account for the savings made to the NHS and criminal justice systems (which are potentially no less substantial) – and of course the devastating impact on the child, the parents, the child's siblings[37] and so on.

There are indeed many other systems loops and perverse incentives. The consequence of authorities categorising this as a simple linear problem – rather than recognising it as the complex and messy problem that it is – impact directly on families creating clusters of problems and blighted lives. The fact that such an approach is also economic madness for the authority and the UK plc – makes this all the more depressing: it is the worst of all worlds.

Inter-agency working and compartmentalising needs

Valuable contextual detail that illuminates the above analysis can be found in a research paper by Cornes et al[38] which considered inter-agency working in relation to the needs of people who were homeless and experiencing 'other facets of deep social exclusion'.

On first contact with a person in this position, the housing officer undertook an assessment of their needs for support to enable them to manage a tenancy (eg securing benefits, paying bills, complying with the terms of the tenancy etc) as well as any need to be referred for 'specialist help with matters such as drugs, alcohol and their own mental health'. However, as the research paper notes:

> Once referrals to other agencies have been made, each agency develops its own 'holistic' support plan, which is rarely shared with other agencies. Each agency sees itself as at the centre and invests some effort in coordinating activities.[39]

This 'compartmentalising needs' approach inevitably creates a number of problems for the individual.[40] Although the housing support workers felt obliged to 'hand over responsibility for the "drink problem", "the drug problem" or the "mental health problem", because these were areas perceived to be outside their professional expertise' they considered this to be particularly problematic as when a crisis arose they found themselves isolated and – in effect – having to pick up the collective pieces.

The research questioned whether the motivation for 'referring on' to other agencies was done in order to meet a disciplinary or 'specialist expertise' need,[41] as these invariably resulted in a number of negatives – for example, they triggered 'many additional veins of assessment and care management and so-called "sign-posting"' and a great deal of duplication in terms of the information being required during these processes – notwithstanding that they purported to be 'holistic' and 'person-centered'.[42] They also added to the case-load pressures of those to whom the referrals were being made.

The research paper provides a clear analysis of the multiple problems that frustrate homeless people who experience deep social exclusion and who seek help from a housing department. To reverse the metaphor of this chapter, they are the pinballs in the pinball machine thrown down the 'shooter alley toward a maze of ramps, bumpers, and traps':[43] ricocheting between the flippers of the mental health and the addiction teams, repulsed by the social security pop bumpers, diverted by the criminal justice playfield magnets – and repeatedly deflected from their goal of attaining a tenancy.

While the paper's description of the system's failure to address the needs of homeless people is convincing, its analysis of what needs to change in consequence is less compelling. This is hardly a criticism – given the complex and messy nature of the clustered problems that people in this situation bring with them when they seek help from the housing department.

The report's authors' conclusions are, in essence, two-fold. The first is a fairly standard cri de coeur for cultural change at 'the very highest levels' to ensure that the specialist organisations work together, share services and costs, and reduce duplication – and a technical fix in terms of adopting standardised assessment tools and more generous eligibility criteria for those in need of support. The second conclusion concerns the need to upskill (and raise the status / confidence of) housing support workers. Both these mechanisms are considered further in the concluding chapter, in the context of effective ways of supporting those who experience clustered injustice. In general terms, however, of the first proposal – it should be said that exhortations of this kind appeared in the Minority Report on the Poor Law in 1909,[44] and have been repeated at regular intervals since that time. While this is not in itself evidence that it is incapable of being an 'operationalised' – incredibly sensible initiatives of this kind, sadly, have a troubled track record.

On the face of it, the second proposal (the upskilling and the raising of the status of housing support workers) would appear to have a greater prospect of providing homeless people with the mean-ingful practical support that they require. Curiously, however, having questioned the value of many of the 'referrals' that such workers felt obliged to make, the research rejected the idea of creating generic care workers[45] and suggested instead[46] a conceptual shift from multi-professional to a non-hierarchical and collegiate inter-professional way of working.

End note

The analysis in this chapter should not be seen as a generalised attack on reductionist approaches to problem-solving. Reductionism works well in many legal contexts and provides a degree of certainty concerning process and outcomes, that is often of vital importance – for example, in relation to commercial transactions and (arguably) the application of criminal law. The point that this chapter, and succeeding chapters, highlight is simply that it is an approach that has its limitations: that in certain contexts its routine application can generate and perpetuate profound injustices (and cause significant collateral harm to public bodies that operate systems of this kind). The adverse impacts of such an approach affects a significant portion of the population: the experience of clustered injustice is not a rare phenomenon (as demonstrated by the pen sketches in the appendix at the end of this book).

In many respects the systems failure at the centre of this analysis results from the state's inability to distinguish between the simple and the complex, and its failure to support the institutions and mechanisms capable of addressing problems of the latter kind – multiple, entangled, messy legal problems. The succeeding chapters consider what effective organisational responses to such challenges might look like.

CHAPTER 4

Juridification and identity laws

Let no one, therefore, expect from us a complete history and theory of the Glass Bead Game. Even authors of higher rank and competence than ourself would not be capable of providing that at the present time. That task must remain reserved to later ages, if the sources and the intellectual prerequisites for the task have not previously been lost. Still less is our essay intended as a text book of the Glass Bead Game; indeed, no such thing will ever be written. The only way to learn the rules of this Game of games is to take the usual prescribed course, which requires many years; and none of the initiates could ever possibly have any interest in making those rules easier to learn.

The Glass Bead Game, Hermann Hesse (p18)

Overview

This chapter considers the complexity of the legal system – which those living with disadvantage must navigate on a daily basis. It is a mass of law – both in terms of its volume and its density – dominated by 'legal process' provisions: procedural hurdles to be crossed before essential social welfare and social justice entitlements can be accessed. Each administrative obstacle creates the potential for a new legal problem: a new need for advice; a new episode for a complaint; a new opportunity for delay. The harm that results from this escalating complexity calls into question not only the validity of the processes that shield these (increasingly degraded) rights, but also the value of some of the 'rights' themselves.

The discussion that follows is premised on the assumption that even if legal complexity of this kind is inevitable in the 21st century, it must be underpinned by a recognition that this is a state-generated phenomenon – and with this recognition, an acceptance that the state is responsible for addressing its consequences. The compensatory measures required of the state are considered in greater detail in the concluding chapter.

There is little doubt that 'process heavy' social welfare law is proliferating. In terms of volume, the total number of pages of UK Acts and statutory instruments (ie regulations, statutory rules and orders) more than doubled between 1986 and 2016.[1] Of the five departments of state most responsible for this increase,[2] three are in the business of creating legal rules that significantly impact on the lives of many people living with disadvantage – the Department of Work and Pensions; the Ministry of Justice; and the Home Office –

regulating, as they do, issues concerning social security, immigration, legal aid, and civil and criminal 'justice'.[3]

Although efforts have been made to curtail the UK's growing statute book – particularly to remove 'unnecessary burdens on citizens and businesses'[4] – it is an open question as to whether these initiatives have in mind those who experience disadvantage. For people in need of state-funded social welfare support, for example, the trend has been one of growing conditionality and complexity: increasingly intricate eligibility criteria, means testing and 'targeting'.

Law has always had its 'own queer, technical language' and has for many been an 'unchartable fourth-dimensional space . . . like Alice's Looking-Glass'.[5] It has, however, become steadily more incomprehensible to non-specialists (and, indeed, many specialists) – particularly in relation to its regulation of social welfare entitlements. Legal complexity per se does not undermine the well-being of those who live with disadvantage, indeed it may be even advantageous in some fields of social welfare law[6] – the harm is caused when the state fails to take responsibility for managing the complexity, when it seeks to transfer that responsibility to the individual.

This chapter considers two closely connected phenomena that have, over the last 50 years, significantly increased the potential for people living with disadvantage to accumulate clusters of legal problems. Both can claim to have been motivated by admirable considerations of social justice – but in both cases, they have generated a degree of legal complexity that has almost certainly undermined that honourable purpose.

The first concerns *juridification*: the sheer amount of 'law' that regulates the lives of the disadvantaged – the 'sharp legal things'[7] that those experiencing disadvantage are forever bumping into. The second concerns the growth in *identity-based rights*. Both phenomena are (as this chapter explains) symptomatic of a political outlook that is closely allied with 'neoliberalism': a broad and ill-defined concept but, for the purposes of this analysis, one that has been characterised as a 'transnational political project aiming to remake the nexus of market, state, and citizenship from above'.[8]

Juridification

Juridification[9] (like neoliberalism) is a contested concept – but broadly it refers to the proliferation of law: both in terms of its volume and its 'reach'. It is a phenomenon that serves several purposes and is not simply a response to the growth in populations and wealth, or the increasingly complex nature of social relations, technology and 'business'. Juridification is essentially a political process by which the law is used to colonise and reshape social norms and attitudes – and one that can relocate troubling issues from the overt political domain – into an ostensibly independent and technical space: the zone of law.[10] In relation to the social welfare rights of particular importance to people living with disadvantage, juridification in its 'liberal-capitalist legal form'[11] has done much to reframe these rights – as rights to 'process' rather than to substance: to independent judges and the adherence of prescribed 'rules' – a form of social justice to be judged solely in terms of the evenness of the playing field.

The use of law to legitimise the contemporary political status quo is not new, but it is a process that capitalism has adopted with vigour – a process that:

> . . . enables laws to appear to be universal and fixed, independent of historical conjuncture and political will, and legal decisions to appear to be technical matters of the interpretation of universal and fixed legal texts in a very formalist sense.[12]

De Shaney v Winnebago County case

Laurence Tribe's critique of an infamous 1989 US Supreme Court judgment[13] provides an arresting and relevant account of the harm that can result from juridification. The case concerned a young child (Joshua) who was so severely and repeatedly beaten by his father that he suffered profound brain injuries. Although the Winnebago County social services authorities were regularly informed about the violence and although they 'kept meticulous, bureaucratically rational records of the child's injuries, they did not lift a finger to help him'.[14] In due course, proceedings were taken against the social services authorities to compensate Joshua for his injuries. The Supreme Court (by a majority) rejected the claim, pointing out that the harm he had suffered was inflicted by his father and not by the social services authorities.

In condemning the court's reasoning, Tribe attacks the suggestion that the social services authorities were detached and in no way legally entangled in the 'sometimes unpleasant natural world, in which the abuse of children is an unfortunate, yet external, ante-legal and pre-political fact of our society'.[15] The reality was that laws protecting children from abuse *changed* the way bystanders behaved: changed what Tribe refers to as 'constitutional space',[16] so that instead of neighbours intervening directly to protect Joshua, the state had created an alternative 'normal': a requirement that suspected abuse had to be reported to the social services authorities. As Tribe argues, the law had effectively warped the legal landscape and deflected the assistance that would otherwise have been available to Joshua.[17]

Abstracting this analysis, Tribe notes that although we are all 'engulfed by, and dependent upon, the structure of the law', we are not all 'rendered equally vulnerable by it'. This unequal vulnerability is, in Tribe's opinion, of central relevance as to 'how the law's shape should be understood': that the social space we occupy has been warped by legal rules and so it is simply not possible for the state to extract itself from responsibility for the 'helplessness of the most vulnerable'[18] regardless of whether that person finds themselves in the public or the private 'sphere'.[19]

The dissenting Supreme Court judgments suggested that it was conceivable that the child protection laws in this case had actually made Joshua *worse off*, because of the failure of the authorities to discharge their responsibilities.[20] This is an issue of importance in the discussion that follows: whether ostensibly benign laws can in fact have a malign impact on people experiencing disadvantage – not only because the necessary support is absent (for example, because of inadequate funding) but also because protections of this kind may have a disproportionately negative impact on people who live with disadvantage and clustered problems.

The juridification of decision-making – case examples

In the UK, the steady increase in 'adult dependency' over the last 35 years[21] has been mirrored by a steady decline in state-funded social care support for elderly, ill and disabled people, and their carers.[22] These cuts to central government social care funding support have had an adverse impact on significant numbers of people who have impaired capacity to make decisions,[23] particularly so in relation to domiciliary care – care to enable people to live independent lives in the community. This has led to a market failure in this sector[24] with the consequence that many people with impaired mental capacity have ended up – in effect – imprisoned within their own homes or institutionalised in care homes and/or hospital wards. The fact that this state of affairs often results in greater expense to the public purse, is simply an unintended consequence: a 'feedback loop' in the complex system that is 'community care'.

In 'systems thinking' terms, a logical response to the increasing need of disabled and older people for support would be to focus on the demand within the system – rather than trying to manage the costs – a point discussed further in the concluding chapter. However, this is not an approach favoured by more recent administrations. When confronted by a social welfare dilemma of this kind, their preferred option has been to enact laws: laws laden with process-heavy 'rights'. And this is exactly the approach that has been taken in relation to the independent living rights of people with impaired mental capacity.

The Bournewood gap

In the example that follows, the story starts in 1997 with a case that is not, in its essentials, about cost-savings but everything to do with the unintended consequences of juridification.

On Tuesday 22 July 1997, a psychiatrist at Bournewood Hospital in Surrey decided to informally detain 'HL', a 48-year-old man with autism and significant learning disabilities. Although HL had spent over 30 years in the same hospital, he had lived for the previous three years in the home of two 'untrained' but dedicated carers.[25] On HL's detention, the hospital denied the carers access to him, and their request that he be allowed to return to live with them was rejected – even though (as the Health Service Ombudsman later concluded) objectively he had a 'significantly better quality of life with them' and it was 'difficult to see why . . . he was not discharged' to their care the following day'.[26] The psychiatric team decided, at an early stage, that there was no need to formally detain HL under the Mental Health Act 1983 as he had impaired mental capacity and was 'compliant' (albeit heavily medicated). In consequence, the team decided that he should be 'informally detained' (under the common law). This meant that there was no effective way for the third parties to challenge his detention (a failing that came to be known as the 'Bournewood gap'). Seven years later, the European Court of Human Rights found unanimously that HL's detention had been unlawful.

The hospital's decision not to formally detain HL under the 1983 Act, probably took – at most – a few minutes to reach. The consequences have (so far[27]) included two major 'deprivation of liberty' (DoL) Acts (with voluminous schedules),[28] extensive statutory instruments, statutory codes and guidance, court rules, an explosion in litigation, an army of social work 'best interests assessors' and advocates, and a cost that can be measured in billions of pounds.[29] Yet a 2014 House of Lords review of the legislative response to the case concluded that the response was 'not fit for purpose' and indeed had not even closed the 'Bournewood gap'.[30]

The point being that the government's reaction to the complex and multiple problems confronting HL and his carers was apply a 'patch' to resolve a technical legal problem. It was not to 'abstract up' and consider the entirety of the system that enveloped HL: his disadvantage; his need to be free from a heavily medicated incarceration; his need for multiple inputs from many agencies to maximise his potential for independent living; his carers' need to challenge his detention – and to safeguard his well-being by negotiating with two (not always co-operative) agencies (social services and the NHS) as well as satisfying the care regulator and to secure his social security entitlements – and so on.

In 2011 (three years before the House of Lords report) evidence emerged concerning the scandalous ill-treatment of people with similar impairments to HL at Winterbourne View (a private hospital).[31] In theory, the patients had the benefit of the mass of law and regulatory structures designed to protect them, including those enacted as a consequence of the *HL* judgment.[32] However – and with strong echoes of Joshua's case, above – the authorities had been notified by third parties of the abuse but had taken no action.[33] In this case (as with Joshua's), despite the abundance of law designed to address these failings, there had been a systems failure to actually protect the individuals. A firm commitment by the government in 2012 that everyone inappropriately in such placements would be moved to community-based support by no later than June 2014 came to nothing,[34] and in 2019 a further scandal came to light at a similar hospital (Whorlton Hall):[35] abuse that had (again) not been picked up by the regulatory bodies despite concerns raised by a whistle-blower.[36]

The point about these cases is that government responses – a proliferation of laws, statutory protection processes and policies – came at great cost, and came at time when the public bodies charged with implementing these policies were making unprecedented cutbacks in terms of the basic care and support needs of those for whom the safeguarding laws are ostensibly directed: people whose care and support needs could have been funded for a fraction of the cost required to sustain the specialist social work and health assessors, the advocates, the lawyers, the court fees, the judges – the bloated apparatus of the law. These responses were political, and designed to demonstrate firmness of purpose, commitment, 'robust' action and so on. Their real purpose, however, was to relocate troubling issues from the overt political domain – into an ostensibly independent and technical space of the law. These problems were caused, not by a lack of law, but by a social welfare systems failure.

The primary reason that legal responses of this kind fail, is not down to a lack of resources (as the above analysis makes plain, these systems are hugely expensive and wasteful): they fail because they treat the system as simple and linear – when it is, in fact, complex, entangled and 'messy'.

Unintended consequences

Legal responses of this kind, purportedly designed to safeguard individuals, ultimately create tortuously complex systems that demonstrably fail in the safeguarding stakes. At a micro scale, the cumulative result of the plethora of processes is the creation of yet more clusters of legal problems to exacerbate the disadvantage of the individuals they are designed to protect. Action of this kind bears an uncanny resemblance to Rachel Carson's 1962 environmental science book, *Silent spring*. In response to an insect problem at Clear Lake in California, a DDT-type pesticide chemical was applied for many years. At the end of this period, the initial problem remained but the unintended adverse environmental costs were found to be truly shocking. Similarly with the Bournewood gap: as a result of a problematic gap in the law, a DoL type law was brought into force and applied for many years. Yet at the end of this period, the initial problem still remained (of individuals being incarcerated unnecessarily and without adequate protection) but the unintended economic costs of the resulting process were demonstrably staggering.

The use of DDT to address the insect problem at Clear Lake and DoLs to address the Bournewood gap are both classic examples of systems failure. In each case the problem was seen as simple (an infection; a legal difficulty) and linear 'solutions' were adopted – spraying to kill the insects, legal process to regularise the detention. However, in both cases, the problems were complex 'messes' not simple difficulties.[37]

Lawful process v just outcome

In relation to the specific example of legislation concerning people considered to lack requisite mental capacity, the proliferation of laws regulating the making of substitute decisions on their behalf can be seen as a direct response to the reduction in state social welfare funding. The deeper the cuts to the substance of social care support (to personal care, supported housing, to welfare entitlements etc), the steeper has been the growth in legal 'process' rights.

A 2016 High Court case[38] that illustrates the vacuous nature of these legal 'process' rights, concerned a challenge[39] to the incarceration of a disabled man with autism, significant learning disabilities, physical and sensory impairments. He had been living in a wholly unsuitable local authority funded flat for many years – which was too small for his wheelchair, such that he had to pull himself along the floor and as a result suffered painful bursitis and leg calluses. The High Court held that it was effectively powerless to decide on the substance of the disabled person's care package[40] – its role was limited to determining whether the *process* that led to his detention in the flat was lawful (which it was). The disabled person was at best a bystander in his own case: a case that had involved 12 hearings over a period of five years, with the estimated costs exceeding £230,000.[41]

Increased costs, increased misery

The extraordinary legal cost of these 'process heavy' mental capacity laws was the focus of a 2014 High Court judgment.[42] It concerned two cases which Mr Justice Peter Jackson considered to be illustrative and in no way exceptional. One had lasted 18 months and incurred legal fees of £140,000; the other had taken five years at a cost of £530,000. The judge referred to the 'human misery' caused by the legal process, as well as the drain on the time and energy of social work and medical professionals. In his opinion, there was a danger that 'we become habituated to . . . "this madness", and that we admire the problem instead of eliminating it'.

This, with respect, misses the point. The very *purpose* of the juridification in this field of social welfare rights, is that 'we' do become habituated to this madness – and that we do learn to admire the problem instead of eliminating it. Eliminating it would – as discussed in the concluding chapter – call for far-reaching change: a change, where we reframe the problem as *political*, not legal. Where we reverse the liberal-capitalist legal formulation of the problem as one of 'process' and identify the problem for what it is – a profound failure of substance – where social justice is not a playing field game.

Juridification and the proliferation of identity rights

During the last 50 years, many 'rights-based' laws have been enacted that might appear incongruous to those unsympathetic to the neoliberal project. One significant example concerns the proliferation of laws prohibiting identity-based discrimination: laws making it unlawful to treat people less favourably because of their 'protected characteristic'. Laws of this nature have been characterised as an example of what has come to be termed 'progressive neoliberalism'.[43] Legislation that clothes the unpleasant exploitive and extractive elements of neoliberal economic policy with ideals such as diversity and empowerment: a progressive politics of recognition that talks 'the talk of diversity, multiculturalism, and women's rights, even while preparing to walk the walk of Goldman Sachs'.[44]

Examples of progressive legislation of this nature are not limited to the realm of non-discrimination law. In relation to social welfare provision, for example, claims by disability groups for cash payments (rather than state-commissioned services) as well as for greater choice and control over health and social care support have, of late, been readily conceded by English right-of-centre governments as they go with the neoliberal 'grain' – advancing as they do the privatisation of welfare state provision, commodification and responsibilisation.[45]

Regardless of the conscious or unconscious motives of such policies, there is no doubting that: (1) many people experiencing disadvantage (and their representative organisations) have actively campaigned for laws that prohibit unfavourable treatment for reasons associated with, for example, race, sex, disability and sexual orientation; and (2) identity-based non-discrimination legislation has proved to be complex (putting it mildly).

Non-discrimination law plays a significant role in addressing prejudicial behaviour and beliefs. As the Race Relations Board stated in its first Annual Report in 1967, law of this kind:[46]

• is an unequivocal declaration of public policy;
• gives support to those who do not wish to discriminate, but who feel compelled to do so by social pressure;
• gives protection and redress to minority groups;
• provides for the peaceful and orderly adjustment of grievances and the release of tensions;
• reduces prejudice by discouraging the behaviour in which prejudice finds expression.

Without in any way questioning the validity of this statement and the objectives of such laws, it important to appreciate their limitations – particularly in respect of their impact on those who live with disadvantage and for whom legal problems do not come singly. Although anti-discrimination law has an incredibly important role in combatting prejudicial behaviour and beliefs, it does not, of itself, address substantive disadvantage. Unfortunately, in the fanfare accompanying its enactment, this fact is often overlooked – providing an opportunity for exploitation at the overtly political level.

The fragmentation of identities

The Race Relations Act 1965 was the first UK statute to prohibit discrimination based on a protected characteristic. Further statutes followed,[47] such that, at the time of writing (August 2020) the Equality Act 2010 list of protected characteristics[48] comprises: age; disability; gender reassignment; marriage and civil partnership; pregnancy and maternity; race; religion or belief; sex; and sexual orientation. There is, however, considerable pressure for the list to be extended – for example, to include 'characteristics' such as: poverty;[49] obesity;[50] genetic identity;[51] former prisoners;[52] and carers.[53]

At the same time, the existing 'protected characteristics' have been progressively *fragmented* – such that adverse treatment based on a person's sex is now to be considered not only in its own right, but is also now to be articulated in terms of gender reassignment; marriage and civil partnership; pregnancy and maternity; sexual orientation, L, G, B, T, Q, I and A. It is then to be classified in *intersectional* terms: the multiple or compound nature of the discrimination – for example, being a black women or being a parent carer, an adult carer, a young carer, a former carer, a young adult carer, an LGBTQIA carer, and so on. Then the *justifications* for adverse treatment need to be separately analysed, as legally they differ depending on whether that treatment concerns race or sex, or one of the less protected characteristics such as age or religion. Then the *nature* of the adverse treatment needs to be categorised in terms of whether it is direct, indirect or associative – or arising from disability; or reverse discrimination; or to be characterised as harassment or victimisation. The language of anti-discrimination law has grown in complexity – like the Tower of Babel – to the point that it has become unintelligible to those for whom the edifice was theoretically constructed. Put simply, the Race Relations Act 1965 was seven pages long – the Equality Act 2010 runs to 251.

Many people whose characteristics are recognised and protected by anti-discrimination laws live with disadvantage, and many experience clusters of legal problems – but many do not. There is therefore a danger in these identity categories becoming 'proxies through which we articulate and understand social inequalities such as poverty and other forms of social disadvantages'.[54] Nevertheless, it is instructive to analyse the extent to which legal recognition can be an effective mechanism in addressing 'poverty and other forms of social disadvantages'.

The analysis that follows considers this question from the perspective of 'carers'. The evidence concerning the clustered injustice experienced by many carers is stark (an overview of the evidence is provided in the appendix at the end of this book). In the opinion of the UN Special Rapporteur on extreme poverty and human rights:[55] 'it is hard to think of a human right that is not potentially affected in some way by the unequal distribution and difficulty of unpaid care work'.

Carers and the failure of identity

In 1963, the Rev Mary Webster felt compelled to give up work to care for her elderly parents and was outraged at the consequent disadvantage she experienced.[56] Shortly thereafter, she founded the 'National Council for the Single Woman and Her Dependents' – an act that many regard as the point of departure (nationally and internationally) for the carers movement.

Mary Webster articulated her disadvantage in terms of her identity – that as a single 'dutiful daughter'[57] she was expected to give up work to care for her elderly parents and as a consequence to cope with the 'financial hardship of loss of income and the prospect of poverty in her own old age'.

Since that time, many carers' organisations have campaigned for the legal recognition of unpaid carers, albeit no longer simply confined to single dutiful daughters. In taking this route, they have followed a path that has led many disadvantaged groups to a much better place.

It is, however, questionable whether self-identifying with a legally defined 'protected characteristic' has the potential to take carers (or indeed other disadvantaged groups) to a 'socially just' destination: in the case of carers, for example, a destination where they are not pressured to fulfil this role – but, where they so choose to do so, they do not in consequence experience multi-dimensional and severe disadvantage.

Identity and recognition

The idea that identity has an objective dimension that may be in stark contrast to the subjective, is no great revelation: I realise that to others I look like an old man, but I seldom think of myself in that way. There is an extensive literature on 'self and identity',[58] as there is on the widespread failure of people who care unpaid to self-identify as carers.[59] As Carers UK notes: 'Despite the large number of people providing care, many who take on caring responsibilities simply do not see themselves as carers':[60] a group that has come to be referred to as 'hidden carers'[61] – namely carers who do not self-identify as carers or who are not recognised as carers by professionals and/or the community.

Putting to one side for the moment, the fact that carers' organisations have spent much time and energy in seeking and gaining state recognition of 'carers' as a distinct status, one has to ask, why the widespread failure of carers to 'self-identify' is considered to be a problem? The answer most readily advanced is that unless carers adopt this identity, they will be unable to unlock the (generally meagre) socio-economic legal entitlements that the law has reserved for them.

O'Connor, for example, notes that a key benefit of identifying as a carer is 'the increased ease with which services could be accessed and utilized';[62] Carers UK states that if you don't see yourself as 'a carer' you will be 'missing out on vital support';[63] and Knowles et al refer to the barriers that prevented a carer 'from identifying as a carer which in turn hindered access to support'.[64] The point being that in many cases it is the law that dictates the identity, not the individual: a situation that Habermas has referred to a 'life-world colonisation' where individuals 'seem to be obliged to define themselves and their life-situation in service system terms and to adapt to service system conditions'.[65]

Carer recognition statutes

Carers have been legally identified for centuries. In England and Wales, the Poor Relief Act 1601 placed a duty on family members to care for their relations[66] and 'liable family rules' of this kind are still to be found in many, if not most, states in the world.[67] It is, however, only in the last 50 years that that provisions have been enacted that frame 'carer recognition' in positive terms – where certain social welfare rights are reserved for those identified as qualifying 'carers'.

The UK's Carers (Recognition and Services) Act 1995 (the world's first 'carer recognition' statute) resulted from a concerted campaign by the Carers National Association (formed in 1988 and renamed Carers UK in 2001).[68] The Act had UK-wide application, and like so many of its subsequent iterations, its focus was on 'process'. Carers[69] were entitled to request an assessment of their needs – but there was no duty on the state to provide them with any support in consequence. Carer-specific statutes[70] and non-statutory 'strategies'[71] have since been enacted in many other jurisdictions.

Most such provisions contain little or nothing of substance for carers: in legal terms they are 'empty vessels' – or indeed flags of considerable convenience for states. They placate carers with the opiate of recognition, crown bestowing states with a virtuous halo and not infrequently mask an ulterior motive. The US model statute – the Caregiver Advise, Record, Enable (CARE) Act [72] – is a case in point. It is a 'recognition' statute that focuses on the 'critical role that family caregivers play in keeping their loved ones out of hospitals'.[73] It provides for a designated family caregiver in the medical record and requires that person to understand 'the medical tasks – such as wound care, injections, medication management' that they 'will perform at home'.[74] The purpose is reasonably plain – namely, to shift responsibility for long-term care (and associated risk) onto unpaid carers. It is little wonder that so many states[75] have been willing to enact this statute, given that in the US '1 of every 8 Medicare beneficiary who leaves the hospital is readmitted in 30 days' and the Medicare cost of avoidable hospital admissions amounts to $17.8 billion.[76]

Mary Webster, as noted above, articulated her disadvantage in terms of discrimination: her adverse treatment on the grounds of being single and female – that she belonged to a category of people on whom the duty to care for parents tended to fall. Webster framed her disadvantage in what we came (25 years later) to express as 'intersectional'.[77] Her campaign was directed at legal change, and in 1967 the law was amended to provide for a dependant relative tax allowance for single women with family caring responsibilities.[78] In due course, this also resulted in a compensatory social security payment (the invalid care allowance[79]) for (among others) unmarried women who cared for their relatives.

Ten years later, Jacqueline Drake gave up work to look after her disabled mother and also, as a consequence, experienced financial hardship. Like Webster, she articulated her disadvantage in terms of discrimination: of being female – but (unlike Webster) she was married and not therefore entitled to the invalid care allowance. Since 'not being single' was not a protected status, the European Court of Justice (ECJ) had to articulate her claim in terms of unlawful sex discrimination – which it did in 1986.[80] Of course, this did not directly address the socio-economic disadvantage that married carers experienced. The UK government could have removed the discriminatory treatment by simply abolishing the invalid care allowance altogether – a course of action it did indeed consider.[81]

Having achieved legal recognition, carers' organisations turned their attention to entrenching this by establishing carers as a group protected in non-discrimination law. An attempt to do this via a private member's bill in 2004[82] was unsuccessful (although other provisions relating to carers did progress when the bill became law as the Carers (Equal Opportunities) Act 2004).

Shortly before the 2004 Act came into force, Sharon Coleman left her employment with a legal firm and submitted a claim that she had been constructively dismissed. Sharon, who cared for her disabled child, argued that she had been treated less favourably than employees with non-disabled children and had been subjected to conduct that created a hostile atmosphere for her.[83] The claim was referred to the ECJ for a preliminary ruling on the interpretation of the 2000 EU Equality Directive.[84] Although Sharon was not a disabled person, she argued that the Directive protected non-disabled employees treated less favourably by reason of the disability of their child, for whom they were the primary care provider.[85] Her claim succeeded, and discrimination of this kind is now generally referred to as 'associative' discrimination.[86]

The 2008 ECJ judgment of *Coleman v Attridge Law*[87] was heralded as a 'radical' legal milestone for carers[88] and received widespread attention in the European press,[89] establishing as it did, the right for carers in the European Union (EU) to challenge their adverse treatment.

2019 research[90] assessed the extent to which the *Coleman* principle has been applied in French, Italian, Spanish, English and Welsh legal decisions in the 10-year period after the judgment (ie 2008–2018). In these six nations (with a total population of over 315 million and upwards of 58 million carers[91]) there were only seven 'carer related' cases where this principle was found to have been cited.

In similar vein, a search of the European Court of Human Rights' database (HUDOC) using the words 'carer' and 'caregiver' reveals only five cases where carers have made complaints which have to a greater or lesser degree, touched upon their caring roles.[92] Five cases from a potential pool of applicants numbering over 800 million[93] and a database of over 20,000 judgments.[94]

It is also significant that a quarter century since the enactment of the Carers (Recognition and Services) Act 1995, the overall well-being of carers in the UK remains far from satisfactory. As the pen sketches in the appendix at the end of this book make clear, the disadvantage experienced by many carers in the UK remains severe: disadvantage that includes poverty, poor physical and mental health and clustered legal problems arising out of difficulties remaining in paid work,[95] difficulties with debts,[96] difficulties accessing healthcare[97] and social care[98] – both for themselves and for the person(s) for whom they care.

Identity recognition and anti-discrimination legislation – wider analysis

The evidence about the poor effectiveness of 'recognition' and anti-discrimination legislation in addressing the severe disadvantage experienced by many carers is mirrored in studies concerning other disadvantaged groups that have obtained formal recognition in anti-discrimination legislation.

Over 40 years ago, David Freeman argued that the principal failure of anti-discrimination legislation was one of perspective. Rather than contesting the negative lived experiences of the victim, it was 'hopelessly embedded in the perpetrator perspective'.[99] It was, in his opinion, 'indifferent' to the experience of victims: indifferent to their disadvantage; indifferent to the 'objective conditions' of their lives – and of their clustered problems caused by 'lack of jobs, lack of money, lack of housing and the consciousness associated with those objective conditions – lack of choice and lack of human individuality'.[100] Instead of focusing on these broad, pervasive and negative experiences, anti-discrimination law simply sought to identify fault and causation: to 'separate from the masses of society those blameworthy individuals who are violating the otherwise shared norm'.[101] In effect, anti-discrimination law simply sought to disaggregate, simplify and adjudicate: to legally categorise discrimination 'not as a social phenomenon, but merely as the misguided conduct of particular actors': its viewpoint is of a world 'where, but for the conduct of these misguided ones, the system of equality of opportunity would work to provide a [fair] distribution of the good things in life'.[102]

Samuel Bagenstos's research[103] concerning the failure of the Americans with Disabilities Act (ADA) 1990 to address the backdrop of structural inequality that frames the lives of many disabled people, adds a practical dimension to Freeman's critique. He describes how the enactment of the ADA 1990 'raised expectations that large numbers of people with disabilities would leave the benefits rolls and enter the workforce' – but his research demonstrates that the Act 'had little, if any, positive effect on the overall employment of people with disabilities', despite it coinciding with a positive economic period in the US. In his opinion, even if one accepts the 'data presented by the statute's most optimistic supporters; the employment provisions of the ADA 1990 have done absolutely nothing to give jobs to the overwhelming majority of people with disabilities'.

Bagenstos's analysis comes to a similar conclusion to Freeman's – namely that governments 'must do more than simply mandate that individual employers cease discriminating and provide accommodations'. Governments 'must adopt more direct and sustained interventions such as the public funding and provision of benefits'. In effect, that *radical social welfare interventions* and not anti-discrimination legislation are the most effective ways of redressing the disadvantage experienced by so many disabled people.

Dean Spade has provided one of the most powerful modern critiques of legal recognition and equality strategies as mechanisms to address disadvantage (specifically from the perspective of the rights of transgender and gender non-conforming people).[104] He argues that 'reconsideration-and-inclusion-focused law reforms' have had 'little impact on the daily lives of the people they purportedly protect'[105] and that instead, there is a need to critically analyse the 'laws and policies that produce systemic norms and regularities that make trans people's lives administratively impossible'.[106] In language that calls to mind the dissenting opinion of Judge Pettiti in *Buckley v UK* (1996)[107] Spade points to the importance of analysing 'how the norms that produce conditions of disparity . . . emerge from multiple, interwoven locations'.[108] For Spade, 'meaningful transformation will not occur through pronouncements of equality from various government institutions' – indeed that for some emergent social groups, 'declarations of universal rights often actually mask and perpetuate and disparity faced by those groups'.[109]

'Vulnerability theory' also questions the potential for anti-discrimination laws to materially advance social justice. For Fineman, 'the trick is how to effect a turn away, not from law, but from identities to institutional structures',[110] and not to fragment 'the legal subject along multiple axes of identity characteristics'.[111] In consequence, she has called for a 'post-identity' inquiry: one that 'is not focused only on discrimination against defined groups, but concerned with privilege and favour conferred on limited segments of the population by the state and broader society through their institution'. Fineman calls for an approach that would take the legal response 'beyond the stifling confines of current discrimination-based models toward a more substantive vision of equality':[112] beyond the process of 'clustering individuals according to one or two characteristics' which then 'become proxies', masking the reality that disadvantage is spread across the whole population.

Vulnerability theory underpins the critiques advanced by Freeman, Bagenstos, Spade and others: that 'it is not multiple identities that intersect to produce compounded inequalities . . . but rather systems of power and privilege that interact to produce webs of advantages and disadvantages'.[113] For Fineman, 'just as privilege is not tethered to identity neither is disadvantage. Vulnerability is universal and, as such, transcends historic categories of impermissible discrimination'.[114]

End note

This chapter has focused on the growing complexity of the law, and in particular the proliferation of 'process heavy' social welfare and identity-based anti-discrimination laws. It points to the risk, that provisions of this kind can act as opiates – by distracting attention away from the realty of the growing socio-economic inequalities within the UK. Indeed, it suggests that in spite of their noble intentions, such laws can actually *increase* the prevalence of clustered injustice.

This critique does not, however, seek to argue that these provisions are worthless. This is clearly not the case, and it is difficult to see how their repeal could be characterised as anything other than a retrospective step. Nevertheless, there can be no doubting that they have added greatly to the complexity of the legal system and that their benefits have, in some contexts, come at a staggering financial cost.

The concluding chapter of this book considers how these conflicting realities can be reconciled. In so doing, it seeks to build on the arguments of Freeman, Bagenstos, Spade and Fineman – that 'more law' is unlikely to be part of the solution and no substitute for radical social welfare interventions and the revitalisation of institutional structures and cultures. The challenge, however, is to identify effective mechanisms that can address the very real problems confronting those experiencing clustered injustice, in the short- and medium-term: the period *before* fundamental reforms of this kind take effect.

CHAPTER 5

Parcelling-out of the soul: public sector bureaucracies

Scrabble

Scrabble is a word game for 2, 3 or 4 players. The play consists of forming interlocking words crossword fashion, on the playing board using letter tiles with the various score values. Each player competes for a high score by using his letters in combinations and locations that take best advantage of letter values in premium squares on the board.

Extract from official Scrabble rules

Introduction

It appears that every family has its own Scrabble rules: who starts; what can be done with blank letters; how letters can be exchanged; player time-limits; whether you can change some (rather than all) of your letters; the consequences when a word is challenged; how a game ends; and so on.

When you were first invited to play Scrabble and admitted to not knowing the rules, someone would have said 'don't worry I'll show you how'. Sadly – that is how many public officers acquired their understanding of their department's legal responsibilities. Public bodies do not generally invest much (if anything) in training their staff about the law.

Bureaucracy is therefore a game with its own familial rules – and for every organisation, the rules are different, even if they conflict with law or central government guidance. Not infrequently people seeking support will be told 'our council doesn't provide that' or 'you can't complain about this in our authority' or 'our trust doesn't consider reports of that kind', and so on and on. Often people who say these things, honestly believe that they are following the correct process. Why should they doubt it? It's how they have always played the game.

The analogy only goes so far, however. At least when someone objects in Scrabble, the rule-book comes out: with public bodies, sadly the law books don't – bureaucracy is not a game played among equals.

Overview

This chapter is concerned with the administrative systems of public bodies: systems that have the ability to both generate and exacerbate the problems experienced by many people who live with disadvantage. It refers to these systems as 'bureaucracies' and in so doing, the word is used technically, casually and colloquially – often as shorthand for systems that create harms of this kind. Bureaucracies are, however, an inevitability of modern life. They are by their very nature, reductionist: designed to smooth the operation of their organisation by reducing complexity; by standardising, subdividing and compartmentalising – not through the machinery of Adam Smith's pin factories, but through the use of processes, procedures, patterns, templates, rules and regulations.

Just as at the micro level conventional legal systems require clusters of intertwined problems to be broken down into individual isolated claims, bureaucratic systems require fragmentation at the macro level – different departments, different authorities and a plethora of different agencies – dealing with different rights, and each with its own operating system: its own familial Scrabble rules – its own budget, its own targets and all the managerial paraphernalia that goes with this.

Weber considered that the bureaucracies were (by their very nature) hierarchical, impersonal and rigid.[1] Although the machinery of such systems filled him despair (iron cages[2] 'filled with nothing but those little cogs, little men clinging to little jobs and striving towards bigger ones'[3]) he nevertheless believed that change was possible: if only to 'keep a portion of mankind free from this parcelling-out of the soul'. He also believed that such systems were 'efficient' – even if only of the cold, hard, impersonal kind.[4]

This chapter's principal focus is directed at the issue of *efficiency*. If administrative systems are an inevitable part of any organisation, then what does an 'efficient' system look like (from the perspective of a person living with disadvantage) and in what ways would it differ from some of the systems that currently operate? If fragmentation and personal indifference are defining characteristics of bureaucracies – how can such systems address the needs of people experiencing clustered injustice – when what they appear to need, are systems that are supportive? How can systems be developed, that are willing (when confronted by complex messy problems) to look at the 'bigger picture' – to 'abstract up', to use the jargon of systems' thinking? How can organisations put to one side their reductionist tendencies and resist the temptation to fragment and to separate, in such cases?

Street-level bureaucrats

Consider, for example, the process of securing a social welfare entitlement. The application must not only be made in the prescribed way, but the claimant must also thereby establish their right to the entitlement. The application process may be simple or labyrinthine depending upon whether (for example) the need is for emergency health care or a social security benefit. If the entitlement is refused, there will be a right to seek a review and again this will need to be framed in the prescribed way.

In order to satisfy the objective demands of accountability, decisions concerning eligibility, or the outcome of disputes, must ultimately be made by people perceived to have some degree of independence (even if there is no requirement that they hold judicial office[5]). Forty years ago, Lipsky coined the term 'street-level bureaucracies' to describe the organisations for whom these people worked: 'schools, police and welfare departments, lower courts, legal services officers, and other agencies whose workers interact with and have wide discretion over the dispensation of benefits or the allocation of public sanctions'.[6] The essential role that these individuals fulfil is:

> ... to make decisions about other people. Street-level bureaucrats have discretion because the nature of service provision calls for human judgment that cannot be programmed and for which machines cannot substitute ... It is the nature of what we call human services that the unique aspects of people and their situations will be apprehended by public service workers and translated into courses of action responsive to each case within (more or less broad) limits imposed by their agencies.[7]

Lipsky argued that for this function to be exercised effectively, such employees had to be accountable both to their employers' preferences and to their clients' claims, and that in order to maintain client confidence (given these twin roles) it was essential that the exercise of discretion was perceived as being independent. This in turn necessitated that street-level bureaucrats be seen to act as 'professionals' when making their decisions: that they took into account of all relevant factors and made rational decisions according to the law (and not the familial Scrabble rules).

Quasi-independent adjudication of this kind is generally seen as a positive characteristic by applicants and complainants – but from the public body's perspective it is problematic. The aura of 'legitimacy' it provides is welcome, but not when this comes at the cost of a loss of control over the process. Employing professionals who are subject to conduct codes outside the narrow 'systems boundary' of the bureaucracy; people with knowledge of the law; and people prepared to consider personal circumstances – does not go with the grain of rigid, hierarchical and impersonal administrative systems.

Loss of 'control' is the Brocken spectre[8] that haunts many public bodies. In this context, however, Lipsky explained that in order to curtail the dangerous tendencies of street-level bureaucrats (to exercise 'judgment'), public bodies, first, introduced the notion of 'accountability' (accountability to the organisation). They then restricted their discretion, by requiring them to follow extensive guidance manuals (that covered almost every contingency); introduced performance auditing and targets (by which they were assessed and sanctioned);[9] and then gave them unmanageable caseloads.

Although Lipsky's account of the role of street-level bureaucrats took place in the relatively early stages of both the broad assault on the professions[10] and the dramatic expansion in the use of information technology (IT) – it still holds true today. The 'control' system he described is generally referred to as 'managerialism'.

Accountability and the rise of managerialism

Managerialism, in one form or another, is almost certainly going to be the administrative system that regulates the way an individual's clustered problems are considered and – if deemed necessary – addressed. It is the most prevalent system used by public bodies and is the one most likely to generate the entangled messy problems that blight the lives of those who live with disadvantage.

Command, control and toxic organisational cultures

Managerialism is generally considered a system where managers 'command and control' the workforce. It is often characterised as a 'top-down management style' where frontline staff are tightly controlled in what they do and how they do it. Staff are closely monitored using performance indicators, audits of their record-keeping with sanctions for those that fail to meet specific targets. It has been described as a 'dumbed-down' systemisation that is ubiquitous in the public sector – where the 'role of the worker is reduced to a powerless doer'.[11]

A paradox within this process concerns the increasing emphasis on qualifications for these front line workers – even though their ability to exercise 'judgment' has been negated by the rigid controls they experience. In contrast, however, it is now not unusual for those who actually exercise real power – the senior managers of (for example) social services, housing, healthcare, education departments – to have little or no background or expertise in these fields.

Forms, templates, targets, standardised measures, prescribed processes and the like are all control measures symptomatic of reductionist approaches and managerialism's obsession with control, which has a particularly adverse impact on those experiencing clustered injustice. As Chapman explains, the 'use of command and control inevitably fails within complex systems and alienates people by treating them instrumentally'.[12] By denying frontline staff any sense of control and by severely constraining what they are permitted to do, managerialism frustrates opportunities for innovation – to work across organisational boundaries with the aim of resolving complex problems. As an administrative system, it has a profoundly demoralising impact on the workforce, creating – in large and small bodies – toxic organisational cultures. Cultures that generally develop incrementally and largely unnoticed – a process characterised as 'change blindness' – or more graphically, by the metaphor of the boiled frog syndrome – whereby incremental changes are accepted to the point that eventual extreme change is also accepted.[13]

Targets – and their unintended consequences

Targets are a key tool of command and control management systems, and there is an extensive literature[14] describing the way individuals and organisations manipulate data, game and cheat in order to hit their targets. The setting of a target creates, therefore, unforeseen and unintended consequences – feedback loops – that result from the targets' impact on the system.

Bevan and Hood[15] have described this as a 'targets-and-terror' system of governance and described how it warps even the 'saints' and 'honest triers' and inexorably turns them into 'reactive gamers' such that it is impossible to know whether improvements in reported performance are genuine or produced by people 'gaming' (aka cheating) the system.[16] Harris[17] speaks of targets (and the associated audits) creating a culture of distrust where 'auditees adapt their behaviour to the audit process, distorting reality so that it conforms to an auditable reality and [becomes] less trustworthy as a result of a process designed to make then more trustworthy'. For Seddon, the issue is simple: targets 'make performance worse: not sometimes, but always. It is in their nature.'[18]

Reductionism

In the context of social work practice, Harris recounts its takeover by a form of managerialism that believes that the lives of those who came into contact with the service can be 'classified into discrete problem categories': a 'reductionist' business model that disregards the 'potential complexity of service user's lives and circumstances that contribute to the "causes" of the problems they present'.[19] Given the new system's aversion to complex messy problems of this kind, Harris argues that it was inevitable that this hostility would also extend to the role of professionals within the service: people who sought to understand the complexity of the lives of those with whom they had contact – in defiance of a new managerial process intent on 'obscuring' this from view.[20]

Harris[21] describes today's social welfare administrative arrangements in terms remarkably similar to those used by Weber. As a process designed to entrench managerial power and in consequence, one that necessitates the 'fragmentation of those processes into smaller, less skilled, tasks that are more susceptible to managerial co-ordination and control'. From the perspective of people who live with disadvantage, the reductionism inherent in this system is the mechanism that generates many of their multiple entangled problems – as the process of simplification erases the critical interconnections that are essential features of their interlinked and compound needs.[22]

A way forward?

Given the problems that traditional forms of managerialism create for many people experiencing clustered injustice, and given its dominance within the public sector, an essential question is whether it is capable of being modified – whether it can be refashioned to enable it to be more effective in dealing with clusters of interlinked problems and able to do this empathetically (a question considered further in the concluding chapter).

On one level, a transformation of this kind would appear to align with some central government pronouncements critical of self-serving impersonal, fragmented and bureaucratic systems. In the context of those who live with disadvantage, two well-publicised initiatives aimed at addressing these problems are of relevance. These can be characterised as: (1) a 'personalisation' programme; and (2) a programme to foster a 'joined up' approach to policy and practice. We will discuss each of these in turn.

Personalisation

The 'personalisation programme' was an English Government initiative launched in 2007 to address perceived failings in the social care support system for disabled people.[23] It was billed as a mechanism to promote choice and expand the competitive market[24] and was underpinned by a 'rhetorical commitment to 'empowerment', co-production' and choice and control'.[25] One of the architects of the programme in the UK hailed it as revolutionary, representing a 'participative approach [that] delivers personalised, lasting solutions to people's needs at lower cost than traditional, inflexible and top-down approaches'.[26] Although the programme was trialled on social care services, it was considered to be appropriate for a much wider range of social welfare services – including maternity services; mental health provision; education; training; school excluded children; drug users; offenders seeking rehabilitation; as well as transport; housing; and healthcare generally.[27]

The essential – if naïve[28] – idea underpinning this programme was that individuals would self-assess and then receive a budget which they could then spend on meeting their needs as they thought best. It was a process that avoided the bureaucracy of assessments, professional paternalism, public sector micromanagement and auditing. Individuals would choose and control how their needs were met, and the process would be cheaper for the state both directly and due to 'the longer-term and indirect savings likely to flow to the public sector as a whole, especially health services'.[29]

Although the programme was overblown in terms of its evangelical[30] rhetoric – of co-production; of person-centredness; of user choice and control; of holistic systems; of consultation – the emphasis on the goal of 'inclusion' can be seen as symptomatic of the failure of the market-led reforms of the 1980s and 90s, to produce the high-quality personal social welfare services it had promised.

From the perspective of many people in need of social welfare support (including individuals with multiple entangled problems) there is much merit in a programme that provides a personalised service capable of engaging with a range of cross-cutting social welfare needs, especially one that can minimise the experience of heavy-handed centralised bureaucratic control.

Sadly, however, there appears to be a general consensus that the personalisation programme has not been the success its architects predicted.[31] A number of factors have contributed to this failure, including:

- the perennial mistake of over-estimating the potential of IT (in this case its ability to generate a realistic 'budget' that each person should receive)[32] – as Lipsky had correctly predicted, this is a process 'that calls for human judgment that cannot be programmed and for which machines cannot substitute';[33]
- the fact that schemes of this kind depend upon there being adequate funding and a functioning 'supply' market so that the personal budget can secure suitable support of adequate quality;[34]
- the need for individuals to have the knowledge and the abilities to identify, commission and manage their own support needs (and to accept the transferred risk this entails – from the state to the individual) 'embed assumptions in their design that privilege higher socio-economic groups';[35] and
- the fact that many people (even if they were prepared to take on the management of their own budget) still had a vital need for ongoing support in relation to new problems, new crisis, changing needs.

Challenging as these failings are, they could probably be addressed if there was a step-change increase in social welfare funding and well-resourced user-support arrangements. There is, however, an overriding problem that confronts personalisation programmes of this kind – and one that is most probably, insuperable – namely managerialism's fundamental and intractable obsession with 'control'.

Joined-up government

As with the personalisation programme, the 'joined-up government' initiative would appear to have offered significant benefits for those who struggle with multiple problems that span different 'silos' of the social welfare system.

In his account of the initiative, Bogdanor notes[36] that the government under Tony Blair's Labour Party decided that 'intractable problems such as social exclusion, drug addiction and crime could not be resolved by a single department of government' and that these had to be addressed by a cross-governmental programme. The initiative was, however, more concerned about the problems of government ('the recognition that some problems of the government do not fit into the neat departmental boundaries'[37]) than the clustered problems of individuals living with disadvantage. The mechanisms adopted to implement the initiative have been characterised as 'top-down',[38] with a particular focus on creating administrative joint planning structures, co-terminosity and other organisational devices to promote joint working.[39]

Unfortunately, without doubting the fine intentions of the programme, there is little evidence to suggest that it materially improved the way that intractable inter-agency problems were addressed – either at the organisation level or at the micro-level of those who experienced the fallout from these demarcation disputes.

Research concerning the necessary ingredients for successful inter-agency working arrangements highlights the challenges posed by organisational cultures, inflexible bureaucratic systems within the siloed agencies[40] and the sheer complexity of such processes. Bryson et al,[41] for example, concluded their extensive review of the literature on joint working arrangements with the comment that 'to say that cross-sector collaborations are complex entities that defy easy generalization is an understatement'. A 2011 paper by O'Flynn et al[42] also identified 'bureaucratic pervasiveness' as a key inhibitor to successful joint working arrangements – the problem of 'deeply embedded bureaucratic characteristics [that] impede attempts at working across boundaries and of connecting outside of silos, to deliver on the joined-up agenda'. In this respect they identified three key factors:[43]

1) the importance of a 'supporting architecture' of trusting relationships and rewards for cooperative behaviour;
2) the problems generated by government targets which invariably focussed on single issue 'silo specific' outcomes; and
3) centralised decision-making.

The concluding chapter of this book considers each of these factors and potential mechanisms to address them.

Organisational cultures

Organisations, like Scrabble-playing families, have their own distinctive character and their own distinctive rules. Organisational cultures develop over time and vary greatly: some benign and some not so benign. As Steinbeck reminds us, even the most well-meaning workforce can co-ordinate senseless and inhumane programmes – such as the eviction of Dust Belt prairie farmers:[44]

> ... every man in a bank hates what the bank does, and yet the bank does it. The bank is something more than men, I tell you. It's the monster.

The analysis so far has been based on the notion that bureaucratic systems are by their nature impersonal and detached. In many contexts, however, the perception of those dealing with such a system, is not one of a neutral administrative 'gaze', but of active indifference that is difficult to distinguish from antagonism. Sometimes, of course, that is the whole point – for example, through the creation of a hostile environment in relation to immigrants,[45] Gypsies and Travellers[46] and for those seeking social security.[47]

A rich literature exists concerning the nature of organisational cultures,[48] which in this context is taken to be the 'values, beliefs and ideologies of the people who make up the organization': their shared ways of 'seeing, thinking and doing'.[49] Thompson et al have described how whole systems management failures can result in defensive, counterproductive and dysfunctional cultures becoming embedded within social services departments – to the extent that the workforce experience 'a form of collective burn out'.[50] These corrosively negative cultures can be deeply unpleasant places in which to work – to the extent that staff become unresponsive and seemingly incapable of engaging in constructive or imaginative problem-solving: lacking in any professional curiosity as to the lives lived by those they are ostensibly there to support (let alone to the requirements of the legal process).

Thompson et al consider that negative cultures of this kind result from over-controlling, highly stressed and coercive managerial regimes[51] which disempower frontline workers, producing a form of 'learned helplessness'[52] that paralyses active decision-making roles: a state described by Klein as 'a passive mindset of just following the steps, and not really thinking about what they are doing'.[53]

Stress creates a hard shell around an organisation and its individual employees that accentuates the difficulties of those seeking to resolve problems. Instead of exploring innovative ways to address these problems (and then applying those that are seen to work), such organisations take refuge in an 'anxiety-avoidance' ritual:[54] an approach that is adopted because it successfully avoids anxiety (for example, by rigidly following the prescribed rule-book) even if it consistently produces negative results – for the organisation, its staff and those who contact it seeking support. Lees et al[55] consider this to be a systems failure to deal positively with the anxiety-provoking and emotionally intense work. The organisation creates a 'series of prescriptive rules, procedures and working practices' that attempts to neutralise the anxieties by (in effect) requiring a mindless 'following the rules' mentality. In other contexts this has been referred to as a 'compliance culture'[56] and a 'compliance addiction'[57] and it is suggested that rather than alleviating 'primary anxiety', defensive approaches of this kind exacerbate the problem by creating 'a set of secondary anxieties'.[58]

This sense of learned helplessness and organisational detachment was identified in 2019 research[59] which concerned social workers who were provided with significant new resources, having experienced a decade of tight budgets, strict eligibility criteria and approval frameworks. The research found that social workers in this position not only had great difficulty on escaping their practice culture 'shaped by a reliance on process and procedure and a reluctance to trust individuals'[60] – but also their internalised lack of trust in themselves to make decisions.

A similar point is also made by Dr Pimenta,[61] a hospital surgeon working during the early stages of the coronavirus outbreak in 2020. He describes how his colleagues were aware of the potential dangers of the epidemic but seemed to think that they were 'prevented by procedure' from putting in place measures that would contain its spread. How, instead of raising concerns about the threat the virus posed they asked, 'Isn't there someone up the chain who should speak out instead?'

Complaints and coercive cultures

People working with unreasonably high caseloads, in chronically underfunded social welfare departments – can find it almost impossible to agree to meet the objective needs of people seeking help. Such systems inevitably generate complaints – 'failure demand' in 'systems thinking' terms. These exacerbate the pressure on staff, as well as having an adverse impact on those who complain.

A 2019 report by the Public Services Ombudsman for Wales provides an insight into the way a council's unhealthy organisational culture impacted on its own staff – even though the impetus for the report was a complaint made by the parents of a disabled young person.[62] The parents had had a previous complaint upheld by the ombudsman, but felt compelled to complain again about a range of additional failures. This was investigated by a complaints manager, who then shared her findings with senior officers. The officers were unhappy with her recommendations, to the extent that she felt she was being bullied. The ombudsman, in upholding her report, was highly critical of the council. This was the second successful ombudsman's complaint made by the family: complaints that spanned nine years and in which the family made it clear that it has lost faith in the council. Having seen how the council treated its own staff member, it takes little imagination to understand the frustration, stress and exhaustion the family must have gone through in the nine-year period – negotiating the many levels of the local complaints process before being able to approach the ombudsman.

It is, therefore, no surprise to find that many people in who live with disadvantage, display a reluctance to complain to statutory agencies. Many lack a support network to help them challenge decisions of this kind; lack an understanding of the law; lack a reserve of energy to persist in the face of the many bureaucratic barriers; and are intimidated by the very real 'power imbalance'[63] that exists in such situations. 'Fear of the consequences' (a fear of retaliatory action)[64] is commonly cited. The fear is not just for the individual but, not infrequently, also for the frontline workers (as the above case illustrates) with whom the complainants may have no complaint.[65]

The reductionism at the heart of most bureaucracies – with their departmental silos and delegated (increasingly privatised) responsibilities – can create significant problems for complainants. It is often far from clear as to which organisation is ultimately responsible – such that multiple complaints have to be made. The difficulty is one that is more acute for those with clusters of problems. Given the successional nature of problems they experience, there will often be a history to each of the resulting complaints: a chronology of concerns spanning months or years. It is not difficult to understand how complainants in this position end up believing that they have been labelled as 'difficult people' by the agencies with whom they interact. Indeed (as discussed in the following chapter) official guidance suggests that people who make multiple complaints, with lengthy supporting documentation, fall into the category of 'unacceptable complainants'.

Complainants may also end up believing that complaints are pointless – a perception highlighted by 2015 research[66] that involved an online survey of almost 2,000 parents concerning diagnosis delays experienced by their disabled child. Three-quarters of respondents had encountered problematic delays for which no explanation had been forthcoming; and three-quarters of them considered that the delay had caused harm. Once a diagnosis had been obtained, most families were either offered no (or inadequate) follow-up support. There were, therefore, very many things on which the families had cause to complain. However, only a quarter of those experiencing delay complained. Of these, the vast majority (in hindsight) considered that complaining had been pointless.[67] From this it could be argued that the sensible thing to do in such cases is not to complain.

This perception has been reinforced by a former Chief Executive of NHS England, who acknowledged that the poor way complaints had been handled created 'a group of individuals who have a problem but choose not to complain' – sometimes referred to as 'silent sufferers'. In his view, this was because complainants considered that processes were 'too complex, involved them having to chase a response and that they fear nothing will change as a result of their complaint'.[68]

Case examples

This sense of the futility is given credence by a number of studies, of which two are of particular relevance.

The first study concerned local authority responses to legal challenges by people threatened with homelessness. It identified 'professional intuition, systemic suspicion, bureaucratic expediency, judgments about the moral desert of applicants, inter-officer relations [and] financial constraints' as some of the values and pressures that shaped how councils responded.[69] It concluded that 'despite extensive and prolonged exposure to judicial scrutiny, unlawful decision-making was rife'. The evidence suggested that legal challenge provoked defensiveness rather than cultural change: organisations continued to make same decisions, but the *process* by which these were made was adapted to 'proof' them against future challenges.[70]

The second study concerned a project by the children's disability charity Cerebra, the Legal Entitlements and Problem-solving (LEaP)[71] study of complaints made by parents who had experienced the same problem with the same council – namely the unilateral withdrawal of support that it was under a statutory duty to provide for their disabled child. The parents had spent a considerable amount of time trying to get the support reinstated but without success. They had all experienced, in consequence, significant hardship including, in a number of cases, immense financial pressure and emotional strain.

The first complaint to the council was rejected, but with help, on review the support was reinstated. Although the council should have learned from this episode, the next family's (effectively identical) complaint was rejected, but once more with help, the council reversed its decision – and on being pressed, it also agreed to amend its defective website statement concerning its legal duties, which it did.

Several months later another parent had the same problem, which was also rejected – but the council then agreed to an independent review hearing. The idea of having to attend such a hearing is daunting and highly stressful for many families. In this case, the parent, having steeled herself for this ordeal – in the late afternoon before the day set for hearing – received a call telling her that her appeal would not be contested. A letter to the council's senior legal officer complaining about the multiple fallings of his authority produced a welcome response accepting fault and agreeing to 'review . . . practice [and] ensure its legality'.

One might conclude from this account, that an effective way of challenging a persistent problem is to get the local policy changed – and ideally to enlist the support of a fair-minded council officer. However, it is not so simple. Almost three years later, the LEaP Project was contacted by another parent in the same council area who had been denied support for the same unlawful reason. The lesson was that changing a local policy changes nothing if officers are not trained in the law, if the old forms are still used and if the organisational culture of saying 'no' persists.

These cases are not atypical: the lack of legal curiosity, the prevalence of delay and the persistence of dysfunctional organisational cultures are reoccurring themes. Winning a case or getting agreement to change a policy does not – in itself – change the way public bodies make decisions. From many other examples, one more suffices.

In 2011 a judicial review of a council's unlawful policy of capping the amount of support for certain social welfare needs was settled by the council agreeing to amend the policy: to make it clear that no such rigid cap existed. The settlement was well publicised.[72] In 2018, the Cerebra LEaP Project was contacted by a family whose support needs had been capped by the same council in the same way. Despite the change in the wording of the policy several years earlier, the automatic cap had in practice continued to be applied.

Child protection, process-led approaches and dysfunctional organisational cultures

Children and their families who live with disadvantage are perhaps the paradigm group of people with clustered problems and for whom the state has unequivocal obligations. As the charity Child Poverty

Action Group explains, the fact that more than one in four children in the UK is growing up in poverty is not inevitable: it is 'low wages, inadequate benefits, expensive housing and childcare, and a lack of decently-paid jobs'. Many children (particularly disabled children) and their families that live with disadvantage are beset by multiple and interlinked legal problems: poor and insecure housing; chronic debt; disturbed education; impaired physical and mental health; higher rates of domestic abuse; and particular difficulties paying for food, rent and utility bills.

It is unclear whether child maltreatment is increasing or decreasing in England and Wales.[73] Between 2014 and 2019 the number of children (aged under 16) being killed by assault or other forms of abuse averaged about one per week.[74] Throughout this period (as before) a number of these deaths have been highly publicised[75] and have led to inquiries that sought to find out what went wrong with the aim of understanding how to better protect children.

In 2010 Professor Eileen Munro was commissioned to undertake an independent review to improve child protection and in 2011 she published an exceptionally insightful report[76] of the review's findings. Her analysis could be applied with equal force to many other sectors of the welfare state – including, of course, adult safeguarding procedures.

Munro identified a key problem as the 'over-bureaucratised' nature of the system: a system where social workers' ability to 'exercise professional judgment in deciding how best to help children and their families' was stifled by a managerial culture whose primary concern was 'compliance': compliance with the auditing requirements of Ofsted (the inspectorate that audits the performance of children's social services). The report describes a process-driven system of performance indicators and targets: a system where records of work had 'acquired a new dominance' which had distorted the priorities of practice – not least the 'emotional dimensions and intellectual nuances of reasoning'. Managerialism of this kind equated 'good' practice' with 'following procedures and keeping records' because – from a management perspective – records could be audited and were 'a way of defending the organisation and fending off criticism.

Munro's report is informed by a 'systems thinking' approach[77] and a recognition that child protection is an incredibly complex area and for which reductionist methods are inappropriate. Simplifying the process to a box-ticking exercise creates unintended consequences – 'feedback loops' in systems thinking terms. Trying to manage anxiety simply creates more anxiety;[78] trying to safeguard children by keeping 'meticulous bureaucratically rational records'[79] does no such thing; and the existence of copious records is seldom a defence when a child is killed.[80]

A process-led approach to child protection assumes that if the process is followed correctly, then children will be safe from harm. Ergo, if a child is harmed it must be due to human failure, not process failure. It is then assumed that the way to address this problem is to stop people making mistakes, which (as the report observes) is addressed through the use of three mechanisms: (1) 'psychological pressure on professionals to try harder'; (2) 'reducing the scope for individual judgment by adding procedures and rules'; and (3) 'increasing the level of monitoring to ensure compliance with them'. These bear a strong resemblance to the mechanisms described by Lipsky to curtail street-level bureaucrats' discretion (see above).

In Munro's opinion, almost every inquiry into a killing of a child has recommended a ratchetting up of one or more of these mechanisms – the cumulative effect of which has been the present dysfunctional and heavily bureaucratised system. One where the unintended consequences of increased proceduralisation was that it had incrementally reduced time with children and families (where some social workers were spending up to 80 per cent of their time on paperwork), less job satisfaction and higher turnover of staff.[81] It was one that:[82]

> ... seems to hold out security but actually creates a feedback loop that reinforces the defensive routine based on a procedural perspective which hampers professional learning.[83] From the perspective of the front line, this has contributed to many feeling that they are working in a compliance culture where meeting performance management demands becomes the dominant focus rather than meeting the needs of children and their families. When these conflict, even the most dedicated child-centred professionals can feel pressured to prioritise the performance demand over the child's needs.

The report proposed an alternative approach – namely that 'when human error is found it is treated as the starting point, not the conclusion of inquiry'.[84] In essence, that human error is inevitable and systems should assume that it will occur. Where a catastrophic event occurs and the sequence of events that led to the tragedy have been identified, it is crucial to 'go behind the label "human error"' and to enable everyone (including the organisation) to better understand the complexity of the work undertaken. Instead of assuming that the unintended consequences mean that the system needs more control and central directives, what actually needs to be done is to recognise that unintended consequences will happen and that they need to be monitored, understood, and if needs be, the system adapted to accommodate these challenges by continually adapting and evolving as the nature of risk changes.

The report endorsed an observation of the House of Commons Health Committee 'that most harm was not done deliberately, negligently or through serious incompetence but through normally competent clinicians working in inadequate systems'[85] and of the need for a 'deeper understanding of why professionals have acted in the way they have, so that any resulting changes are grounded in practice realities'.[86] It also endorsed the following submission it had received during its review process:

> Managers should use their leadership role to monitor and improve (i) the way the system continually learns and adapts; (ii) what the system requires of frontline workers; and (iii) how healthy and free of toxicity is the work environment. They will need a high level of awareness of how organisations perform as systems.[87]

End note

This much I think we learn from the analysis in this and the preceding chapters.

All public bodies must have administrative systems, and currently these are almost always reductionist in their approach. In classical bureaucratic terms, their role is to smooth the operation of their organisation through standardising and subdividing administrative roles. This does not, however, mean that these systems have to be so rigid and centrally controlled that front-line workers cannot exercise significant autonomy in the decision-making process. In the NHS, for example, GPs still retain not insignificant decision-making power of this kind.

Unfortunately, managerialism is the operating system for nearly all public bodies (including most of the NHS). This system, with its obsessional control of its workers, creates most of the clustered problems experienced by those who live with disadvantage and is the single greatest impediment to the effective resolution of their problems. It is a system plagued by damaging unintended consequences, feedback loops and 'failure demand'.

It is possible to have an effective system of administration that can be proactive when confronted by individuals who have needs across multiple branches of the social welfare system – and it is equally possible for that system to have effective reactive mechanisms to resolve problems when things go wrong. There is strong evidence to suggest that a responsive system of this kind would be more efficient – from the perspective of the individual experiencing clustered injustice; from the perspective of the well-being of those who work within it; and from the perspective of the public body's financial balance sheet.

The concluding chapter considers further what such a system might look like.

Harm

Snakes and Ladders

Each player puts their counter on the space that says 'start here'. Take it in turns to roll the dice. Move your counter forward the number of spaces shown on the dice. If your counter lands at the bottom of a ladder, you can move up to the top of the ladder. If your counter lands on the head of a snake, you must slide down to the bottom of the snake. The first player to get to the space that says 'home' is the winner.

British Council 'LearnEnglish Kids'[1]

Introduction

It appears that Snakes and Ladders derives from an ancient Indian board game 'Moksha Patam'. It was a morality game, concerned with the player's destiny and the role that virtue (ladders) and vice (snakes) play in life's journey. Generally, there were fewer ladders than snakes and the roll of the dice (the making of a key decision) could bring positive or negative consequences – highlighting the role of karma and of fate.

On the back page of a guide published by the disabled children's charity Cerebra,[2] we have a game for families to play. It is called 'Real Snakes and Fantasy Ladders' and it reflects the lived reality for many families with disabled children. People with clustered problems are generally being thwarted by the system: one step forward, and the inevitability, at some stage, of there being setbacks – sometimes right back to square one. It is a not a morality story or a fairy tale of golden stairways: it is a tragedy. It is Sisyphus forever pushing the stone up the hill – with the added anxiety of knowing that there will be another stone (another problem) arriving soon.

Overview

Living with disadvantage and weighed down by the baggage of unresolved legal problems is, in itself, a disabling and chronic condition: stressful, depressive and always on the mind – an ever-present dark cloud.

In the context of this study, a relevant and prevalent consequential harm has been variously described as 'cognitive overload', 'restricted cognitive bandwidth', 'attentional capture',[3] and 'depleted reserves of mental effort'. In short, that people become so preoccupied with daily struggles of living with disadvantage that this severely reduces their ability to find the mental space to make prudent decisions on not only critical but also on peripheral (albeit important) issues. Although this is a phenomena that is applicable to many forms of disadvant- age[4] (and inevitably intensified by multiple experiences of disadvant- age), most of the relevant research has concerned the impact that the experience of poverty has on decision-making.

Daniel Kahneman[5] has described two different ways that we reach decisions. One is instinctive, impulsive and intuitive – done without real thought and where the answer comes effortlessly. He labels this 'fast thinking'. The other – 'slow thinking' – is a 'more deliberate and effortful form of thinking'. Most of what we do is governed by fast thinking – although, as Kahneman explains, the slow thinking mode is also active, but in 'a comfortable low-effort mode' endorsing the many 'impressions, intuitions, intentions and, feelings' that the fast thinking mode generates. However, when the fast thinking mode runs into difficulty, the slow thinking mode has to power up. This requires 'cognitive effort' – and sometimes demands our whole atten- tion, such that we have to sit down and 'turn off' all fast thinking and concentrate. For people living with the constant preoccupations that result from many forms of disadvantage, it is not always possible to find this mental space – and in consequence, their ability to make 'make rational choices or see a bigger picture' is materially impaired.[6] It has, for example, been argued that for those living with poverty and/or with ever-present debt, that the load these constant distrac- tions impose on cognitive functioning is similar to that which results from losing a full night of sleep.[7]

As Gandy et al[8] explain, 'the multiple dimensions of poverty and disadvantage – including financial worries, time pressures, coping with stereotypes and emotional distress – sap our mental processing capacity, which in turn affects our judgement and decisions'.

Mullainathan and Shafir[9] describe the problems caused by the lack of mental space (to practice 'slow thinking') in terms of 'scarcity' – which they consider to be a clustering of several important concerns, not least those of money and time. People on low-wage, zero hours contracts often fall into this category – of which care workers provide a clear illustration. Increasingly, such workers are subject to telephone-based electronic monitoring systems that track their loca- tion, their arrival and departure times when making home care visits: visits that often require multiple and complex caring tasks. The system financially penalises the workers if the tasks in their pre-set rota are not completed within the specified period. In her research concerning this system, Hayes includes a case example of a worker constantly preoccupied by the contract time, the needs of the people she visits and the needs of her children at home – as well as the ever-present problems resulting from her poverty.[10]

In this situation, people often lack the ability to think clearly and carefully, and instead take refuge in 'fast thinking': in 'impulsive and intuitive behaviors that eventually cumulate producing poor economic decisions, thus leading to a vicious cycle of poverty-inducing behaviors'.[11] In 'systems thinking' terms, this vicious cycle is a feedback loop 'in which poverty reinforces itself through exerting an influence on psychological outcomes, which may then lead to economic behaviours that are potentially disadvantageous' such as time-discounting[12] where the focus is solely 'on immediate and safe payoffs'.[13]

Warrior mothers and fathers

For those of us who do not live with disadvantage and who have the space to practice 'slow thinking', one of its invaluable benefits (through its continuous monitoring of our behaviour) is that it keeps us polite when we are in fact very angry – and stops us blurting out distasteful remarks or using offensive language.[14] Slow thinking provides us with 'resistance to self-destructive temptation'[15] and in times of stress, it stops us snapping and saying what we are actually thinking. For lawyers, slow thinking does not stop us writing the furious and exceedingly blunt email, but it does stop us pressing the send button (generally). We know that we need to calm down, review and tone it down the next day when we have regained some sense of self-control. However, if you live with disadvantage 24/7 and are hemmed in by clusters of problems – your reserves of 'mental effort' may be so depleted that you just press that button.[16]

For the last 40 years, my work has brought me into close contact with many people who have severe cognitive overload: people juggling multiple synchronous legal problems; people dealing with inept public bodies and well beyond their wits end: 'ill-used people' to use the language of George Bernard Shaw.[17] Not infrequently, when I have asked a public body, informally, why it behaved in the way it did to one of my clients, the response has been – 'you know she is a very difficult person, don't you?' In truth I am generally well aware that they are difficult – sometimes very difficult – but I also know *why* they are difficult. They may have been born to considerable disadvantage, or encountered this at some point in their lives – but this did not make them 'difficult'. Being enmeshed in a dysfunctional social justice system – ostensibly created to support them – is what has made them difficult. What is so troubling is the lack of insight by those responsible for shaping these systems: systems that create difficult, angry people who have no compunction about pressing the 'send button' at 2am of a morning; people who do not like the combative person they have become; people who are suffering a form of post-traumatic stress disorder (PTSD) created by years of sleepless nights and being shell-shocked by the behaviour of a heartless system.

This (for me) is particularly so for carers, for example parents of disabled children – sometimes children with expected 'short lives'. Families who are pushed beyond endurance – beyond extreme anxiety for their child, and have absolutely no qualms about saying exactly what they think. As one such mother recently explained to me:

> If you take everything away from a person in my position when the only thing you have left to lose is your loved one, your sanity and your reputation, we have nothing left and we become very dangerous as I think nothing about sending letters and emails trying to tell our life as it's not a story.

Although there are 'warrior parents' of both sexes, mothers in partic-ular, experience hostility when they push back strongly against incompetent, unresponsive public sector systems. All too commonly this is categorised as 'unwomanly', hysterical and as raising troubling questions about their ability to be 'fit' parents. Helen Lewis uses the phrase 'difficult women' and, from my experience, provides a much more accurate assessment of their nature and their approach:

> The Difficult Woman is not rude, petty or mean. She is simply willing to be awkward, if the situation demands it; demanding, if the occasion requires it; and obstinate, if someone tries to fob her off. She does not care if 'that's the way it's always been done'. She is unmoved by the suggestion that it's 'natural' for women to act a certain way or accept a lower status.[18]

Of course, there are many mothers who lack the skills and networks necessary to enable them to secure their children's essential needs. In this context, Janet Read has described the constant danger of marginalisation that 'poor women' and mothers from minority ethnic communities experience when fighting to have their disabled children's needs fully represented – but who lack the necessary skills to do this and 'have to live with the knowledge that they could not make it happen no matter how hard they tried'.[19]

Consider not the mother as the epicentre of the injustice: nor the various identities she has – but the environment that she inhabits.

Just as space is distorted by an object, so should justice (the playing field) bend to accommodate her and the disadvantage she encounters.

The problem lies not in the individual, but in the way that the multiple agencies of the state interact with that person. The image of a body (a small silver sphere) moving serenely through space and, as Einstein tells us, distorting the space-time continuum (indeed, multiple continuums) is how the theoretical legal person is supposed to interact with the legal system as they progress through their ideal-ised life: a will here, a divorce there, a mortgage here and a small claim there. But that is a false metaphor for a person experiencing disadvantage and clusters of legal problems. To grasp their reality, you must load that silver sphere into a much abused pin-ball machine, turn the music up, turn down the lights and pull the trigger – and you have some idea of what it feels like to be trying to address the multiple rebuffs she experiences when trying to access the essential legal entitlements that she, and maybe her child, needs in order to function. But she is not a silver ball, she is flesh and blood rammed, repulsed and ricocheting within not one unfeeling hard machine, but in multiple machines in multiple directions – and of course, once one issue has been resolved, the ball is reloaded for the new chal-lenge that has arisen – and so it goes.

'Unacceptable behaviour' and 'difficult people'

What the state views as 'unacceptable'

There is a fascinating practice manual (now in its second edition) issued to frontline staff working for the Australian New South Wales (NSW) Ombudsman's office: 'Managing unreasonable complainant conduct'.[20] It cites at the outset a senior judge's comments concern-ing the problem of 'the chronic complainer': people who can cause 'disproportionate disruption' to the work of the ombudsman and 'his staff'.[21] The guidance refers on a number of occasions to the fact that this is a growing problem, and gives a range of reasons why some complainants behave 'unreasonably' – all of which locate the fault with the complainant (as they must, having framed the problem this way). It helpfully states that although 'psychiatrists and psychologists may have reasons to focus on the causes behind a person's behaviour (to assess their mental state or make a psychological diagnosis), it is generally not' the ombudsman's problem.

There are two pages of bullet points listing behaviours, which are suggestive of 'unreasonable' complainants. Although these do not mention pressing the 'send' button at 2am, they do include:

- having made a number of previous complaints;
- having made contact with various other government agencies, MPs, ministers or oversight bodies about their issue;
- being dissatisfied with the outcome or level of attention they were given;
- having a history of mental health issues;
- using text that is uppercase or underlined (etc);
- using inappropriate legal terminology;
- using excessively dramatic language;
- using an excessive number of pages;
- being rude, confrontational, angry, aggressive or unusually frustrated.

Although it cannot be doubted that some people are very difficult to deal with, it is curious that their numbers should be increasing – or at least, curious that the NSW ombudsman shows no curiosity about the reasons for this.

Similar, but less extensive, guidance exists in England from the Local Government and Social Care Ombudsman on the 'management of unreasonable complainant behaviour'.[22] It explains that the ombudsman will not tolerate 'abusive, offensive, threatening or other forms of unacceptable behaviour from complainants' but fails to explain the principles by which it decides what is transgressive in this context or acknowledge the sometimes appalling stress complainants may be under. It does, however, echo the views of the NSW Ombudsman in identifying as unreasonable behaviour people who:

- make excessive demands on the time and resources of staff with lengthy phone calls, emails to numerous council staff, or detailed letters every few days, and expecting immediate responses;
- adopt a 'scatter gun' approach: pursuing parallel complaints on the same issue with various organisations.

In relation to the assertion that some complainants make excessive demands on council resources – the suggestion appears to be that it is the complaints' handlers that decide what is excessive. A 2004 case[23] illustrates the dangers of this approach. A council argued that it had been unable to respond sensibly to a complaint's lawyer because of the excessive volume and persistence of her letters. In the judge's view, the problem was, however 'the conjunction of a highly efficient solicitor and of a very hard-pressed local authority unable to articulate full and speedy responses' which resulted in it becoming 'defensive and unconstructive'.

There is also a strong argument to suggest that many of the workload problems stem from the increasingly impersonal and digitalised complaints systems developed by public bodies. Instead of face-to-face meetings to resolve problems, complaints systems have become a formalised bureaucracy with all that inevitably flows in its wake. The problem of 'excessive demands' cuts both ways. It is not unheard of for a public body to respond to a complaint by overwhelming the complainant with reams of largely irrelevant material and commentary: maladministration by not being succinct.

As noted in the proceeding chapter, concern has been expressed about the fragmented nature of social welfare systems[24] such that it is often necessary to make multiple complaints to various bodies – particularly so for those with clusters of overlapping problems. The ombudsmen's proposition suggests that it is unreasonable not to understand the intricacies of public services functions: something that is – I would venture – above the comprehension of most people. How many people understand what an NHS trust does; what functions a clinical commissioning group discharges; what NHS England's role is; which public body is responsible for public health; which department of the NHS or social services is responsible for drug rehabilitation and occupational therapy; whether a complaint concerning a care home failure is something that can be considered by a local authority or the care home or the Care Quality Commission; and so on. In the context of myriad fragmented, euphemistically labelled publicly funded entities, each with a role in the social welfare system – a 'scatter gun' approach to complaining would appear to make eminent sense – except, it seems, to public bodies and the ombudsmen.

For people who lack the cognitive bandwidth to sit down and distil the grounds for a multi-stranded complaint (and for whom no empathetic advocate or friend is on hand) the approach personified by the ombudsmen is straightforward: if you cannot exercise control (like 'normal people') then your complaint risks not being considered.

'Unacceptable behaviour' policies in practice

There is abundant evidence that 'unacceptable behaviour' policies are applied in practice.[25] Many of these cases involve complaints alleging a serious failure to support a third party, for example an elderly parent or a child. Exasperated complainants are then incendi-arised by an inflammatory comment made by the public body, which is then used as evidence of their unreasonableness. In essence, having lit the blue touch-paper, the public body then stands back and condemns the ensuing fireworks.

One illustrative example concerns a parent, whom the court considered to be 'measured, courteous [and] reflective', who became increasingly angry with a local authority's failings – not least its abject failure to safeguard his two children. The council responded by using his anger to justify its refusal to communicate with him. In a wither-ing judgment, the court accepted that there were 'many occasions when the father's irritations have been ventilated trenchantly and unambiguously' but that it was 'by no means difficult to empathise with the depth of his frustration'.[26]

Retaliatory action of this kind can go wider than merely blacklist-ing exasperated individuals by alleging 'unacceptable behaviour'.

In 2018 the BBC aired three programmes[27] concerning the exper-iences of 12 families who had asked their council for social care support for a disabled child and/or made a complaint about its failing to provide this support. In each case they had then been accused of fabricating the extent of their child's impairment. Fabrication of this kind used to be called 'Munchausen syndrome by proxy', but is now generally referred to as FII – 'fabricated or induced illness'. The BBC obtained expert advice which indicated that within the council in question, the expected incidence of FII would be one case every two years. Following the programmes, it appeared that accusations of this kind made by councils were not unusual,[28] and as one respond-ent observed, 'only parents who have been accused of fabricated and/ or induced illness can really say how far-reaching and completely devastating these accusations are'.

In addition to troubling evidence of this kind, there is well-documented evidence of care homes threatening to evict residents as a reprisal for their families making complaints.[29]

In similar vein, there are many examples where local authority 'safeguarding' powers have been misused. These include making a disabled child the subject of a child protection plan merely because the council was in dispute with his parents as to where he should live – parents who 'had done all they could reasonably do'.[30] Another example is a decision by a council to take adult protection measures in relation to a disabled young man because it was in dispute with his family over aspects of his care plan. In the ombudsman's opinion, it was action that 'beggars belief'.[31]

One of the most shocking examples, however, concerns a council's description of a mother of five severely disabled children as 'abusive'. Due to her 'totally inappropriate accommodation', the children could not be adequately bathed. Despite desperate representations, the council refused to provide assistance. This meant that the oldest child often had faeces spread across his body and his mother 'had no option but to hose him down in the back garden', sometimes in the middle of the night. Instead of providing the support needed, the council told her that if this continued it would be dealt with as child abuse. Noting that the mother's parenting skills and her commitment to care for her sons had never been in question, the ombudsman considered that the authority's comments were of 'breathtaking insensitivity' caused by 'ineffective management that can fairly be described as "institutionalised indifference" '.[32]

Chronic stress and cognitive overload

Although cognitive overload is generally perceived as stressful – it is not 'stress' itself that creates the cognitive overload difficulties of those who live with disadvantage.[33] Some stress can be viewed as positive and indeed can increase working memory – for example, the stress experienced by 'time poor' executives.[34] The two conditions are, however, closely related – particularly for those whose clusters of concerns include being 'money poor'.[35]

The research evidence concerning the harm caused by the *chronic* stress that attends those who live with disadvantage, is extensive. Chronic stress is considered to be the main environmental risk factor for mental illness, particularly major depressive disorders.[36] It can result in impaired immunity – not least to influenza[37] – atherosclerosis, obesity, bone demineralisation and atrophy of nerve cells in the brain, as well as chronic anxiety disorders.[38] Chronic stress can result from all manner of negative interactions and experiences – including persistent incivility – which can lead to individuals suffering from 'rumination' where they find it difficult to stop thinking about a past event or worrying about future interactions – leading to sleep loss and eventual disease: for example, clinical depression.[39]

As Nikolas Rose has observed 'we have scarcely begun to really tackle the question of the complexity of the entanglements that lead any individual to mental distress':[40] that 'the level, frequency and duration of stressful experiences and the extent to which they are buffered by social supports in the community' suggest that those 'lower on the social hierarchy are more likely to be subject to such experiences and have access to fewer buffers and supports'.[41]

End note

Distressing, avoidable and shaming as is the harm inflicted on those who experience clustered injustice, it is only one aspect of the negative impact that results from the way social welfare systems are currently configured.

As the analysis in the preceding chapters demonstrates, the losses and disbenefits for the state are also substantial. Not funding simple preventive measures (such as adaptation grants or support for children living on the cliff-edge) can have a severe financial impact on the resources of UK plc; can demoralise staff working in the social welfare sectors; can result in costly and high staff turnovers; can create 'failure demand' through the stifling of innovation by front-line workers; can foster expensive anxiety avoidance rituals; and on and on.

Sadly, this is something that needs to be emphasised, since there is a view – widespread perhaps – that regrettable as it may be, the harm suffered by those experiencing clustered injustice is a price worth paying for the convenience of the many. In truth, the dominant managerialist approach to the administration of public bodies is not convenient for anyone. It is simply that it is not so debilitating for those who do not live with disadvantage – those who are not forever bumping into its sharp edges – as to provoke the moral outrage that it should.

CHAPTER 7

Doing justice

Couldn't help but make me feel ashamed to live in a land
Where justice is a game.

Hurricane, Bob Dylan and Jacques Levy

Introduction

The multiple, entangled legal problems that blight the lives of those who live with disadvantage are symptomatic markers of a failed system of social justice. Fixing this broken system calls for a radical programme of reform: reform not only of the way social welfare programmes are funded, but also in the way in which we conceptualise disadvantage and justify privilege.

Effective action of this kind is plainly feasible. As Keynes observed during a not dissimilar period of uncertainty, 'the difficulty lies not so much in developing new ideas as in escaping from old ones, which ramify, for those brought up as most of us have been, into every corner of our minds'.[1] Radical reform will, however, take time: not least the time to put in place an adequate supply of decent social welfare supports.

There must be hope that this can come to pass. The coronavirus epidemic of 2020 has laid bare how incredibly expensive it is not to have such a system, just as the 2007/08 financial crisis demonstrated how incredibly expensive it was to have unregulated financial markets. Expensive, not just in financial terms – but in terms of human suffering and the increasing social instability generated by gross inequalities of this kind.

A reformed and properly funded social welfare system would drastically reduce the numbers of people experiencing clustered injustice. However, adequate funding alone cannot hope to eradicate the phenomenon, particularly if the new funding simply resources the failed systems of, for example, reductionism, compartmentalism, juridification, bureaucracy and the process-led approaches described in earlier chapters.

Action to address the inherent biases within the law would also reduce the scale and severity of the impact of clustered injustice – but meaningful reform of this kind will be incremental and be measured in decades and generations. In the shorter term, all we can hope for is a greater appreciation by lawyers and judges of these biases: that they pause before trotting out some apt maxim they learned as uncritical students; that at some fundamental level they come to understand what it is like to be a person who lives with disadvantage – despite the fact that they inhabit a different planet.[2]

Overview

Rather than focus on the macro challenges of securing adequate social welfare reform, this chapter concentrates instead on practical and more immediate measures that can be taken to address the harm experienced by those who live with clustered injustice.

In this context, the first requirement is, as noted throughout this book, an acceptance by the state[3] of responsibility for the creation of the problem. The state has, through the development of its legal and administrative systems, artificially compartmentalised almost every aspect of civic life. Sometimes this has been done out of objective necessity, but not infrequently the sole justification appears to 'administrative convenience'. Whatever the motivation, this fragmentation of responsibility has a disproportionate impact on those who experience clustered injustice.

With this recognition comes the obligation on the state (analogous to the 'polluter pays' principle) to take effective steps to address it. This will include using its best endeavours to avoid the creation of complexity in the first place, and where complexity is unavoidable, to take responsibility for managing that complexity (rather than simply exporting it to the individual experiencing disadvantage). It is a duty that rests with every state actor, albeit that overall accountability rests with central government.

The principal focus of the analysis that follows concerns the *proactive* measures that would reduce the prevalence of clustered injustice. In addition, it considers (briefly) some *reactive* measures that would reduce the severity of its impact. The analysis opens, however, by highlighting an over-arching factor, of relevance to both contexts: the importance of support.

The importance of support

The research programme that has occupied much of my time for the last decade – the Legal Entitlements and Problem-solving (LEaP) project funded by Cerebra, a disabled children's research charity[4] – has concerned legal problem-solving for families with disabled children. Families struggling with the dysfunctional systems of multiple, underfunded agencies protecting their budgets and – in practice – displaying little ability to 'work together': families for whom the phenomenon of clustered injustice is very real indeed.

The programme has identified one factor more than any other that is essential to enable families to persevere and to cope with the consequential stress and anxieties they experience. That factor is 'support': emotional support from people who are – or have been – in a similar position. For many, living with clustered injustice is going to be a long-term experience for which there are no magic wands, no vaccines, no 'solutions'. Although there will often be a need for additional practical, technical and legal support – having the emotional resilience to embark on this journey will often be decisive.

Small, local and independent support

Support groups

The support that is considered of greatest value to those encountered in the Cerebra LEap research, is support from people who have personal experience of trying to work through the same impossibly messy problems – complex administrative public sector challenges that may materialise as a result of the most simple of requests for assistance. External support of this kind not only provides those in need with practical advice on how to proceed, it also gives them a sense of 'external validation' – that (for example) they are right to trust their senses: right to feel that they have been treated badly by the system. In so doing, it empowers individuals to persevere – to believe that they are not being unrealistic. In this context, Wolff and De-Shalit[5] speak of the value of 'affiliation': of how this provides a sense of 'belonging' to a wider group and enables the person to 'feel more self-assured about their ability to handle negotiations with authorities'. Knowing that other people have experienced the same problem and considered it unreasonable, can challenge a sense of isolation: a realisation that they are not alone and not the first to encounter this particular problem.[6]

There is considerable research that demonstrates that the high value placed on independent support groups is not unique to disabled children and their families – that this view is shared by (for example) carers generally,[7] people with mental health difficulties,[8] disabled people,[9] people who have experienced domestic violence[10] and people who are homeless or threatened with homelessness.[11]

In psychological terms, there is good evidence to suggest that sustained emotional support engendering a sense of well-being[12] can counteract the negative effects of cognitive overload.[13] It can, in particular, enable individuals: to be more creative;[14] to have the space to see the 'bigger picture'; to be 'integrative' (to be able to think across systems boundaries and consider a broader range of materials); to be more efficient; to be more open to information; and can 'fuel psychological resilience'.[15] In a similar vein, research suggests that a negative sense of well-being narrows people's attention; narrows their ideas about possible courses of action; makes them 'miss the forest for the trees'; and is most probably an 'evolutionarily adaptive' response – for example, by focussing and mobilising action to escape when the individual feels threatened.[16]

Small, local independent user-led groups are valued because of their authenticity: as one member of a mental health user group has explained – it is about 'sisterhood, connections, emotional support, relationships, advice, information and guidance, lifeline, trust, safe space et al.'[17]

Given that 'independence' is one of the most highly valued characteristics of user-led support groups, it might appear that the state has only a limited ability to nurture their development. This perception is open to challenge on a number of counts, but in the context of those experiencing clustered injustice there is perhaps one thing above all others that public bodies can do. It is to find some way to understand, at a fundamental level, how institutionally unreceptive their systems are to independent voices of this kind; how wilfully deaf they are to evidence of 'systems failures'; and how hostile they can be to those that have the temerity to deliver this news.

Instead of nurturing and valuing independent support groups, the approach of many public bodies can be characterised as exploitative, to the extent that (objectively) they actively undermine their values and independence. As the National Council for Voluntary Organisations (NCVO) has observed, groups developing close working relationships with government can find themselves compromised, and state funding can create 'pressure for self-censorship'.[18]

An influential 2013 report highlighted the particular importance of state funding to independent organisations 'working with disadvantaged groups' – namely those 'working with socially excluded and vulnerable people; offenders and their families; people with mental health needs; parents and carers; people with substance abuse problems; lesbian, gay and bisexual people; homeless people; victims of crime and their families; and asylum seekers'.[19] It then stated:

> The evidence is that [the government] is not doing enough to recognise or safeguard the sector's independence. It is particularly surprising to see direct attacks by Government and others on the freedom of expression of voluntary bodies working with the state. Self-censorship

by voluntary bodies is also a problem because some fear losing vital and increasingly scarce state funding if they challenge the status quo. There is widespread non-compliance by central and local government with measures to protect independence.[20]

In 'systems thinking' terms, the disdainful, controlling approach that many public bodies have towards small, independent support groups makes no economic or administrative sense – let alone sense in terms of advancing the well-being of those they support. Chapman refers to this as the presumption of 'knowing best': an approach that 'completely closes the door to any learning experience – if one already knows the answer or knows best there is no need to learn anything'.[21] Even with public bodies who claim to have an open-door policy, all too often there is only the pretence of listening and 'learning': of going through the motions of 'consultations' peppered with rhetorical protestations of 'co-producing' and joint working'.

Input from frontline staff

Improvements in the effectiveness of public sector systems also depend on public bodies listening to and taking on board feedback from their frontline staff as to what works, what does not and what unintended consequences need to be ironed out. Such an approach, in systems thinking terms, provides:

> . . . a framework within which most or all of the participants can agree an agenda for improvement or a process for moving forward. This is actually the best that can be achieved when dealing with messes, but it may still appear inadequate to someone wedded to the idea of an instant solution.[22]

Making public bodies open to such insights requires – first and foremost – that they reject managerialism as an administrative system and in so doing, that they commit to a continual process of improving their organisations' 'culture' by – among other things – listening to and empowering their frontline workers those for whom they serve.

Legislative change

Legislative change may also have a role to play – for example, through a fundamental reform to commissioning – of a kind described by Hudson as 'commissioning local and small'.[23] Hudson advocates an expansive use of the Public Services (Social Value) Act 2012 to 'embed social value into the design of services and decision-making criteria, rather than concentrating solely on cost and efficiencies'. In this respect he echoes key aspects of systems thinking, that 'counter-intuitively, focussing on cost drives costs up'[24] – and that when it comes to provision of public services, the idea of 'economies of scale' in the form of 'industrialised services based on service centres and back offices, built around controls on activity and cost'[25] is a myth.

Hudson, like many systems thinking analysts, argues that the people most likely to design systems that are effective in delivering decent co-ordinated social welfare support for marginalised groups are 'front-line workers and the people with whom they work'.[26]

The Social Services and Well-being (Wales) Act 2014 s16 also provides an example of the role that legislation may be able to play in bringing about positive change. It places a duty on councils to promote the development of 'social enterprises, co-operatives, user led services and the third sector'. Although there is only 'patchy' evidence so far of the impact of this provision, academic commentators have suggested that it has the potential to contribute in meaningful ways 'to the delivery of high quality user-oriented services that also entail a variety of social and local economic benefits'.[27]

Large, national and complicated support

Charities and not-for-profit organisations running state-funded services

The above analysis places considerable emphasis on 'smallness' – or perhaps more aptly, the absence of 'largeness'. Although there is clearly a role for larger organisations in the process of addressing the phenomenon of clustered injustice, for many people with this problem the early support of a small, local and genuinely independent user-led group is considered to be of greatest value.

There are many reasons why size appears to matter. Most obviously, that the multiple, successional, messy problems that blight the lives of people in this position, are overwhelmingly created by large organisations – by the bureaucratic, impersonal, Procrustean operating systems that so many of them employ. Size creates complexity and complexity generates unforeseen consequences. This is as true for charitable and not-for-profit organisations as it is public sector bodies. Another not insignificant factor concerns the extent to which some large charities have found themselves compromised by their contractual relationships *with* central and local government.

It is, of course, understandable that charities may choose to run state-funded services for those for whom they advocate – believing (often with good reason) that they can do this better than the public or 'for profit' sectors. This, however, carries risks – including the perception of being 'captured' by the very commercial forces that prompted them to enter the market in the first place.

Case example – care workers

In many respects, the case of *Royal Mencap Society v Tomlinson-Blake*[28] provides the starkest illustration of this potentially destructive relationship. As I write, this case is on appeal to the Supreme Court, but the final decision is, in many respects, immaterial for the purposes of this analysis (but not, of course, for care workers at the centre of the dispute).

The case involved Mencap, a charity which seeks to improve the lives of people with a learning disability. In 2019, over 80 per cent of its annual income (of over £200 million) came from the provision of social care services, of which a large part derived from central and local government contracts.[29]

It is well established that there is a market failure in the UK for social care services funded by the state,[30] with many commercial organisations providing such care at significant risk of insolvency.[31] In workforce terms, care workers are the lowest paid sector in the UK[32] with a staff turnover rate (in 2019) of 40 per cent:[33] almost three times higher than the UK average. Turnover is a particular problem for many disabled and elderly people for whom continuity of care worker (having consistent care from a person they have come to know and trust) can be particularly important.[34] There is the additional (but closely associated) problem of severe staff shortages. At any one time, in adult social care, there are over 120,000 unfilled posts.[35] It appears that most observers believe that low pay is the critical factor in both the recruitment and retention crisis affecting this sector.[36]

Mencap employs a large number of care workers, many of whom 'sleep over' as part of their caring role. Because of the financial constraints imposed by central and local government contracts, Mencap found itself challenging the right of care workers to be paid the national minimum wage when their work required them to 'sleep over' at the home of the person for whom they cared. Mencap succeeded in the Court of Appeal, which it appears, saved charities £400 million.[37] Conversely, of course, it meant that care workers were denied this sum – and in addition, the 'tens if not hundreds of thousands of low paid sleep-in workers' that had been paid the minimum wage for this work were at risk of having their hourly rate cut to £3.23.[38] Mencap stressed that it 'did not want to bring this case, but had to because the prospect of having to make large unfunded back payments threatened to bankrupt many providers'.[39]

Sustaining the precarious, low paid conditions of care workers not only undermines the quality of the care and support packages of people with learning disabilities, it also generates many other adverse (and unintended) consequences – some of which have become apparent during the coronavirus emergency of 2020. For example, in order to earn a breadline wage, many care workers have multiple jobs in multiple care settings. It appears that this factor significantly contributed to the virus's disproportionate impact on disabled and elderly people.[40]

The paradox of a highly respected charity finding itself – in essence – taking legal proceedings to shore up such a broken state system creates dilemmas for those in need of straightforward, unqualified and independent support. It points to reasons why the support of small, unquestionably independent, local user-led not-for-profit organisations is so highly valued: the small charitable organisations 'with little profile but high energy, real street credibility and beneficiary involvement' to quote Peter Beresford.[41]

There is, however, no denying the valuable work done by many larger charities, and their support will often be pivotal when the option of small, locally based user-led support does not exist or does not appeal to the person experiencing clustered injustice. Hybrid support mechanisms can also be of considerable value – ie where a public body commissions a charity to develop an 'intentional peer support group': one that then recruits 'peers with experience' to support people who are homeless or in other particularly complex and precarious situation. The literature suggests[42] that these artificial user-support entities have the potential to provide valuable support – by building mutual trust and empathetic relationships – although this is dependent in large measure on the willingness of the public body to be open to collaborative and innovative models of working.[43]

Proactive measures

Although emotional support and good local advice is often of fundamental importance in sustaining people experiencing clustered injustice, ultimately their ability to live less troubled lives depends on the responsiveness of the relevant public bodies. In general, the extent to which such bodies are willing (or are capable of being coerced) to take appropriate action will be dictated by two interconnected factors: (1) their managerial administrative system; and (2) the state of their organisational culture.

Reforming managerialism

Chapter 5 has considered the harmful effects of 'command and control' managerial administrative systems on individuals experiencing clustered injustice. The language of managerialism[44] is the language of control, of targets and of change: of 'aiming higher'; 'driving forward'; and endless reorganisations. In relation to the harm it is causing the national health service, a former Chief Executive of NHS England has referred to it[45] as a 'pace-setting' approach which:

> . . . is about getting stuff done, setting targets, hitting them and then getting the next one and driving the organisation forward. If you look at NHS management, it is predominantly pace-setting, when in fact, to deal with the world that we are talking about in the future, being responsive to patients, engaging with local populations and creating services around individual patients, there are different styles that you need. We have got a major task to shift NHS leadership from the predominantly pace-setting to something else.

It is indeed difficult to think of any public sector workplace that has not been 'restructured' on multiple occasions over the last 20 years – and difficult to remember any that have led to a material improvement in the quality of the organisation's service (before another reorganisation came along).

'Systems thinking' theorists are not hostile to change – merely to change driven 'top-down'. For Seddon, positive change (like a positive organisational culture) develops when frontline workers are given the freedom to think about how the quality of the organisation's work can be improved and how the range of different challenges that arise can be addressed ('problem-solved') effectively.[46]

Case example – health and social care inter-agency working

Many years ago, a colleague and I were asked to look at the way health and social services co-operated with each other in Wales.[47] Inter-agency disputes between health and social services bodies blight the lives of many people who experience clustered injustice, and this is hardly surprising: at what point a 'free of the point of need' health need becomes a 'means tested' social care need is practically and legally unfathomable.[48]

My colleague and I travelled throughout Wales searching for good practice and interviewing many key players in this game: the game of 'pass the parcel'. Initially we focused on the centres of power – meeting senior officers in their headquarters: finding plenty of problems there, but few examples of relationships that worked well. We then started looking further afield.

What we discovered was that the further you moved away from these centres, the more likely you were to encounter constructive joint working. Indeed, one of the most positive examples we encountered was in the delightful and relatively isolated town of Tregaron in West Wales. The point being that in Tregaron, pretty well everyone seemed to know each other – and these relationships transcended their differences (such as whether they worked for the NHS or the local council). If they encountered someone with a complex messy problem, they would simply discuss this with their colleague in the other organisation and work out a way of addressing the problem – without necessarily feeling obliged to follow the detailed procedures in their rule-books.[49] All around them, Welsh public sector bodies were being reorganised and, as one interviewee commented, it was 'almost impossible to overstate the problem that this was causing'.[50]

The research concluded that the 'establishment of good personal relationships between key health and social services officers is the single most important factor facilitating constructive inter-agency collaboration'. It recommended that in future, organisational upheavals should be kept to the absolute minimum: that the 'ability of health and social services to harmonise their planning and commissioning functions is inversely proportional to the degree of organisational upheaval they experience'. In effect, we recommended that the government do something revolutionary (something it had not attempted before) – namely that it should *do nothing*.

Inevitably, of course, the report was ignored.[51]

Personal relationships, trust and organisational turbulence

Personal relationships and trust are crucial to effective inter-agency joint working – particularly 'prior relationships [and] existing networks'.[52] Relationships and trust take time to develop: the longer the relationship the greater the likelihood that the partners will gain a mutual understanding and with this learn to trust each other.[53]

Organisational turbulence fractures these relationships – key workers get relocated; they have to re-apply for their jobs; they may see their roles disappear; they will often leave in despair; and so on.

The harm this causes has a disproportionate impact on people who experience clustered injustice because their problems almost invariably straddle more than one public sector silo.

Creating problem-solving organisational cultures

The cumulative impact of managerialism's control fixation is the creation of the poisonous organisational cultures that not uncommonly confront those experiencing clustered injustice (considered in chapter 5 above). The creation of workforces with a 'sense of futility and pessimism . . . long before they enter the problem-solving arena': workforces that 'simply give up trying; the energy and will to resolve problems and attain goals drains away'.[54] Organisations with a 'culture of stress' that harms not only those seeking support but also their staff and 'the organization as a whole'.[55] A situation that has been described as a 'toxic cocktail' that combines both a 'reluctance on the part of citizens "to express their concerns or complaints" and a defensiveness on the part of services "to hear and address concerns"'.[56]

We learn from the above analysis that frontline workers play a critical role when those experiencing clustered injustice approach a public body for assistance. We learn that for the process to be effective, these workers need to have sufficient autonomy to be able to work across boundaries; to forge relationships of trust with those in need of support and with other key players; and to be able to make significant decisions. We learn that arrangements of this kind are much more likely to occur in public bodies with positive organisational cultures: positive both for those within and those without the system.

Key workers

In identifying what needs to be done, it is best to start with people. What does a person who experiences clustered injustice need when they make contact with a public body? The answer is that they need to be listened to by someone with experience and with knowledge of how things work in their locality; someone with the ability to effect change; someone who can see the bigger picture and who is able to work across boundaries. The job title of this person is irrelevant, but they must be able to exercise power on behalf of the organisation. In the section that follows, such people are referred to simply as 'key workers' – people with experience and (ideally) with anarchic tendencies.[57]

When confronted by a cluster of messy problems, key workers have the ability to go up a level of abstraction – and to avoid the bureaucratic temptation of separating, labelling, compartmentalising and then assigning each discrete problem to other offices. By seeing the bigger picture, they are able to warn the individual of future challenges that may be encountered, as well as other – seemingly unconnected – action that needs to be taken. They may be experts in one field or another (for example, housing officers, social workers, substance misuse workers, probation officers) but their USP will be that they are excellent generalists; comfortable working across systems boundaries and making judgment calls as to which battles have to be fought and which can be skirted. They will have a 'backpack' of practical experience to draw on: what works, who can be trusted, which levers to pull and when to pull them. They will know in their bones that rules are made for the guidance of the wise and the blind adherence of the stupid.

There is no shortage of people with these qualities working in the public sector[58] – it is simply that in command and control regimes, skills of this kind are unlikely to result in career progression. Indeed, the extent to which large organisations value such key workers will be directly proportional to their efficiency and their decency. In toxic organisations, they are the first group to be offered early retirement and (sadly but understandably) the first to grasp that opportunity.

Unfortunately, it is seldom that someone experiencing clustered injustice encounters a person with these qualities on first contact with a public body. As a general rule, their first contact will usual be with a call centre (or with a one-stop shop or 'reception' that is, by any other name, a call centre).

The 'call centre approach' is considered at chapter 3 and for those experiencing clustered injustice it constitutes another senseless barrier to be negotiated. Although the theory of call centres is that they cut costs by (among other things) hiding specialist workers in the back office, 'systems thinking' theory argues that this is not the case[59] – and that 'instead of the front-end being "dumb", the place where people first present should be staffed by people who have the expertise to understand their'[60] needs and what it will take to meet them.

This, in effect, requires that the back office of skilled key workers be placed in the front office: to be available at the first point of contact for those seeking help. A situation, of course, not a million miles from the process that is supposed to operate in the primary health service – of making contact with a G P. It is an approach that rejects the one-size-fits all 'simplification by fragmentation' mindset and requires flexibility within the system to enable an individual's complex needs (that will often span multiple organisational silos) to be addressed by such workers with sensitivity to their actual living conditions.[61]

By listening to and analysing what is being said, key workers can, if needs be, go up a level of abstraction and then initiate and co-ordinate the provision of multi-layered and multi-dimensional support across many agencies and networks in order to effectively deal with clustered problems.[62] For example, a housing officer who can propose spending above their budget, to avoid a fivefold 'hit' to the social services budget;[63] or one who is trying to accommodate a homeless person who is not only able to assess the support the person needs in order to be able to manage the tenancy but is also able to co-ordinate the support the person needs to address their substance abuse and mental health difficulties.[64]

The value of key workers for people experiencing clustered injustice has been highlighted by many studies.[65] Research by Wodchis et al,[66] for example, reviewed 30 integrated health and social care programs in high-income countries and identified the benefits of key workers empowered to 'problem solve' across these boundaries and the importance of the close involvement of local organisations in these systems (as well as full support at the strategic senior manager level).

Key workers, when co-ordinating action to address the needs of those at risk of experiencing clustered injustice, will often require specialist input from a range of disciplines (for example, social workers, nurses, doctors, occupational therapists etc) – although (as noted in chapter 3) it may be open to question whether this input is objectively necessary in every case.[67]

Arrangements of this kind – with the removal of over-controlling, highly stressed and coercive managerial regimes – should, in theory, result in the emergence of more positive and innovative organisational cultures where there are rewards for co-operative behaviour and where trusting relationships can in time develop. The evidence suggests that such systems are likely to be significantly more efficient[68] in reducing the numbers of individuals experiencing clustered injustice and to be cost-effective from the perspective of the U K plc. Of course, there is no certainty that this transition from a problem-causing to a problem-preventing system will happen effortlessly – it is indeed likely that systems change of this nature will produce unintended consequences – unforeseen feedback loops.

Without creating any targets, performance indicators or other trappings of managerialism, mechanisms will need to be developed to ensure that positive 'person-centred' environments replace the current unhealthy regimes: environments that are accessible, inclusive, sensitive, flexible and enabling.[69] Whatever shape these mechanisms take, it will be essential that they be underpinned by measures that reflect the priorities and sentiments of those who experience clustered disadvantage – as well as the knowledge and insights of those who work at the coal-face of the relevant public bodies.

A connected and perhaps controversial aspect of reforms of this kind, concerns the extent to which they are capable of marginalising or offsetting the negative consequences that have resulted from the excessive juridification of social welfare law considered in chapter 4. In the case studies considered in that chapter, the negative consequences involved disproportionate expenditure on legal fees (in the case of mental capacity legislation) and misdirection and distraction (in the case of identity recognition legislation).

There is good reason to believe that one of the consequences of a reform programme leading to the adequate funding of the social welfare system will be that these complex 'process-heavy' laws become largely obsolete. The experience of the health service is instructive in this respect. The NHS is (by comparison to the other pillars of our welfare state) relatively well-funded. Its main underpinning statute, the NHS Act 2006, contains hardly any specifically enforceable substantive or process rights, and there is no loud clamour for this to change. In contrast, the poorly funded social care system simply bristles with such rights, and the clamour for change in this sector has resulted, not in better funding, but in an ever-greater proliferation of process-heavy rights. This suggests that in relation to socio-economic rights – the trick is to focus on the adequacy of the budget and not to be distracted by the magniloquence of the law.

Until such time as we have radical, progressive and well-funded social welfare interventions, it is decidedly unattractive to advocate the repeal of these progressive neoliberal measures, notwithstanding their questionable efficacy in addressing the mischief that was used to justify their enactment. Paraphrasing Laurie,[70] although 'it is not in the public interest that an excessive proportion of the social welfare budget is spent on administration and legal disputes', it is neither in the public interest that public bodies be given the benefit of the doubt when the right to fundamental socio-economic support is at stake – particularly when the level of state funding for that support is patently inadequate.

All that can be suggested, in relation to these organisational measures, is that – subject to one major caveat – *more* of the heavy lifting be done by social care professionals[71] and *less* by lawyers. The caveat is, of course, that this takes place within a non-managerialist administrative system.

Form-filling

Form filling is something that almost everyone finds tedious, but is a process that dominates the lives of many people who live with disadvantage.[72] It is all the more tiresome when the information demanded has nothing to do with the individual's specific need and/or is information that the public body has been given many times before. Putting key workers 'front of house' should mean that only strictly relevant information is captured – as is the case in the average GP's practice. However, 'acting like this challenges the regime's requirements for 'complete' and standardised information'[73] and sadly, despite endless exhortations to public bodies to develop 'tell us once' policies, that is not how it works.

Even in their most elementary and seemingly innocuous of contexts, form-filling requirements can be highly revealing of an organisation's approach: a litmus test as to their accessibility and inclusion agendas. An elderly man is sitting at the back of a charity's reception area, holding a brown envelope, a blank questionnaire and looking bewildered. On being approached by a concerned visitor he explains that he came to ask for help with a letter he had received – and at the reception desk was handed a form to complete so that the adviser had his basic details. Instead of going through their standard 'script' – the receptionist might instead have 'listened': might have asked him why he needed help with the letter he had brought with him. Had this been done, the elderly man could have explained that he was unable to read.

The template form-filling process can also be deeply humiliating, not just for those for whom reading or writing in English may be a challenge. Not infrequently, when a parent of a disabled child, for example, approaches an English local authority asking for assistance, they are subjected to exactly the same process as parents considered to be neglecting or abusing their child.[74] The reason that authorities take this approach, appears to be (in large measure) to enable them provide the regulator (Ofsted) with data that scores highly in the auditing process[75] – where (to quote Munro[76]) records have 'acquired a new dominance' and 'good practice' is equated with 'keeping records'.[77] Lane et al[78] refer to this as 'compliance addiction' where professional practice and judgement are 'compromised by an over-complicated, lengthy and tick-box assessment and recording system'.[79]

Completing endless and complex forms is not only frustrating, it adds to the cognitive overload of those who experience clustered injustice[80] (discussed in the previous chapter). Gandy et al[81] describe how even 'seemingly small barriers to accessing social welfare entitlements – such as lengthy or complex applications – can affect an individual's decision to apply and may be sufficient to deter those . . . in greatest need'.[82] A number of commentators consider that this insight has important implications for policy-makers, who should focus on reducing the requirement that people in this position have to complete (for example) long forms and decipher new rules[83] as well as 'bundling application processes and eligibility requirements across programmes'.[84]

Reactive measures

Legal aid

If the focus of this book was simply disadvantage or injustice or the holding the state to account – then much of this final chapter would, perforce, be devoted to the importance of legal aid: to the need to reverse the savage cuts; to the repairing of the damage it has suffered through endless, crass reorganisations; to its disfigurement by decades of poisonous managerialism.[85]

The focus of this book is, however, the harm caused by *clustered injustice* – and it would be disingenuous to claim either that the erosion of legal aid is the cause of this phenomenon; or that if adequately funded, legal aid would constitute an effective mechanism for addressing it.

For many people living with disadvantage, the accumulation of multiple and synchronous legal problems is not (to paraphrase Freeman[86]) due to the 'misguided conduct of particular actors' – rather, it is a social phenomenon: a systems failure and one that cannot be resolved simply by disaggregation, simplification and adjudication.

Of course legal aid has an important part to play in addressing many of the distinct legal problems people living with disadvantage experience, and on occasions it can fund strategic action that removes a log jam, that can prove to be a pivotal moment in a person's life. However, that will be the exception, not the rule. For most people experiencing clustered injustice, 'the law school model of personal legal problems, of solving them and returning the client to the smooth and orderly world in television advertisements, doesn't apply'.[87]

Historically, many legal aid lawyers have functioned as generalist key workers, having experience and skills across the *social welfare legal spectrum*: social security, debt, housing, health and social care, as well having as key fields of *private law*, such as family; and often with an adequate understanding of *criminal law*, or at least access to criminal defence practitioners in their organisation. This was particularly so in relation to law centres and not-for-profit advice centres. As chapter 3 notes, half of all such centres have closed in the last eight years. At the same time, legal aid has – in effect – ceased to be available in benefits, debt, employment, non-asylum immigration, private family and child welfare law matters (legal aid remains available for care proceedings and domestic violence cases) and many areas of housing; and in those fields where legal aid is still available, there are fewer such contracts, and it is increasingly rare for providers to have contracts across the range of available disciplines. This means that lawyers are no longer available to act as generalist key workers for people experiencing clustered injustice. It might be argued that this makes sense, as having lawyers in the role of key workers is an unnecessary expense. To make this argument, it would of course be necessary to understand how much legal aid lawyers are actually paid.[88]

Public services ombudsmen

The value of the ombudsmen process for those experiencing clustered injustice

The public services ombudsmen process[89] provides the public with free, independent and impartial reviews of complaints about public services. It has, in theory, many characteristics of value in addressing significant aspects of the harm suffered by those experiencing clustered injustice. Many ombudsman reports consider a wide range of disparate and interlinked failings by public bodies. The ombudsmen are empowered to investigate (among other things) 'alleged or apparent maladministration'[90] by public bodies – and 'maladministration' is an admirably ambiguous concept. A former ombudsman considered that maladministration included (among other things):[91]

> ... bias, neglect, inattention, delay, incompetence, ineptitude, perversity, turpitude, arbitrariness, rudeness, refusal to answer reasonable questions, knowingly giving advice which is misleading or inadequate, ignoring valid advice or overruling considerations which would produce an uncomfortable result for the overruler, offering no redress or manifestly disproportionate redress, showing bias whether because of colour, sex or any other grounds, faulty procedures, failure by management to monitor compliance with adequate procedures, cavalier disregard of guidance which is intended to be followed in the interest of equitable treatment of those who use the service, partiality; and failure to mitigate the effects of rigid adherence to the letter of the law where that produces manifestly inequitable treatment.

This extraordinary list of unreasonable behaviours by public bodies is broad enough to encompass almost all of the difficulties encountered by those who experience clustered disadvantage – and the ombudsmen's case-loads are of an order that one could envisage it being of material benefit to those in this situation. In 2018/19, for example, that Parliamentary and Health Services Ombudsman (PHSO) handled 29,841 complaints (and made decisions on 5,658);[92] and in the same period the Local Government and Social Care Ombudsman (LGSCO) handled 16,899 complaints, of which 4,232 were investigated in detail, and of these 58 per cent were upheld.[93] By comparison, in the same period there were 3,600 applications for judicial review, of which only a small proportion made any progress (see chapter 2 above).

Practical problems with the ombudsmen process

The public services ombudsman process is generally a lawyer-free zone and has considerable potential as a mechanism for redress when things have gone seriously wrong. There are, however, a number of practical problems with the process.

First, the ombudsmen are all seriously under-funded. Considering the LGSCO, for example, the number of complaints it has received has grown five-fold in the last 10 years, during which time its budget has (in real terms) halved.[94] The substantial rise in complaints has been mirrored by increasingly severe restrictions on the availability of publicly funded legal advice and support (indeed, the legal aid cutbacks may have contributed to this increase[95]).

Second, the ombudsmen lack the power to hand down binding decisions. They make 'findings' and 'recommend' remedies (including the payment of compensation) but public bodies do not have to comply with these recommendations. This has led – in some respects – to a negative spiral. The ombudsmen become hesitant to recommend appropriate compensation in severe cases of maladministration – fearing that this will increase the likelihood of non-compliance by public bodies, which in turn means that there are no significant sanctions to deter the badly behaved – which then prompts the compliant public bodies to question the affordability of good behaviour.[96]

2019 research[97] illustrates this point. It analysed over 1,500 decisions of the LGSCO concerning 'children and education' with a view to understanding how it dealt with councils that had significantly delayed complaints investigations. Delay is one of the most neglected of all legal harms confronting those who live with disadvantage. For those with clusters of problems, delay in resolving a complaint will increase the likelihood of their cluster expanding – as new problems arise before existing ones are resolved. Delay is an especial problem for children: children don't get a second chance at childhood; and children can't stop their needs changing while they hang around waiting for a public body to get its act together.[98]

The research found that a relatively small number of councils accounted for a significant proportion of the complaints concerning delay and that in over 60 per cent of all cases (where the ombudsman found fault) the case was remitted back to the council without a recommendation for compensation for the delay – despite the average delay being almost a year. In the remainder of cases, where compensation was recommended, it amounted to 30p per day on average.

The take-away lesson from this process is that badly behaving councils face few (if any) adverse consequences for ignoring the law; for fostering legal illiteracy among their staff (eg as the statutory timescales for complaints investigations); for failing to invest in well-trained complaints teams; and for failing to learn the lessons when things go wrong. Indeed, for a cash-strapped council, having a dysfunctional complaints policy can be highly cost-effective.

Third, a further, and significant failing of the ombudsmen process concerns its increasing reliance on mechanisms associated with managerialism – including the use of performance indicators and targets.[99] The result is that many complaints are now rejected for the procedural reasons, few if any investigations involve face to face meet-

ings with complainants and all the worst effects of targets are introduced into a system that is in many other respects has many merits.

A way forward

These defects are all remediable. There is no reason why the system
could not be properly funded; no reason why it cannot impose
enforceable and seriously dissuasive penalties for bad behaviour; no
reason why it should not shed its damaging managerialist tendencies.[100] If this occurs, the process would be of considerable value for
those seeking to challenge the clustered injustice they experience. It
would, however, remain a largely reactive process – one that kicks in
when serious problems have already arisen.[101]

The Equality and Human Rights Commission

As with the public services ombudsmen, the Equality and Human
Rights Commission (EHRC) has many powers that could make it a
potent force addressing aspects of the harm suffered by those experiencing clustered injustice. People with protected characteristics are
disproportionately at risk of experiencing clustered injustice: women,
people with a BAME identity and disabled people, for example. The
Commission has the power: to provide assistance to victims of
discrimination; to intervene in court proceedings in human rights
and equality cases; and to take proceedings where public bodies have
acted in a way that breaches the Equality Act 2010 or the Human
Rights Act 1998. Notwithstanding the limitations of identity-based
rights laws (considered in chapter 4 above), these are valuable and
potentially formidable powers.

However, as with the ombudsmen, the EHRC has experienced
devastating cuts to its funding, such that its budget in 2020 was
barely a quarter of that in 2012.[102] In the light of the appalling and
disproportionate harm inflicted by the coronavirus epidemic on
communities with protected characteristics, there must be hope that
the EHRC will receive the funding that is needed to enable it to fulfil
its important role.

The role of information technology

Seddon et al, in describing how public sector systems can better
meet the needs of those for whom they ostensibly exist, emphasise
that 'IT should come last'.[103] In keeping with this observation, this

chapter concludes by considering the role that IT has to play in addressing the needs of those who experience clustered injustice.

There is no doubting that some legal procedures lend themselves to digitalisation – for example, processes that are well-established and involve the completion of standard forms, such as applications for probate, for a divorce or to instigate a small claim in the county court. What appears to be an essential (but often forgotten) element in the digitalisation process, is that the system should first be perfected before there is any consideration as whether an IT 'transformation' might offer significant additional benefits.

IT makeovers are most likely to be effective when they are applied to systems that are governed by relatively simple rules and have few (if any) 'feedback loops'. In essence, systems that can operate through the application of a reductionist approach: systems that break each stage of the process into separate sub-units which can then be 'digitalised' before their reassembly – as cogs in a clockwork clock.

The process by which entangled messy problems are addressed requires the development of responsive systems that can accommodate complexity: systems that can learn from the unintended consequences that they generate. Systems of this complexity are not promising candidates for IT 'silver bullet transformations', and the literature describing the collapse of IT projects bears this out.[104] One of the reoccurring factors identified in many IT failures concerns the extent to which the problems presented by complex systems are underestimated.[105] The National Audit Office[106] has referred to this as the long-standing problem of 'optimism bias' and Kahenman and Tversky[107] refer to this as 'delusional optimism' where executives fail to act on the basis of the 'rational weighting of gains, losses, and probabilities'. The recent failures have been well publicised – including, for example, the failure of the 'IT in the NHS' project; of home energy 'smart meters'; of the IT signalling in CrossRail; of universal credit; of the COVID-19 'track and trace' app; and on and on.

Despite all the evidence to the contrary, public bodies continue to put their faith in IT – as a mechanism for addressing workload challenges regardless of their complexity. Problematically, a number of larger charities are also exploring IT's potential to address similar workload issues. Increasingly, research in this sector has all the appearance of being 'IT first' – rather than 'perfecting problem-solving first' before undertaking an assessment of whether there is scope for the process then to be digitalised.

The evidence to date suggests that chatbots, 'smart apps' and other IT widgets hold little or no promise for those experiencing clustered injustice – apart from yet greater isolation on the wrong side of a 'digital divide'.[108] Indeed, mechanisms of this kind are arguably even more alienating than call centres – where at least there is the prospect of conversing with a human being. It is not difficult, however, to see their attraction for public bodies and large charities – promising as they do pandemic-proofed, human-free systems where all 'failure demand' is billed to the disadvantaged person's mobile calling plan.

End note

Even in the best of social welfare systems, there will be failures – even in systems where resources are devoted to the building of the resilience of the many and to challenging the inequitable distribution of privilege among the few. Even in the best of welfare states the experience of clustered injustice will fall, disproportionately, on those who live with disadvantage.

The best of welfare states anticipate that their systems will fail, from time to time, and provide effective safety nets – soft places to fall and mechanisms to help lift the fallen back up again. The best of welfare states have adequately resourced institutions that react: that compensate and put things right for those that have been failed; that ensure that lessons are learned and systems improved; that impose seriously dissuasive penalties on public bodies that fail to maintain effective preventative systems.

But in the UK – we do not live in the best of welfare states; but then again, we do not live in the worst of all worlds either. For sure our social welfare institutions are seriously underfunded and for the most part badly run. For sure there is indefensible inequality and grotesque examples of both disadvantage and undue privilege. For sure the organisational culture of many public bodies materially harms those they are (theoretically) there to serve, as well as their own workers.

However, many of our systems and our institutions are capable of being effective: capable of being 'personalised'; capable of being far more effective for those they serve and for those they employ; and capable of using their resources far more efficiently and productively.

As a nation, we have the infrastructure of a social welfare state that has much to recommend it and one that employs very large numbers of people with desire and potential to do good – if only they are empowered to do just that.

We are also living at a pivotal moment – when the art of the politically possible has utterly changed.

At what feels to be an incredibly bleak time – we must not only 'hope', we must also demand a system of social justice for which we can be proud – and not one that is 'a disgrace ... a social equality and economic disaster rolled into one'. [109]

Disadvantage

Introduction

This section contains brief pen sketches of various groups for whom clustered injustice is a common experience. The examples are illustrative and by no means exhaustive.

1) asylum-seekers and people in breach of immigration controls;
2) disabled adults;
3) disabled children and their families;
4) Gypsies and Travelling people;
5) homeless people;
6) people at risk of domestic abuse;
7) people enmeshed in the criminal justice system;
8) people in precarious tenancies;
9) people who experience poverty and debt;
10) unpaid carers.

Asylum-seekers and people in breach of immigration controls

In 2017 it was estimated that there were between 800,000 and 1.2 million unauthorised (or 'irregular') migrants living in the UK.[1] This figure includes about 250,000[2] children (of which over half were born in the UK to irregular migrant parents). In 2018 there were, in addition, over 45,000 people awaiting the outcome of their asylum applications.[3]

The ever-present risk of irregular migrants and their children[4] to detention and deportation places them at considerable danger of a wide range of abuse and exploitation including domestic violence,[5] trafficking and forced labour.[6] In addition, by being excluded from almost all forms of social welfare support they find themselves at significant risk of experiencing a broad cluster of legal problems, including – for example – difficulties in obtaining and retaining accommodation, homelessness, access to healthcare support, poverty and debt.

The experiences of many irregular migrants render them highly susceptible to developing mental health problems.[7] As with all healthcare difficulties, this problem exacerbated by the fear of being reported and deported if they do seek health care support (even – as in the case of those seeking asylum – when legally this fear is not well-founded).[8] In this context, a 2011 report noted that 'all migrants face particular problems accessing health care due to language barriers, lack of knowledge of the NHS, institutional racism, and the lack of cultural competence of the NHS systems and staff'.[9] For both asylum-seekers and those in breach of immigration controls, public services can be intimidating, and the consequent failure to seek help, can create other problems that further intensify their pre-existing disadvantage.

Detention can also trigger or aggravate the development of mental health difficulties, in particular when the detention may be for an indefinite period and there are significant difficulties accessing and receiving appropriate legal advice.[10]

Evidence of the clustered injustice experienced by immigration detainees was cited by 2016 Shaw Report[11] – namely that 'detainees held in the prison estate suffer from multiple, systemic, and compounding barriers to accessing justice, with an often devastating effect on their ability to progress their immigration case, seek independent scrutiny of their ongoing detention from the courts and tribunals, and seek release from detention, as well as on their physical and mental wellbeing'.[12]

Asylum-seekers and irregular migrants are not legally entitled to work; thus, poverty and debt may drive people to work illegally, opening them up for financial and physical abuse. Research has shown that undocumented workers are working for up to 12-hour days, for around £40 a day,[13] putting their earning substantially below the national minimum wage. In extremes, people in this situation may be driven to criminal activity, for example theft, which then enmeshes them in the criminal justice system with all the consequential and negative impacts that this entails.

As at April 2020, asylum-seekers were entitled to £37.75 per person a week to cover all expenses (other than housing) and 2012 research reported that 'the majority of our respondents struggled to feed themselves and their children and afford essential items including clothes, shoes or medicines'.[14]

Access to accommodation is a significant problem for many British nationals and this difficulty is much more acute for many asylum-seekers and irregular migrants. The Immigration Act 2014 severely restricted access to rented accommodation for individuals who lacked a passport or other relevant credentials by imposing significant penalties on landlords who failed to make relevant checks of this kind.[15] The net effect of this legislation was (and indeed was intended to be) a hostile environment in which the threat of homelessness was deployed as a coercive measure.

People enmeshed in the criminal justice system

In 2019, 1.59 million individuals were dealt with by the criminal justice system in England and Wales.[16] Offenders with repeated involvement in the system accounted for nearly two-fifths of the offending population, with 48 per cent of adults being reconvicted of another offence within one year of release from prison,[17] meaning for many their lives are effectively trapped within the revolving door of conviction, detention, release and reconviction.[18]

Pre-existing disadvantage is the single greatest determinant of a person's risk of becoming enmeshed within the system: for example, a childhood within the public care system, childhood poverty, mental health difficulties and homelessness. For Wacquant the impoverished nature of social welfare systems and 'incarceration' are neoliberal 'tools for managing the unruly poor' and best 'understood by paying attention to the structural, functional, and cultural similarities between workfare and prisonfare as "people-processing institutions"'.[19]

Young people in care represent a disproportionate percentage of those trapped in the criminal justice system: fewer than 1 per cent of all children are in care,[20] but two-fifths of children in secure training centres and young offenders' institutions have been in care[21] and young people in care are six times more likely to be cautioned or convicted of a crime than the general population.[22] In similar terms, high numbers of people with mental health difficulties become enmeshed in the criminal justice system, with 26 per cent of women and 16 per cent of men reporting that they received treatment for a mental health problem in the year before their custody.[23] Once detained, it appears that one in five of those diagnosed with a mental health problem receive no care from a mental health professional in prison.[24]

Disadvantage is not, of course, only a causal factor in precipitating an individual's entanglement with the criminal justice system – it is very frequently also a consequence. A high proportion of those who enter the system end up living in poverty.[25] Prisoners are unable to claim for universal credit until release[26] and entitlement to housing benefit stops for those expected to be in prison for more than 13 weeks,[27] meaning many people are unable to retain their tenancy. Unsurprisingly, therefore, one in five people (serving sentences of less than six months) who left prison in the year to March 2018 were homeless.[28] Combined with these financial difficulties, many prisoners are released with debts which have built up during their sentence, often for things as mundane as phone bills.[29] Prisoners often have issues finding employment to alleviate such debts, with only 17 per cent of people in PAYE employment a year after leaving prison,[30] as well as the stigma of imprisonment causing a long-term wage gap – equivalent to around £60 a month.[31]

The clustered injustice that tracks those enmeshed within the criminal justice system is well established. People 'with convictions face many years, if not a lifetime of struggle – in employment, housing, insurance . . . to name a few'.[32] It is a 'revolving door' phenomenon that dominates the lives of many people who experience 'poor mental health, drug and /or alcohol misuse, homelessness, poverty and debt. Each of these difficulties feed into and exacerbates the others, creating a downward spiral that brings people into frequent contact with the criminal justice system'.[33]

Disabled adults

In 2016/17 it was estimated that 22 per cent of the UK population were disabled people.[34]

Like other groups that experience disproportionate disadvantaged, disabled people often experience clusters of legal problems of which the most common problem is poverty. Poverty and disability are mutually reinforcing: a two-way relationship in which disability adds to the risk of poverty, and conditions of poverty add to the risk of disability.[35] Almost half of all people in poverty in the UK are living in families with a disabled person[36] and two-thirds of disabled people living alone are in poverty.[37] Although the high levels of unemployment experienced by disabled people have been identified as the principal cause of their high levels of poverty, their poverty could equally well be attributed to the inadequacy of their social security support entitlements.[38]

In 2017, only 50 per cent of disabled people of working age in the UK were in employment[39] compared to 80 per cent for non-disabled people of working age.[40] The 'stigma and discrimination that touch nearly all aspects of the lives of persons with disabilities'[41] is evident in the perceptions of many employers. 2019 research revealed that one in five employers openly admitted to being less likely to hire a disabled person, than a non-disabled person[42] and even within employment, disabled people are at significant risk of poverty with full-time disabled workers earning on average more than 10 per cent less than full-time non-disabled people,[43] a disadvantage is felt most acutely by those that combined disadvantage of both ethnicity and disability (disabled Bangladeshi and Pakistani men in particular) and those with a mental health problem: the largest proportion of workers paid below the living wage (35 per cent) being those living with a mental impairment.[44]

Research suggests that disabled people's day-to-day living costs are typically 25 per cent higher than those of non-disabled people,[45] with disabled people spending an average of £550 a month on costs related to their disability (such as specialist home equipment/higher insurance premiums).[46]

Poverty and unemployment (as well as disability itself) are all factors that draw disabled people into contact with the Department of Work and Pensions: opening the door to the many opportunities this provides for adverse decisions, perverse revisions: requirements for constant reporting, online form filling, and the resulting need for appeals and tribunal hearings.

Disabled people are more at risk of falling into debt – being more than twice as likely to have unsecured debt totalling more than half of their household income.[47] Having debt of this nature can trigger additional disadvantage, such as housing problems, entanglement with the criminal justice system and an increased susceptibility to poor mental health[48] which brings with it (for example) a yet further risk of the loss of employment.[49] In similar vein, many disabled people also have need of support from social services with all the challenges this poses – in assessments, unfavourable eligibility decisions, inadequate care packages, social care charges appropriating a substantial portion of their social security benefits, reviews, cutbacks, complaints, ombudsman challenges and so on and so on.

Disabled people, particularly for those with mental disabilities, experience high rates of domestic abuse. Research suggests that more than one in three people with mental illness have experienced domestic abuse in the past year (an incidences four times higher than in the general population).[50] In England, it appears that disabled people experience twice the rate of sexual assault, domestic abuse and stalking than non-disabled people.[51] 2015 research, for example, recognised that 'not only do disabled people experience higher rates of domestic abuse, they also experience more barriers to accessing support, such as health and social care services and domestic abuse services'.[52] This can be due to a lack of awareness of their rights, the inability to defend themselves, or sometimes simply lacking the finances to escape from the abuser, who more often than not, holds a coercive position of power.[53]

Disabled children and their families

The Department for Work and Pensions estimates that there are 1.1 million disabled children in the UK or approximately eight per cent of the population under 18 years old.[54] A 2010 study found that many disabled children have difficulties in more than one area of 'daily living' and that almost a third experienced between two and four difficulties and more than 10 per cent experience five or more difficulties.[55]

The last four decades have seen an increase in the numbers of disabled children with multiple and complex impairments being cared for at home. This is due, in part, to 'improved survival rates for low-birth-weight and extremely pre-term babies'.[56] The intensive (and increasing) caring roles of families with disabled children are particularly evident for the 40,000 children and young people estimated to be living in England with a life-limiting condition.[57]

Separately, it has been estimated that in England one in eight children aged between five and 19 (1.25 million people) have a mental disorder[58] and that the Child and Adolescent Mental Health Services (CAMHS) are – in the opinion of the Royal College of Psychiatrists – in a state of 'crisis'.[59]

Children with disabilities commonly experience clusters of other problems associated with (or compounding) the difficulties of dealing with their disability. Childhood disability has been described as a 'trigger event' for poverty as a result of additional costs, family break up and unemployment.[60] Consequently, children with a disability are more likely to be living in poverty and consequently in poor housing than their non-disabled peers, with families with a disabled child being 50 per cent more likely than other families to live in over-crowded accommodation; to rate their home as being in a poor state of repair; and to report problems with wiring, draughts and damp in the child's bedroom.[61] In addition, children with disabilities, were found to be four to five more likely to have a diagnosable psychiatric problem than children without a learning disability.[62] As a result of the combination of poverty, poor housing, mental health issues as well as the initial disability, in 2018 only 13.5 per cent of young people with special educational needs achieved English and Maths at grades 9–5 compared to 48.3 per cent of their peers with no identified special education need.[63] This attainment gap can compound the disadvantages for the disabled child in the future; 29 per cent of disabled young adults aged 16–24 years were not in any form of education, employment or training, compared to nine per cent of other young adults.[64]

A 2013 government report summed up this clustered disadvantage, noting that the association between poverty and child disability meant that disabled children are more likely than their peers to live in conditions which are shown to impede development and educational attainment, as well as increasing social exclusion and poor health.[65]

The evidence suggests that children and young people with mental health difficulties also experience clusters of additional problems 'such as abuse, neglect or child sexual exploitation' and for those that don't have the support their families 'to help them navigate a complex system or ensure that they attend appointments, there is a risk that they can fall between services'.[66]

Parents and families of disabled children also experience clustered disadvantage. Caring for a disabled child can often be an extremely intensive role, with 20 per cent of people caring for disabled children under 16 reporting to having left employment[67] and 46 per cent reporting it having effects on their employment;[68] 24 per cent of parent carers provide over 100 hours of care per week,[69] demonstrating the extreme intensity of the caring role, which contributes hugely to unemployment within families of disabled children. As Gandy et al have commented:

> The complexity of juggling these demands with parental responsibilities can lead to cognitive overload, limiting parents' attention and self-control, and making it hard for them to make effective decisions, let alone set aside time to support their child's learning and development.[70]

Additionally, a greater proportion of disabled children live in lone-parent households than non-disabled children,[71] meaning the intensive caring role is even more concentrated. Although a causal relationship is not entirely clear, changes to family composition and marital status may be due to socio-economic strain, rather than the disability itself.[72] The level of unemployment is clearly partially responsible for the high proportion of families with disabled children who live in poverty (27 per cent of families with a disabled child are living in poverty).[73] However, families with disabled children also face average extra costs of £581 a month,[74] with almost a quarter of these families having extra costs of over £1,000.[75] Although social security benefits are available for some families to provide additional support (ie disability living allowance, carers' allowance etc), this is often insufficient, with 56 per cent of families saying that the extra costs of having a disabled child are only partly covered by their disability benefits.[76]

In addition to the caring responsibilities of having a disabled child, families often have to 'wade through a treacle of bureaucracy'[77] in order to get the help/support their child is entitled to. In 2019 the Education Select Committee expressed grave concern about the many legal problems family encountered – referring to the 'complex, awful and often unnecessarily antagonistic experience for parents [that] can prevent them from accessing their entitlements'.[78] The Committee argued that this complexity and bureaucracy exacerbates disadvantage further, as it often means that a child's access to support is determined by parents' legal expertise, education and personal resilience, often meaning those with less social capital/fewer contacts within the system end up with the least help.[79] This complexity in accessing the necessary support often compounds the initial disadvantage faced by such families, as the isolation and stress can cause mental health issues, which could potentially make the family even less resilient to other disadvantage; mothers consistently report big impacts on their mental health/wellbeing that come as a result of having a disabled child,[80] with 33 per cent of carers of a disabled child under 16 reporting being unable to socialise and 46 per cent of this group being simply too tired to go out.[81] This intense pressure of having a disabled child, combined with the financial struggles (so severe as to mean that one in five families reported cutting back on food as a result of the costs of bringing up a disabled child)[82] makes it clear that consequent mental health struggles and social isolation of carers will inevitably add to the clustered disadvantage of families of disabled children.

Gypsies and Travelling people

In the 2011 Census, 63,000 people in the UK identified themselves as a member of either a Gypsy, Traveller or Irish Traveller community.[83] However, other sources suggest that the 2011 figure may be an underestimate, with the Council of Europe estimating the actual population at between 150,000 and 300,000.[84]

2015 research by the Equality and Human Rights Commission found that many Gypsies (including Roma) and Travellers faced 'multiple disadvantages' in education, health, the workplace and the justice system:[85] disadvantages that are tightly interdependent and often result in the development of clusters of legal problems.

A significant difficulty experienced by many Gypsies and Travelling people concerns income instability due to their low rates of employment: the 2011 Census identifying them as the ethnic group with the lowest employment rates and highest levels of economic inactivity.[86] This is attributable in part to the discrimination they face in employment (with a survey conducted in 2016/2017 showing that 49 per cent of Gypsy/Traveller respondents experienced discrimination in employment[87]) as well as low literacy rates stemming from the barriers they encounter in accessing mainstream schooling.[88] Low literacy rates have the ability to exacerbate many legal problems, particularly those arising from difficulties in reading and completing forms (for example, welfare benefits claim forms) – whether in manuscript or in digital formats. As research by Cemlyn et al identified, 'for highly mobile individuals and families, the requirement to prove their previous addresses or sufficient credit-worthiness to obtain a bank account can be an enormous hurdle'.[89]

The unstable and often unfit accommodation arrangements of many Gypsies and Travellers can trigger health problems. Research by Morris and Clements referred to the 'appalling' site conditions and locations of many of the 350 public Gypsy sites in England and Wales, frequently located 'in locations deemed unsuitable for any other development; on old waste tips, beside (or even underneath) motorways, far removed from shops and other amenities, often with one or two taps serving perhaps 20 or so families and with no foul drainage; muddy quagmires in the winter and dust bowls in the summer'.[90] In this context, the Equality and Human Rights Commission has referred to the approach of successive governments to the accommodation needs of Gypsies and Travellers as 'a hostile environment policy'.[91]

Studies have reported higher infection rates in such sites, linked to poor sanitation and poor access to clean water.[92] As a consequence of their multiple disadvantages, life expectancy for Gypsy and Traveller men and women is 10 years lower than the national average and Gypsy and Traveller mothers are 20 times more likely than the rest of the population to have experienced the death of a child.[93] Even by comparison to other marginalised groups, Gypsies and Travellers have been found to have materially poorer health.[94]

The evidence suggests that many Gypsies' and Travellers' experiences with public services are poor and that this contributes to their hesitancy in seeking assistance. The resulting lack of knowledge of and scepticism surrounding public services can lead to victims of domestic abuse within the Gypsy and Traveller communities failing to seek help.[95] Additionally (among other factors) the size of some families[96] can also be a barrier preventing victims of domestic abuse seeking help: nationally, refuges for domestic abuse are generally only licensed for one with women with up to three children.[97]

Despite evidence that crime levels are similar in Traveller and non-Traveller populations,[98] five per cent of the prison population identified as Gypsy, Roma or Traveller in 2013,[99] whereas only 0.1 per cent of the population had identified as such in the 2011 census.[100] These statistics partially explain the hostility towards authority felt by many Gypsies and Travellers and point to overzealous, institutionally racist policing: 'the last bastion of racism' as one former officer has described it.[101] Traumatic and unnecessary detentions contribute to high levels of mental ill-health; Gypsies and Travellers have greatly raised rates of depression and anxiety, with relative risks 20 and 8.5 times higher than the normal population.[102] Furthermore, incarceration damages employment chances, which in turn exacerbates poverty.

Homeless people

In 2019 Shelter,[103] the national charity for homeless people, reported that 280,000 people in England were recorded as homeless and that almost 220,000 were threatened with homelessness. In 2018 a total of 4,677 people were counted or estimated by local authorities to be sleeping rough in England on any one night[104] (more than double the number estimated in 2010[105]). It appears, however, that the actual numbers may be considerably greater: BBC research, for example, has suggested that in 2019 there were five times as many people sleeping rough as reported in official figures.[106] In 2018, there were an estimated 726 deaths of homeless people in England and Wales – an increase of over 20 per cent on the previous year.[107]

People who are homeless or at risk of homelessness often have clusters of legal problems arising out of a complex mix of 'multiple (often inter-related and multi-directional)'[108] causes – causes that include: poverty; the breakdown of family and other 'anchor' social relationships; traumatic experiences during childhood; domestic violence; substance misuse; mental or physical health problems; leaving care; anti-social behaviour or crime; overcrowded housing; debt; and financial problems caused by benefits reduction.[109]

The legal problems that homeless people may have, range widely and may include difficulties in accessing: social security entitlements; housing services; healthcare (including mental health and addiction management support); social care supports; protection from domestic violence; representation in criminal proceedings; debt advice, and so on.

Research by Bramley and others[110] considered adults in England whose 'severe and multiple disadvantage' could be measured in terms of three 'key manifestations' – namely homelessness, substance misuse and involvement in the criminal justice system. In addition to these severe problems, 'poverty was an almost universal, and mental ill-health a common, complicating factor'. The research found that each year, over a quarter of a million people have contact with at least two out of three of the key manifestations, and that at least 58,000 people have contact with all three – and that people in this situation 'fall between the gaps' in policy and services altogether, or were viewed through a succession of separate and uncoordinated 'professional lenses'.[111]

Levels of homelessness are 'strongly associated' with reductions in spending on social welfare by councils and central government[112] in the UK and (unsurprisingly) that 'even in the most difficult structural contexts, targeted interventions can protect at-risk groups from homelessness'.[113]

People at risk of domestic abuse

The evidence suggests that in 2019 over five per cent of adults in the England and Wales (2.4 million people) experienced domestic abuse – and in that year, the police these two nations responded to over 1.3 million domestic abuse-related incidents.[114] It is generally considered that the scale of the problem is not fully reflected in these figures, with research suggesting that, on average, there will have been 35 assaults before victims call the police.[115]

Victims of domestic abuse often simultaneously suffer from other socio-legal problems. The trauma of domestic abuse has been shown to lead to severe mental health difficulties with 2017–18 data suggesting that over 40 per cent of people accessing domestic abuse services had had mental health problems in the past 12 months.[116] This trauma can also manifest itself in substance abuse, with research finding that 'women who have been abused are 15 times more likely to abuse alcohol and 9 times more likely to abuse drugs than those without a history of abuse'.[117] Substance abuse of this kind increases the likelihood of the victim becoming enmeshed in the criminal justice system – a relationship that has been characterised as 'bidirectional',[118] suggesting that either of these problems increase the risk of the other.

The cluster of socio-legal legal problems experienced by those suffering from domestic abuse commonly include poverty and homelessness. The evidence suggests that 22 per cent of all women experience 'persistent low income'[119] – a problem severely exacerbated when women in coercive relationships are often not given access to finances. Over 20 per cent of respondents to a 2018 survey[120] who had left an abusive relationship said that their partner had retained documentation the survivor needed to move on (for example, to get a tenancy, apply for welfare benefits or a job),[121] meaning victims of abuse are often left unable to restart their lives independently. Inevitably this situation creates problems for women in finding alternative accommodation to an abuser – with the attendant risks of homelessness. This risk has been highlighted by a number of studies,[122] with Margulies pointing to the commonly faced pairing of domestic abuse and homelessness, and noting that for 'domestic violence survivors, shortages in affordable housing can mean staying with an abusive partner and risking injury or even death'.[123] Poverty and homelessness can of course result in problem of debt – which in turn can entrench poverty and increase the likelihood of homelessness. A 2018 domestic abuse survey found that over 40 per cent of respondents reported that they were in debt as a result of their abuse.[124]

An additional problem sometimes encountered by victims of domestic abuse concerns the harm inflicted on them by the sharp edges of immigration law. Those who have been brought to the UK before being forced into a marriage are particularly vulnerable; often faced with deportation, sometimes lacking language abilities and unable to access social security or other public funds – and for whom there is all too often no escape route due to the complex intersection of their problems.[125] Survivors of domestic abuse with insecure immigration status may additionally face economic challenges in receiving medical care, sometimes having to pay a healthcare surcharge before accessing the NHS.[126]

People in precarious tenancies

The number of households in the private rented sector in England increased by 60 per cent between 2007 and 2017 – in which year there were 4.7 million households in privately rented accommodation.[127] 2017 data from the English Housing Survey suggests that just under a quarter of current tenants (ie over 1 million) reported that their last move from private rented properties was forced in some way, and 'was not because they wanted to move',[128] evidencing the lack of housing choice and control that confronts many people.

In 2019, Shelter's review of government data indicated that almost 220,000 people in England were threatened with homelessness.[129]

Over 80 per cent of the increase in repossessions in recent years has been attributed to the use of 'no fault' evictions:[130] Housing Act 1988 s21 enables private landlords to repossess their properties from assured shorthold tenants without having to establish fault on the part of the tenant.[131]

Irrespective of the use of the 'no fault' eviction power, the knowledge that it could be used at any point is detrimental to the sense of well-being of many tenants – creating what has been referred to as 'constant anxiety and insecurity'.[132] Unsurprisingly, therefore, many studies have shown links between precarious tenancies and mental health problems:[133] problems that are particularly prevalent for those in temporary accommodation especially in multi-occupation buildings.[134] Collectively, this evidence demonstrates how precarious housing can be instrumental in triggering and exacerbating mental health conditions, which in turn can aggravate a person's housing and other difficulties, not least by compounding their money management abilities and their lines of communication with the local authorities.[135]

The structural unavailability of secure housing plays a significant role in entrenching poverty.[136] Precarious tenancies lead to frequent moves and the not insignificant costs of moving[137] are borne by tenants.[138] A further complication is that the relationship between housing and poverty is bidirectional – as precarious housing can be instrumental in pushing tenants into poverty. Additionally, those already in poverty and reliant on housing benefits may be barely able to afford the housing they are in, which by default makes the housing 'precarious', as any minimal rise in rent or living costs may not be covered by their benefits. 2012 research found that the unaffordability of housing is most acute among the lowest income quintile, with 38 per cent of this group spending more than one third of their income on housing (in contrast only two per cent of the richest fifth of the working-age population spent this proportion of their income on housing costs),[139] evidencing how vulnerable those living in poverty are to precarious housing, where they are on the threshold of their rent budget.

Other dimensions to the 'housing / poverty' interrelationship concern the heightened risk of unemployment (the loss of work when forced to move)[140] and the refusal of some landlords to rent to those in receipt of housing benefit. A 2016 study found that 42 per cent of landlords refused to let to housing benefits claimants and a further 21 per cent would prefer not to have done.[141] This reluctance is often exacerbated by administrative issues associated with the processing of housing benefit payments. Rent arrears which inevitably make a tenancy precarious were found to be most often caused by problems with housing benefits, including delays in payments:[142] for those in poverty, managing their money and tenancy is consequently sometimes out of their control.

Precarious tenancies (and the stress these engender in tenants) have been shown to increase instances of domestic violence.[143] Many perpetrators of this abuse remain in the family home while the victim and any children move between temporary and unsuitable housing.[144] 2015 research found that immediately after leaving an abusive partner, 49.6 per cent of women lived in temporary accommodation.[145] For many women, as well as the trauma this causes, having to find new/temporary accommodation can often push victims further into poverty; for 67 per cent of women who had left an abusive situation, housing costs increased after separation,[146] evidencing how the combination of poverty, domestic abuse and precarious housing can compound an individual's disadvantage.

People who experience poverty and debt

Poverty is a huge problem in the UK. In 2018 it was estimated that 14.2 million people were living in poverty and that more than 4 million people were trapped in 'deep poverty' (meaning their income was at least 50 per cent below the official breadline) triggering weekly struggles to buy even the most basic essentials.[147] This acute poverty is often associated with debt, as many of those in poverty are forced to take out loans in order to make ends meet in the short term. Additionally, in the wake of the coronavirus emergency, it is forecast that many more will fall into poverty, triggering unprecedented applications for welfare benefits.

Those in poverty often face many clusters of disadvantages simultaneously. Darton and Strelitz have referred to the 'far reaching consequences of poverty: health, education and crime. In today's Britain the least affluent suffer most on all three fronts'.[148]

In relation to individual health, it is well established that for those in poverty it is generally worse than those within the general population. Children born into poverty are more likely to suffer from chronic diseases such as asthma, as well as diet related problems such as tooth decay, malnutrition, obesity and diabetes.[149] This problem continues throughout life, with prescription charges sometimes deter those in poverty and debt from getting treatment, meaning conditions are often allowed to worsen.[150]

There are also clear links between poverty and poor mental health; nearly a quarter of adults in the poorest fifth of the population experience depression and anxiety – more than twice the number in the richest two-fifths of the population.[151] The administration the welfare benefits system is itself a significant component in the mental stress experienced by those in receipt of benefits: Craig and Katikireddi, for example, have noted that the way claims are assessed, benefits are paid and what conditions/sanctions are imposed can have a significant impact on an individual's health and wellbeing.[152]

Other poverty-related issues, such as being unable to buy good quality food and live in environmentally benign areas also contribute to the disparity between life expectancy of those in poverty and more affluent people. In England in 2013, the life expectancy for those in the most deprived areas compared to the least deprived areas was 7.9 years higher for men and 5.9 years for women.[153] A 2017 British Medical Association report has described the relationship between poverty and ill-health as bidirectional stating 'unemployment and poverty can contribute to poor health ... but poor physical health also increases the likelihood of unemployment and the two can become mutually reinforcing'.[154]

The unemployment resulting from poor health can create a range of other clustered legal disadvantages. Unemployment can force individuals to take out loans, which can then create long term debt. As well as often causing chronic stress, issues with debt repayment can also lead to a person becoming enmeshed in the criminal justice system. Such debts are not just from perceived 'loan sharks' but from mundane bills such as council tax. About 100 people are jailed each year in the UK for non-payment of council tax bills, with 5,000 people a year being taken to court or threatened with prison.[155] As well as the devastating effect incarceration can have on a person already in poverty, the simple threat of it can lead to people in financial difficulties being more reluctant to seek help, not just in terms of finances, but in relation to their housing and healthcare needs. The National Audit Office estimated in 2018 that £18 billion of debt was owed to government, utility companies, landlords and housing associations:[156] debts held disproportionately by those receiving universal credit and with 25 per cent of such debtors facing serious debt problems (compared to eight per cent of the general population). It appears that approximately 600,000 people need debt advice but are unable to access it[157] and those most likely to be in debt are often those least able to access help.

Poverty has been shown to lead to lower educational attainment, with less than a quarter of 'disadvantaged' children (those in receipt of free school meals or in local authority care) achieving a pass grade at GCSE maths and English.[158] The clear correlation between school attainment and future earnings potential means that for a young person, the experience of childhood poverty is likely to cast a life-long shadow of disadvantage.

Poverty and increasing inequalities are thought to increase 'risky behaviour'[159] by those living with disadvantage, with the effect that – among other things – those living in disadvantaged communities are exposed to greater levels of crime and vandalism.[160] Webster and Kingston have analysed the crime / poverty inter-relationship – in the sense that poverty both increases the risks of a person being the victim of crime as well as a person (particularly a young person) feeling they have little to lose by resorting to risky behaviour. As they observe, on the one hand poverty 'generates conditions that make delinquent and criminal "solutions" more likely than would otherwise be the case'[161] evidencing how simultaneous disadvantages faced by those in poverty can push a person in situations of financial desperation towards becoming enmeshed in the criminal justice system creating a further dimension of legal difficulty. On the other hand, as 'public housing has become more 'residual' and poverty has grown more spatially concentrated, crime victimisation has come to mirror socioeconomic deprivation and both poverty and crime have concentrated in fewer areas.[162]

As noted elsewhere in this section, poverty is an aggravating factor in most clusters of legal problems. But, of course, not everyone is at equal risk of poverty. Almost 50 percent of those in poverty are living in families with a disabled person;[163] the allowances available to asylum-seekers put them almost 75 percent below the poverty line;[164] and over two million unpaid carers in the UK live below the poverty line.[165] Privilege and disadvantage are unequally and unfairly distributed, and as Wexler tells us, poverty 'creates an abrasive interface with society'[166] with the result that for those who experience disadvantage it is ever present, dark and cold anxiety – sapping their every thought process and leaving them vulnerable to making poor decisions: decisions that can then deepen poverty.[167]

Unpaid carers

In 2016 it was estimated that there were at least 5.3 million informal (unpaid) carers in the UK,[168] although recent estimates now put this figure at 8.8 million.[169] While some of these carers are undertaking minimally intensive roles, it appears that 38 per cent provide at least 20 hours per week of support, including (in 2016) 710,000 who care for at least 50 hours.[170] This devotion of time by unpaid carers constitutes our primary social care system – with informal carers providing 80 per cent of long-term care within Europe.[171]

Despite the fundamental role played by unpaid carers, they often face many clustered problems. One disadvantage that frequently arises as a result of being an unpaid carer is poverty, with 2.1 million of the unpaid carers in the UK living below the poverty line.[172] The poverty faced by a substantial number of carers appears to be caused by two main factors: the extra costs they incur in ensuring that the person(s) for whom they care have the necessary support, equipment and home adaptations[173] and the adverse impact that providing unpaid care has on their ability to undertake paid work. The employment rate of working-age carers is 64 per cent compared to the national average of 74 per cent.[174] Additionally, as care levels increase, employment decreases, with a clear impact on full time employment. Among working-age people caring for 35 hours of more each week, just 40 per cent are in employment.[175] This inability to work as a result of caring, combined with the upfront financial costs, means that many carers are substantially worse off, with one in three carers reporting that they are over £20,000 a year worse off as a result of caring.[176] For over a quarter of carers, state or private pensions are the main source of income.[177] However, for those whose caring role begun before pension age, poverty is more likely and with it the probability of the 'accrual of lower pension entitlements' and in consequence putting such carers at an increased risk of old-age poverty.[178] In this context, only 17 per cent of carers in a 2018 study considered that their ability to plan/save for retirement had not been affected by caring.[179]

Even if the caring role a person takes on is not long term, the influences on their employment prospects and finances in the future can be disastrous. A report by Carers UK referenced difficulties returning to the labour market after a caring role has ended, with the peak age for caring often coinciding with the peak of an individual's career (50–64)[180] meaning that returning to the labour market is often particularly difficult.

In addition, reports have recognised that young carers[181] face 'stig-matization' at school and as a result of their intense caring roles have 'difficulties [following] a standard educational curriculum'.[182] This can mean young carers tend to leave school earlier,[183] which could partly explain the lower number of unpaid carers with qualifications – with 70 per cent of those caring for 20 hours or more a week having no or low qualifications compared to less than half for non-carers.[184] Combining qualification issues and timing, a relatively short period of caring can still have devastating impacts on a person's employment prospects, and thus further increase their likelihood of ending up in poverty.

Poverty itself can create more complex money issues, which require further assistance; for instance, almost half of carers (44 per cent) report having ended up in debt, using credit cards or an over-draft to make ends meet.[185] The debt itself has the potential to trigger other problems – for example housing/eviction concerns.

The poverty and debt associated with caring can lead to physical and mental health issues, with 72 per cent of UK carers reporting mental ill-health (most commonly chronic stress, anxiety and depression) and 61 per cent reporting physical ill-health as a result of caring. Physical ill-health has been attributed to (among other factors) carers economising on basic necessities as a result of financial worries, with 45 per cent of UK carers reporting cutting down on food and 44 per cent on heating to try and make ends meet.[186] An additional problem concerns the difficulty many carers experience in finding the time to maintain their own health, due to the strenuous demands of caring for another. A 2019 briefing noted the common problem of carers being 'unable to find time for medical treatment for themselves, with two in five carers saying they are forced to put off treatment for them-selves because of their caring responsibilities.[187]

Research from Carers UK included cases of carers discharging themselves from hospital because of a lack of alternative care options.[188] Equally, unpaid caring, and the associated poverty, debt and stress has been shown to lead to mental health problems. Part of this stress is thought to come from having to navigate the complex health, social care, social security and housing systems in order to access benefits they are entitled to; many carers report struggling to understand what they are entitled to, and 42 per cent report having missed out on financial support to which they were entitled.[189]

Carers' legal problems are also compounded by not only having to navigate the 'system' in order to claim support to mitigate their own (adverse) health and wealth impacts, but also having to fulfil this role for the person for whom they care. Many carers feel unsupported during this process, with over 80 per cent reporting feeling lonely or socially isolated.[190] Vitaliano describes this sense of isolation and exhaustion as 'having all the features of a chronic stress experience'.[191] Schulz and Sherwood have, in turn, argued that 'caregiver distress leads to depression which in turn makes caregivers more susceptible to illness, all potentially leading to an early death',[192] evidencing the devastating physical and mental health impacts unpaid caring can have.

Notes

1 Introduction

1   The Cerebra Legal Entitlements and Problem-solving (LEaP) Research Project.
2   In this context, see in particular, J Read, *Disability, the family and society: listening to mothers*, Open University Press, 2000, p119.
3   This is of course overly simplistic. During the research, we have encountered barristers who have disabled children and who have admitted to finding it almost impossible to navigate the system in order to access their children's legal entitlements.
4   I should state that Cerebra is an enlightened funder and fully appreciates the challenges research of this nature has in measuring 'outcomes'.
5   J Tunstill and J Blewett, 'Mapping the journey: outcome-focused practice and the role of interim outcomes in family support services', *Child and Family Social Work* (2015) 20, pp234–243.
6   'Systems thinking' theory is considered further in chapter 3.
7   The harm experienced by those with 'cognitive overload' is considered further in chapter 6.
8   See generally, A Currie, *The legal problems of everyday life. the nature, extent and consequences of justiciable problems experienced by Canadians*, Department of Justice, Canada, 2007, p52 'Problem clusters based on trigger problems'.
9   K Duffy, *Social exclusion and human dignity in Europe*, Council of Europe, 1995; A Giddens, *The third way*, Polity Press, 1998, p104; and see generally, R Levitas, *The inclusive society? Social exclusion and New Labour*, Palgrave, 1998. However, the Social Exclusion Unit's definition of social exclusion as 'a shorthand term for what can happen when people or areas suffer from a combination of linked problems such as unemployment, poor skills, low income, poor housing, high crime, bad health and family breakdown' is clearly closer to the concept of 'disadvantage' adopted for the purposes of this study – see Social Exclusion Unit, *Preventing social exclusion*, The Stationery Office, 2001, p10.

10 Jonathan Wolff and Avner De-Shalit speak of this obligation in terms of the 'capability approach' – of the availability of genuine opportunities for individuals to achieve a 'functioning' and hence a 'capability' – see J Wolff and A De-Shalit, *Disadvantage*, OUP, 2007, chapter 4. Martha Fineman describes this obligation in terms of states ensuring the existence of responsive structures that empower the vulnerable subject – see, for example, M A Fineman, 'The vulnerable subject and the responsive state' (2010) 60 Emory LJ 251 – discussed further below.

11 See, for example, H Genn, *Paths to justice: what people do and think about going to law*, Hart, 1999; and P Pleasence, N Balmer and R Sandefur, *Paths to justice: a past, present and future roadmap*, UCL Centre for Empirical Legal Studies, 2013.

12 K N Llewellyn, *The Cheyenne Way*, University of Oklahoma Press, 1941, p41.

13 See in particular, Z Bankowski and G Mungham, *Images of law*, Routledge & Keegan, 1976, pp38–39; and P Morris, R White and P Lewis, *Social needs and legal action*, Martin Robertson, 1973, pp75, 79.

14 Z Bankowski and G Mungham, *Images of law*, Routledge & Keegan, 1976, p39.

15 See, for example, H Genn, *Paths to justice: what people do and think about going to law*, Hart, 1999; A Currie, *The legal problems of everyday life. the nature, extent and consequences of justiciable problems experienced by Canadians*, Department of Justice, Canada, 2007; P Pleasence, N Balmer and R Sandefur, *Paths to justice a past, present and future roadmap*, UCL Centre for Empirical Legal Studies, 2013; and R Franklyn, T Budd, R Verrill and M Willoughby, *Legal problem and resolution survey*, Ministry of Justice, 2017, available at: www.gov.uk/government/publications/legal-problem-and-resolution-survey-2014-to-2015.

16 H Genn, *Paths to justice: what people do and think about going to law*, Hart, 1999, at p35.

17 A Currie, *The legal problems of everyday life. the nature, extent and consequences of justiciable problems experienced by Canadians*, Department of Justice, Canada, 2007, p42.

18 R Franklyn, T Budd, R Verrill and M Willoughby, *Legal problem and resolution survey*, Ministry of Justice, 2017, p15.

19 R Franklyn, T Budd, R Verrill and M Willoughby, *Legal problem and resolution survey*, Ministry of Justice, 2017, pp16–17 and Appendix C, Table C5.

20 A Currie, *The legal problems of everyday life. the nature, extent and consequences of justiciable problems experienced by Canadians*, Department of Justice, Canada, 2007, p45.

21 A Currie, *The legal problems of everyday life. the nature, extent and consequences of justiciable problems experienced by Canadians*, Department of Justice, Canada, 2007, p44.

22 A Currie, *The legal problems of everyday life. the nature, extent and consequences of justiciable problems experienced by Canadians*, Department of Justice, Canada, 2007, pp46–47.

23 A Currie, *The legal problems of everyday life. the nature, extent and consequences of justiciable problems experienced by Canadians*, Department of Justice, Canada, 2007, p43.

24 *Statement on visit to the United Kingdom*, by Professor Philip Alston, United Nations Special Rapporteur on extreme poverty and human rights, London, 16 November 2018; available at: www.ohchr.org/en/NewsEvents/Pages/DisplayNews.aspx?NewsID=23881.

25 United Nations General Assembly, Human Rights Council, Forty-first session, 24 June-12 July 2019, Agenda item 3, 'Promotion and protection of all human rights, civil, political, economic, social and cultural rights, including the right to development', Visit to the United Kingdom of Great Britain and Northern Ireland, Report of the Special Rapporteur on extreme poverty and human rights, A/HRC/41/39/Add.1, 23 April 2019 at para 3. Available at: https://undocs.org/A/HRC/41/39/Add.1.

26 Para 95.

27 R Booth, 'Amber Rudd to lodge complaint over UN's austerity report', *Guardian*, 22 May 2019.

28 F Snowdon, *Epidemics and society*, Yale University Press, 2019.

29 See, for example, S Caul, *Deaths involving COVID-19 by local area and socioeconomic deprivation: deaths occurring between 1 March and 31 May 2020*, Office for National Statistics, June 2020 (www.ons.gov.uk/peoplepopulationandcommunity/birthsdeathsandmarriages/deaths/bulletins/deathsinvolvingcovid19bylocalareasanddeprivation/deathsoccurringbetween1marchand31may2020): 'people living in more deprived areas have continued to experience COVID-19 mortality rates more than double those living in less deprived areas'; and *Coronavirus (COVID-19) related deaths by ethnic group, England and Wales: 2 March 2020 to 10 April 2020*, Office for National Statistics, May 2020 (www.ons.gov.uk/peoplepopulationandcommunity/birthsdeathsandmarriages/deaths/articles/coronavirusrelateddeathsbyethnicgroupenglandandwales/2march2020to10april2020): 'Black males are 4.2 times more likely to die from a COVID-19-related death and Black females are 4.3 times more likely than White ethnicity males and females'.

30 M Fraser, 'The disease map of rural America', *Dissent*, Summer 2020.

31 M Fraser, 'The disease map of rural America', *Dissent*, Summer 2020 – the other listed risks being: population growth, climate change, rapid means of transportation, the proliferation of megacities with inadequate urban infrastructures and warfare.

32 M A Fineman, 'The vulnerable subject and the responsive state', 60 Emory LJ (2010) 251–275 at 253.

33 M A Fineman, 'The vulnerable subject and the responsive state', 60 Emory LJ (2010) 251–275 at 253.

34 MA Fineman, 'The vulnerable subject and the responsive state', 60 Emory LJ (2010) 251–275 at 253.

35 MA Fineman, 'The vunerable subject and the responsive state', 60 Emory LJ (2010) 251–275 at 267.

36 MA Fineman, 'The vulnerable subject and the responsive state', 60 Emory LJ (2010) 251–275 at 268.

37 MA Fineman, 'Beyond identities: the limits of an antidiscrimination approach to equality', (2012) 92 Boston University Law Review 1713–1770 at 1762–1763.

38 The Health Select Committee estimated that the cut to the public health budget between 2014 and 2020 amounted to almost 15 per cent, describing it as a 'false economy, creating avoidable additional costs in the future': House of Commons Health Select Committee, *Impact of the spending review on health and social care*, HC 139, House of Commons, 2016, para 93.

39 Between 2010 and 2019, funding for adult social care in England was cut by £7 billion – *Association of Directors of Adult Social Services budget survey: human cost of failing to address the crisis in adult social care*, 2019; and see also P Simpson, *Public spending on adult social care in England*, Briefing Note BN200, Institute of Fiscal Studies, 2017.

40 Fineman accepts the inevitability (indeed necessity) in certain situations for there to be inequality – for the unequal distribution of privilege (for example, in relation to the parent/infant relationship and the employer/employee relationship – and for her analysis of this issue see MA Fineman, 'Vulnerability and inevitable inequality' (2017) 4 *Oslo Law Review*, 133–149.

41 MA Fineman, 'Vulnerability and inevitable inequality', (2017) 4 *Oslo Law Review*, 133–149, at 142.

42 MA Fineman, 'The vulnerable subject and the responsive state', 60 Emory LJ (2010) 251–275 at 269.

43 See, for example, L Kuenssberg, 'Covid: Casey's poverty warning difficult to ignore', BBC, 15 October 2020.

44 A Smith, *The wealth of nations*, first published 1776, OUP, 1904, Book 1, Chapter 6, p55.

45 'There are two ways that people can acquire wealth. There is production and there is plunder.' Winston Churchill (1907) cited in M Daunton, *Trusting Leviathan*, Cambridge University Press, 2001, p363.

46 B Disraeli, *Sybil, or The Two Nations*, Henry Colburn, 1845, Book 2, Chapter 5.

47 For deaths involving the coronavirus, the rate for the least deprived area was 25.3 deaths per 100,000 population and the rate in the most deprived area was 55.1 deaths per 100,000 population – *Deaths involving COVID-19 by local area and socioeconomic deprivation: deaths occurring between 1 March and 17 April 2020*, Office for National Statistics, 1 May 2020, p10.

48 See, for example, S Bagenstos, 'The future of disability law', *Yale Law Journal* (2004) 114.1; and D Spade, *Normal life*, Duke University Press, 2015.

2 The grain of the law

1 From: www.bowls.org.uk/flat-green.
2 B Disraeli, *Sybil or The two nations*, 1844; and G Orwell, *The road to Wigan Pier*, Victor Gollancz, 1937.
3 H Garfinkel, 'Conditions of successful degradation ceremonies', *American Journal of Sociology*, vol 61, No 5 (March 1956) 420–424.
4 Z Bankowski and G Mungham, *Images of law*, Routledge & Keegan, 1976.
5 Perhaps more accurately, the 'law'.
6 H Laski, *The grammar of politics. the works of harold Laski*, Routledge, 2015, p157.
7 A Smith (1776), *Wealth of nations*, OUP World Classics [1904], Oxford Volume II Book V, Chapter I, Part II, p341.
8 Attributed to Louis D Brandeis in an article in the *Cleveland Plain Dealer* (a Cleveland, Ohio newspaper) dated 15 October 1912; and see also L Scharf, 'The great uprising in Cleveland: when sisterhood failed' in JM Jensen and S Davidson, *A needle, a bobbin, a strike*, Temple University Press, 1984.
9 This process is further considered in the chapter that follows – and see generally, J Chapman, *System failure. Why governments must learn to think differently*, 2nd edn, Demos, 2014, at 35.
10 See, for example, AT Kronman, 'Contract law and distributive justice', *Yale Law Journal* (1980) 89 pp472–511 (considered further below); and TC Grey, 'Property and need: the welfare state and theories of distributive justice', *Stanford Law Review* (1976) 28 pp877–902.
11 'One may say there is a force like a hundred thousand wedges trying [to] force every kind of adapted structure into the gaps in the economy of nature, or rather forming gaps by thrusting out weaker ones': Charles Darwin, Notebook D 135e, 28 September 1838.
12 Lord Westbury, HL Debates vol 201 col 1573, 30 May 1870.
13 AC Hutchinson, 'Practising law for rich and poor people: towards a more progressive approach', *Legal Ethics* (2020), DOI: 10.1080/1460728x.2020.1799302, p9.
14 T Hobbes, 'Behemoth: the history of the causes of the civil wars of England, and of the counsels and artifices by which they were carried on from the year 1640 to the year 1660', Part III, p312 in W Molesworth (ed), *The English works of Thomas Hobbes, vol 6 (Dialogue, Behemoth, Rhetoric)*, Bohn, 1839–45.
15 J Smith, 'The use of maxims in jurisprudence', *Harvard Law Review*, Vol 9, No 1 (25 April 1895), pp13–26 at 24.
16 HS Maine, *Ancient law: its connection to the history of early society* (first published 1861), Dent, 1917, p538.
17 HS Maine, *Ancient law: its connection to the history of early society* (first published 1861), Dent, 1917, p538.

18 Maxim 1: 'In jure non remota causa, sed proxima spectatur' – see
JC Hogan and MD Schwartz, 'A translation of Bacon's Maxims of the
Common Law', 77 *Law Library Journal* 707 (1984–1985).

19 It appears, however, that there is little evidence to suggest that this is
what the maxim meant – see PJ Kelley (1991), 'Proximate cause in
negligence law: history, theory, and the present darkness', *Washington
University Law Quarterly*, v69 pp49–105 at 56.

20 *Liesbosch Dredger v SS Edison* [1933] AC 449 at 460 (per Lord Wright).

21 Considered further in the appendix at the end of this book.

22 J Wolff and A De-Shalit, *Disadvantage*, OUP, 2007, p120.

23 23 EHRR 101.

24 23 EHRR 101 at 137.

25 See, for example, H Genn, *Paths to justice: what people do and think
about going to law*, Hart, 1999; A Currie, *The legal problems of everyday
life. the nature, extent and consequences of justiciable problems experienced
by Canadians*, Department of Justice, Canada, 2007 (www.justice.gc.ca/
eng/rp-pr/csj-sjc/jsp-sjp/rr07_la1-rr07_aj1/rr07_la1.pdf); P Pleasence,
N Balmer and R Sandefur, *Paths to justice: a past, present and future
roadmap*, UCL Centre for Empirical Legal Studies, 2013; and
R Franklyn, T Budd, R Verrill and M Willoughby, *Legal problem and
resolution survey*, Ministry of Justice, 2017 (www.gov.uk/government/
publications/legal-problem-and-resolution-survey-2014-to-2015).

26 *Liesbosch Dredger v SS Edison* [1933] AC 449: the defendants had
negligently sunk the plaintiff's dredger – causing them also to lose the
income. Although another dredger could have purchased without difficulty
or delay, the plaintiffs did not have the available money to do this.

27 In relation to negligence claims, this principle was modified by *Lagden
v O'Connor* [2003] UKHL 64; see D Tompkinson 'Thin skulls and thin
wallets' NLJ 2004, 154(7120), 424–425.

28 See, for example, W Friedmann (1951–1952) 'Changing functions of
contract in common law', *University of Toronto Law Journal* (1951–1952)
pp15–41 at p17; and G Van Bueren, 'Falling behind – the United
Kingdom and human rights for the poor', *British Institute for Human
Rights Newsletter*, Winter 2009, p17.

29 *Liesbosch Dredger v SS Edison* [1933] AC 449 at 460 (per Lord Wright).

30 *Liesbosch Dredger v SS Edison* [1933] AC 449 at 460 (per Lord Wright).

31 L Clements and A L Aiello, *Unacceptable delay: complaints procedures for
disabled children and their families*, Cerebra, 2019, para 6.06.

32 JA King, 'The pervasiveness of polycentricity', *Public Law*, Spring 2008,
101–124.

33 JA King, 'The pervasiveness of polycentricity', *Public Law*, Spring 2008 at
102, citing L Fuller, 'The forms and limits of adjudication' (1978–1979)
92 *Harvard Law Review* 353 at 397.

34 JA King 'The pervasiveness of polycentricity', *Public Law*, Spring 2008,
101–124 at 113.

35 JA King 'The pervasiveness of polycentricity', *Public Law*, Spring 2008, at 112.

36 In *Winnik v Dick (Winnik)* 1984 SC 48 Lord Hunter refers to it as such.

37 J Mance, '*Ex turpi causa* – when Latin avoids liability', *The Edinburgh Law Review* 18.2 (2014): 175–192 at 175.

38 *Everet v Williams* (1725) 104 ER 725.

39 See, for example, *Moore Stephens v Stone & Rolls* [2009] 1 AC 1391; and J Mance, '*Ex turpi causa* – when Latin avoids liability', *The Edinburgh Law Review* 18.2 (2014): 175–192 at 175.

40 J Mance, '*Ex turpi causa* – when Latin avoids liability', *The Edinburgh Law Review* 18.2 (2014): 175–192 at 176: 'it is of course an invitation to fast-thinking of the type that the Nobel prize-winner Daniel Kahnemann has in his book *Thinking Fast and Slow* so tellingly – and, for decision-makers like myself, alarmingly – described. It suggests easy answers, but is entirely fallacious in so doing.'

41 *R v Hereford and Worcester County Council, ex p Smith*, Court of Appeal, 7 April 1993; a case considered by A Beale and R Geary, *Abolition of an unenforced duty*, NLJ 1995, 145(6679), 47–48, 61; and also in L Clements, 'Dirty Gypsies – ex turpi causa and human rights', *Human Rights* (2002) December 204–212.

42 Highways Act 1980 s137.

43 EP Thompson, *Whigs and hunters*, Allen Lane, 1975, p265.

44 EP Thompson, *Whigs and hunters*, Allen Lane, 1975, p266.

45 L Clements, 'Dirty Gypsies – ex turpi causa and human rights', *Human Rights* (2002) December 204–212 at 209.

46 Caravan Sites Act 1968 s6.

47 J-P Liégeois, *Gypsies and Travellers*, Council of Europe, 1987, p111.

48 European Court of Human Rights, App No 27238/95, 18 January 2001.

49 Caravan Sites Act 1968 s6.

50 *280,000 people in England are homeless, with thousands more at risk*, Shelter, 2019.

51 *Rough Sleeping Statistics*, Homeless link, 2019.

52 D Wainwright, *Homelessness: Councils record 28,000 on the streets over a year*, BBC, 26 February 2020.

53 H Cromarty, G Sturge and D Pyper, *Rough sleepers and anti-social behaviour (England)*, House of Commons Library Briefing Paper No 07836, 2 April 2019.

54 R Loopstra, A Reeves, B Barr, D Taylor-Robinson, M McKee and Stuckler, 'The impact of economic downturns and budget cuts on homelessness claim rates across 323 local authorities in England 2004–12' *Journal of Public Health* (2016) 38, 417–425.

55 G Bramley and S Fitzpatrick, 'Homelessness in the UK: who is most at risk?', *Housing Studies* (2017) 33, 96–116 at 98.

56 G Bramley and S Fitzpatrick, 'Homelessness in the UK: who is most at risk?', *Housing Studies* (2017) 33, 96–116 at 98; S Fitzpatrick, H Pawson,

G Bramley, S Wilcox, B Watts and J Wood, *The homelessness monitor: England 2019*, Crisis, 2018, p2; Alma Economics, *Homelessness. causes of homelessness and rough sleeping. Rapid evidence assessment*, Ministry of Housing Communities and Local Government and the Department for Work and Pensions, 2019; and R Loopstra, A Reeves, B Barr, D Taylor-Robinson, M McKee and Stuckler, 'The impact of economic downturns and budget cuts on homelessness claim rates across 323 local authorities in England 2004–12', *Journal of Public Health* (2016) 38, 417–425.

57 H Cromarty, G Sturge and D Pyper, *Rough sleepers and anti-social behaviour (England)*, House of Commons Library Briefing Paper, No 07836, 2 April 2019.

58 Vagrancy Act 1824 s3.

59 Vagrancy Act 1824 s4.

60 H Cromarty, G Sturge and D Pyper, *Rough sleepers and anti-social behaviour (England)*, House of Commons Library Briefing Paper, No 07836, 2 April 2019.

61 Section 67.

62 P Greenfield and S Marsh, 'Rising number of councils issuing fines for rough sleeping', *Guardian*, 7 March 2019.

63 23 Edw 3, c1 (1349); 25 Edw 3, c1 (1350).

64 D Baker, 'A critical evaluation of the historical and contemporary justifications for criminalising begging', *Journal of Criminal Law* (2009) 73 pp212–240 at 215; and see generally, P Lawrence, 'The Vagrancy Act (1824) and the persistence of pre-emptive policing in England since 1750', *The British Journal of Criminology*, Vol 57, Issue 3, 1 May 2017, pp513–531.

65 D Baker, 'A critical evaluation of the historical and contemporary justifications for criminalising begging', *Journal of Criminal Law* (2009) 73 pp212–240 at 217.

66 405 US 156 (1972).

67 Citing *Edwards v California*, 314 US 160, 174 Douglas J agreed that 'the theory of the Elizabethan poor laws no longer fits the facts'.

68 H Hershkoff and AS Cohen, 'Begging to differ: the First Amendment and the right to beg', *Harvard Law Review* (1990–1991) 896–916 at 901.

69 H Hershkoff et al cite M Walzer, *Spheres of justice. a defence of pluralism and equality*, Basic Books, 1983, p94: 'No community can allow its members to starve to death when there is food available to feed them; no government can stand passively by at such a time – not if it claims to be a government of or by or for the community.'

70 H Hershkoff and AS Cohen, 'Begging to differ: the First Amendment and the right to beg', *Harvard Law Review* (1990–1991) 896–916 at 906.

71 He however argues that the resemblance is entirely superficial as '[b]egging involves a request for assistance and a claim of need that cannot be to fit into a model of a commercial transaction' (p42).

72 E McCarraher, *The enchantments of Mammon*, Belknap Press, 2019, p5.

73 Principally, *McDonald's Corporation and McDonald's Restaurants Ltd v Steel and Morris* [1997] EWHC QB 366; and *Steel and Morris v McDonald's Corporation and McDonald's Restaurants Ltd* [1999] EWCA Civ 114.

74 *Steel and Morris v UK* App No 68416/01 15 Feb 2005.

75 Paraphrasing Bankowski and Mungham's observation that 'although the system might administer justice impartially, "justice itself is partial" ' – see Z Bankowski and G Mungham, *Images of law*, Routledge & Keegan, 1976.

76 See generally F Donson, *Legal intimidation*, Free Association Books, 2000.

77 There are of course rational arguments for (and against) corporations for having a right to sue in such cases – see A Mullis and A Scott, 'Something rotten in the state of English libel law? A rejoinder to the clamour for reform of defamation', *Communications Law* (2009) 14 (6). pp173–183.

78 For example, through the use of intimidatory SLAPP injunctions (strategic lawsuits against public participation).

79 S Sedley, 'A bill of rights for Britain', EHRLR (1997) 5, pp458–465 at 464.

80 The rules that determine whether a person (including a corporation) has the right to commence legal proceedings – sometimes referred to as the rules concerning 'sufficient standing'.

81 C Dickens, *Bleak House*, 1853, Ch 1: 'Jarndyce and Jarndyce still drags its dreary length before the Court, perennially hopeless.'

82 RH Tawney, *Equality*, George Allen & Unwin, 1964, p116.

83 Although arguably less privileged than corporations. International human rights treaties protect corporations – as they are deemed to be 'persons' at law – but not public bodies (such as the BBC or the Food Standards Agency) even though the revenue earned by many corporations far exceeds the gross domestic product (GDP) of many nation states (see, for example, *Ending corporate impunity*, Global Justice, 2018; and in the UK public bodies cannot be legally defamed – *Derbyshire CC v Times Newspapers* [1993] AC 534.

84 Senior Courts Act 1981 s31(3).

85 See, for example, *R v Greater London Council, ex p Blackburn* [1976] 3 All ER 184.

86 *R v Monopolies and Mergers Commission, ex p Argyll Group Ltd* 1986 1 WLR 763 [1986] 2 All ER 257.

87 *R v Somerset CC and ARC Southern Ltd ex p Dixon* [1997] JPL 1030; and see also *Walton v Scottish Ministers* [2012] UKSC 44.

88 *Civil justice statistics quarterly, England and Wales, January to March 2020 (provisional)*, Ministry of Justice, 2019.

89 *Civil justice statistics quarterly, England and Wales, January to March 2020 (provisional)*, Ministry of Justice, 2019.

90 In the last 10 years the legal aid budget has been reduced by 75 per cent – a factor considered further in the chapter that follows.

91 *Progress on socio-economic rights in Great Britain. Update report on Great Britain's implementation of the International Covenant on Economic, Social and Cultural Rights*, Equality and Human Rights Commission, 2018, p7.

92   See, for example, S Halliday, 'The influence of judicial review on bureaucratic decision-making' (2000) *Public Law* 110–122, 112.

93   P Scraton, 'Policing with contempt: The degrading of truth and denial of justice in the aftermath of the Hillsborough disaster', *Journal of Law and Society* (1999) 26(3) p 273–297, 295.

94   W Macpherson, *The Stephen Lawrence Inquiry*, The Stationery Office, 1999, para 6.32.

95   W Williams, *Windrush lessons learned review*, HC 93 (House of Commons, 2020) at 137.

96   R Francis, *Report of the Mid Staffordshire NHS Foundation Trust Public Inquiry – Executive summary* HC 947 (House of Commons, 2003) para 1.116.

97   See chapter 1.

98   C Dickens, *Great Expectations*, 1861.

99   Private law is the law that regulates the relationships between individuals – remembering, of course, that in the UK a company or corporation is considered to be legal 'person'. Private law includes the laws of property, contract, family and employment.

100 AC Hutchinson, 'Practising law for rich and poor people: towards a more progressive approach', *Legal Ethics* (2020), DOI: 10.1080/1460728x.2020.1799302, p9; Hutchinson added, however: 'to be frank this pretense of being apolitical and non-committed, fools only the complicit'.

101 N Hayes, *The book of trespass*, Bloomsbury, 2020; and see also R Cooke, 'Forgive us our trespasses: forbidden rambles with a right-to-roam campaigner', *The Observer New Review*, 9 August 2020, pp8–11.

102 AC Hutchinson, 'Practising law for rich and poor people: towards a more progressive approach', *Legal Ethics* (2020), DOI: 10.1080/1460728x.2020.1799302, p8.

103 MA Fineman, 'The vulnerable subject: anchoring equality in the human condition', *Yale J of Law and Feminism* (2008) 20(1) p10.

104 MA Fineman, 'Vulnerability and inevitable inequality', *Oslo Law Review* (2017) 4(3) 133–149 at 136.

105 For example, if it was concluded because of threats of physical violence or other forms of coercion, fraud or deceit: or if it is for immoral purposes of one party is a youth, or lacks the requisite mental incapacity. See generally D Campbell, H Collins and J Wightman (eds), *Implicit dimensions of contract: discrete, relational, and network contracts. International studies in the theory of private law*, Hart Publishing, 2003.

106 AT Kronman, 'Contract law and distributive justice', *Yale Law Journal* (1980) 89 pp472–511 at 496.

107 California's Penal Code s396, for example, makes it illegal to increase the price of a product or service item more than 10 percent in times of emergency and Florida Statute 501.160 prohibition against

unconscionable prices during emergencies – and see generally, MJ Sandel, *Justice*, Penguin, 2009, pp3–5.

108 As Dawson notes, the imperative for judicial intervention in such cases being reasonably clear – namely 'to preserve for a dominant class the economic resources on which its prestige and power depended – see JP Dawson, 'Economic duress – an essay in perspective' (1947) 45 Mich L Rev 253 at 268.

109 JP Dawson, 'Economic duress – an essay in perspective' (1947) 45 Mich L Rev 253 at 273.

110 *Clark v Malpas*, 25 April 1862: (1862) 4 De GF & J 401, [1862] Eng R 604, (1862) 31 Beav 80, (1862) 54 ER 1067.

111 *Proof v Hines*, Cases Temp Talbot 111 (1735).

112 *Proof v Hines*, Cases Temp Talbot 111 (1735).

113 *Baker v Monk*, 4 De Gek., J&S 388 (1864).

114 *Fry v Lane*, 40 Chan Div 312 (1888).

115 *James v Kerr*, 40 Chan Div 449 (1889).

116 *Alec Lobb (Garages) Ltd v Total Oil Ltd*, QBD [1983] 1 All ER 944; [1983] 1 WLR 87; and *Portman Building Society v Dusangh and others* [2000] EWCA Civ 142 CA.

117 Kronman has, for example, argued that advantage-taking should only be allowed if the 'person who has been taken advantage of in a particular way will be better off in the long run if the kind of advantage-taking in question is allowed than he would be if it were prohibited' – see AT Kronman, 'Contract law and distributive justice', *Yale Law Journal* (1980) 89 pp472–511.

3 What's your problem? Personal legal problems as singular

1 'How Pinball Machines Work' at: https://electronics.howstuffworks. com/pinball-machine1.htm.

2 J Chapman, *System failure: why governments must learn to think differently*, 2nd edn, Demos, 2004, p35.

3 J Chapman, *System failure: why governments must learn to think differently*, 2nd edn, Demos, 2004, p35.

4 House of Commons 'Law Centres: Written question (by Richard Burgon MP) 273435 Answer Paul Maynard MP', 11 July 2019; and see also O Bowcott, 'Legal advice centres in England and Wales halved since 2013–14', *Guardian*, 15 July 2019.

5 The legal aid budget stood at £2.2 billion in 2012, and in 2018 it had been reduced to £678 million (an inflation-adjusted cut of 75 per cent) and during this period, each year a million fewer claims for legal aid were processed. In the year before the Legal Aid, Sentencing and Punishment of Offenders Act (LASPO) 2012 came into force, 91,000

people received legal advice for welfare benefits cases; whereas in the year following, this fell by 99 per cent to just 478 people – see J Organ and J Sigafoos, The impact of *LASPO on routes to justice*, EHRC, 2018; D Newman and F Gordon 'Legal aid at 70: how decades of cuts have diminished the right to legal equality', *The Conversation*, 29 July 2019; and O Bowcott, 'Legal advice centres in England and Wales halved since 2013–14', *Guardian*, 15 July 2019.

6   See, for example, H Sommerlad, S Harris-Short, S Vaughan and R Young, *The futures of legal education and the legal profession*, Hart Publishing, 2015.

7   Richard Susskind, for example, gives a range of legal matters on which 'individual citizens' may require assistance – identifying variously unpaid debts, employment contracts, wills, loan documents, landlord and tenancy agreements, conveyancing, probate, personal injury, or pursing some personal injury claim. These are of course all 'private law' matters and the only reference to disadvantage appears to be is 'coping with debt' (p4) – a subject that (beyond this reference) is not covered further – see R Susskind, *Tomorrow's lawyers*, OUP, 2013.

8   R Susskind and D Susskind, *The future of the professions*, OUP, 2017.

9   R Susskind and D Susskind, *The future of the professions*, OUP, 2017, p198.

10 R Susskind and D Susskind, *The future of the professions*, OUP, 2017, p212.

11 Where 'square pegs may be thrust into round holes' – William L Andrews, ' "Baxter's Procrustes": some more light on the biographical connection', *Black American Literature Forum* Vol 11, No 3 (Autumn 1977), pp75–78 at 77 reviewing a story by Charles Chesnutt, 'Baxter's Procrustes' that appeared in the *Atlantic Monthly*, 93 (June 1904), 823–30.

12 For a review of the background to systems thinking see, for example, D Lane, E Munro and E Husemann, 'Blending systems thinking approaches for organisational analysis: Reviewing child protection in England', *European Journal of Operational Research* 251 (2016) 613–623 at 614–615.

13 V Anderson and L Johnson, *Systems thinking basics: from concepts to causal loop*, Pegasus Communications, 1997, 17–36 at 19.

14 J Chapman, *System failure. Why governments must learn to think differently*, 2nd edn, Demos, 2014, at 35.

15 J Chapman, *System failure. Why governments must learn to think differently*, 2nd edn, Demos, 2014, at 35.

16 J Chapman, *System failure. Why governments must learn to think differently*, 2nd edn, Demos, 2014, at 35.

17 See the *DeShaney v Winnebago County* case considered in chapter 4.

18 An apocryphal story demonstrating how an attempted solution to a problem can actually make the problem worse, where – in order to

eradicate cobras in Delhi – a reward was paid for every dead one delivered to the authorities. The programme worked in the short term, but in due course it led to the breeding of cobras as this provided a source of income. In response, the government stopped the programme. The cobra breeders then released their worthless snakes, causing a dramatic increase in the numbers of cobras.

19 N Harris, 'Complexity in the law and administration of social security: is it really a problem?', *Journal of Social Welfare and Family Law*, (2015) 37:2, 209–227 at 224.

20 N Harris, 'Complexity in the law and administration of social security: is it really a problem?', *Journal of Social Welfare and Family Law*, (2015) 37:2, 209–227, citing P Spicker *How social security works: An introduction to benefits in Britain*, Policy Press, 2011, at 204.

21 R Susskind and D Susskind, *The future of the professions*, OUP, 2017, p212.

22 A paralegal is someone who (although not a qualified solicitor or barrister) undertakes legal work supervised by a solicitor or barrister, and is often someone with a law degree who has been unable to secure a training contract or pupillage.

23 R Susskind and D Susskind, *The future of the professions*, OUP, 2017, p121.

24 J Seddon, *Systems thinking in the public sector*, Triarchy Press, 2008, at p135.

25 J Seddon, *Systems thinking in the public sector*, Triarchy Press, 2008, at p51.

26 J Seddon, *Systems thinking in the public sector*, Triarchy Press, 2008, at p134.

27 J Seddon, *Systems thinking in the public sector*, Triarchy Press, 2008, at p 134.

28 J Seddon, *Systems thinking in the public sector*, Triarchy Press, 2008, at p135.

29 J Chapman, *System failure. Why governments must learn to think differently*, 2nd edn, Demos, 2014, p19.

30 J Corner in the 'Foreword' to G Bramley and S Fitzpatrick, *Hard edges. Mapping severe and multiple disadvantage*, The Lankelly Chase Foundation, 2015.

31 J Chapman, *System failure. Why governments must learn to think differently*, 2nd edn, Demos, 2014, at p11.

32 See p 4 above in chapter 1.

33 L Clements and S McCormack, *Disabled children and the cost effectiveness of home adaptations & disabled facilities grants*, Cerebra, 2017.

34 See, for example, K Zokaei, S Elias, B O'Donovan, D Samuel, B Evans and J Goodfellow, *Report for the Wales Audit Office: Lean and systems thinking in the public sector in Wales*, Lean Enterprise Research Centre, 2010, pp15–16, which suggested that for an investment of just over £1 million the local authority saved over £12.5 million; and A Barnes, *Isle of Wight Council DFG cost savings research*, 2016, cited in L Clements

and S McCormack, *Disabled children and the cost effectiveness of home adaptations & disabled facilities grants*, Cerebra, 2017 at para 4.06 which calculated that the net annual savings resulting from DFGs amounted to over £13.5 million.

35 *R v Birmingham CC ex p Taj Mohammed* (1998) 1 CCLR 441.

36 Adding 'And that's what you have to do sometimes, or . . . you keep quiet' – J O'Flynn, F Buick, D Blackman and J Halligan, 'You win some, you lose some: Experiments with joined-up government', *International Journal of Public Administration*, (2011) 34, 244–254 at 249.

37 L Clements, 'Why investing £60k in home adaptations saves public money', *Guardian*, 26 July 2017.

38 M Cornes, L Joly, J Manthorpe, S O'Halloran and R Smyth, 'Working together to address multiple exclusion homelessness', *Social Policy and Society*, (2011) 10: 513–522.

39 M Cornes, L Joly, J Manthorpe, S O'Halloran and R Smyth, 'Working together to address multiple exclusion homelessness', *Social Policy and Society*, (2011) 10: 513–522 at 516.

40 M Cornes, L Joly, J Manthorpe, S O'Halloran and R Smyth, 'Working together to address multiple exclusion homelessness', *Social Policy and Society*, (2011) 10: pp 513–522 at 519.

41 M Cornes, L Joly, J Manthorpe, S O'Halloran and R Smyth, 'Working together to address multiple exclusion homelessness', *Social Policy and Society*, (2011) 10: 513–522 at 519.

42 M Cornes, L Joly, J Manthorpe, S O'Halloran and R Smyth, 'Working together to address multiple exclusion homelessness', *Social Policy and Society*, (2011) 10: 513–522 at 519.

43 L Stinson, 'Anatomy of a pinball machine', *topic Magazine*, Issue No 9, March 2018.

44 The report, for example, bemoaned the fragmentation of social welfare responsibilities: 'the overlapping, confusion and waste that result from the provision for each separate class [of categorised need] being undertaken, in one and the same district by [multiple authorities]' – see H Wakefield Russell, F Chandler, G Lansbury and B Webb, *Minority Report of the Royal Commission on the Poor Law 1905–1909*, HMSO, 1909, p395.

45 Citing McGarth's critique of approaches that fudged 'the boundaries between the professions and trying to create a generic care worker' – M McGrath, *Multidisciplinary teamwork*, Avebury, 1991.

46 Citing M McGrath, *Multidisciplinary teamwork*, Avebury, 1991.

4 Juridification and identity

1 P Loft, *Acts and Statutory Instruments: the volume of UK legislation 1850 to 2019*, Briefing Paper CBP 7438, House of Commons Library, 2019, p19.

2   The Treasury, the Department for Work and Pensions (DWP), the Department for Business, Innovation and Skills (BIS), the Ministry of Justice (MoJ) and the Home Office (HO) (respectively) – see J Blackwell and R Fox, 'Parliament and delegated legislation in the 2015–16 Session', Hansard Society, 2017, p13.

3   During the first eight years of the Blair Government an additional 3,023 criminal offences were created – see N Morris, 'Blair's "frenzied law making" ', *Independent*, 16 August 2006.

4   See, for example, 'The Red Tape Challenge' pioneered by the Department of Business Innovation and Skills between 2011 and 2014 and the 'One in, two out' approach introduced in 2013 and included in the *Cabinet Office Better Regulation Framework Manual*, Department for Business, Innovation and Skills, 2013.

5   KN Llewellyn, *The Cheyenne Way*, University of Oklahoma Press, 1941, p41.

6   'Simplification may help citizens understand their rights and administrators to uphold them, but it may erode those same rights' – see N Harris, 'Complexity in the law and administration of social security: is it really a problem?', *Journal of Social Welfare and Family Law* (2015) 37:2, 209–227 at 222.

7   S Wexler, 'Practising law for poor people', *The Yale Law Journal* (1969–1970) 79 pp1049–1968 at 1050.

8   L Wacquant, 'Crafting the neoliberal state: workfare, prisonfare, and social insecurity', *Sociological Forum*, Vol 25, No 2, June 2010 p197–220 at 213: a project that 'entails not simply the reassertion of the prerogatives of capital and the promotion of the marketplace, but the close articulation of four institutional logics' namely: (1) economic deregulation; (2) welfare state devolution – 'retraction, and recomposition designed to facilitate the expansion and support the intensification of commodification and, in particular, to submit reticent individuals to desocialized wage labor via variants of "workfare" '; (3) an 'expansive, intrusive, and proactive penal apparatus'; and (4) the 'cultural trope of individual responsibility'.

9   Juridification is an altogether more exotic concept – first coined by Jürgen Habermas in his *The theory of communicative action*, translated by T McCarthy, Beacon Press, 1984–1987; and see generally M Deflem, 'The legal theory of Jürgen Habermas' in R Banakar and M Travers (eds), *Law and social theory*, 2nd edn, Hart, 2013; and D Loick, 'Juridification and politics: from the dilemma of juridification to the paradoxes of right', *Philosophy and Social Criticism*, 2014, Vol 40(8) 757–778.

10   For David Benbow, 'Governments within the neo-liberal era have attempted to naturalise their reforms by endeavouring to remove them from political contestation' – see DI Benbow, 'Juridification, new constitutionalism and market reforms to the English NHS', *Capital & Class* (2019) 43(2) pp 293–313 at 295.

11 H Brabazon, 'Dissent in a juridified political sphere' in H Brabazon
(ed), *Neoliberal legality: understanding the role of law in the neoliberal
project*, Routledge, 2018, pp167–189.

12 H Brabazon, 'Dissent in a juridified political sphere' in H Brabazon
(ed), *Neoliberal legality: understanding the role of law in the neoliberal
project*, Routledge, 2018, pp167–189.

13 *DeShaney v Winnebago County Department of Social Services*, 109 S Ct
998, 1002 (1989).

14 L Tribe, 'The curvature of constitutional space: what lawyers can learn
from modern physics', *Harvard Law Review* (1989) 103(1) pp1–39 at p8.

15 L Tribe, 'The curvature of constitutional space: what lawyers can learn
from modern physics', *Harvard Law Review* Vol 103:1–39 at p10.

16 In much the same way that general relativity argues that mass warps
the space-time continuum.

17 L Tribe, 'The curvature of constitutional space: what lawyers can learn
from modern physics', *Harvard Law Review* Vol 103:1–39 at p11.

18 L Tribe, 'The curvature of constitutional space: what lawyers can learn
from modern physics', *Harvard Law Review* Vol 103:1–39 at p13z.

19 N Rose, 'Beyond the public/private division: law, power and the family'
(1987) 14 *Journal of Law and Society* 1, 61.

20 *DeShaney v Winnebago County Department of Social Services*, 109 S
Ct 998, 1001 (1989).

21 CR Gale, C Cooper and AA Sayer, 'Prevalence of frailty and disability:
findings from the English longitudinal study of ageing' (2015) 44(1)
pp162–165; and *Living longer: how our population is changing and why it
matters*, Office for National Statistics, 2018.

22 Between 2010 and 2019, funding for adult social care in England was
been cut by £7 billion – *Association of Directors of Adult Social Services
budget survey: human cost of failing to address the crisis in adult social care*,
ADASS, 2019; and see also P Simpson, *Public spending on adult social
care in England*, Briefing Note BN200, Institute of Fiscal Studies, 2017.

23 L Clements, *Community care and the law*, Legal Action Group, 2019,
para 11.4.

24 Care Quality Commission, *The state of health care and adult social care in
England 2018/19*, HC 9, House of Commons, 2019.

25 Graham and Wendy Enderby – see P Fennel, 'Graham Enderby
obituary', *Guardian*, 2 May 2020, p8.

26 European Court of Human Rights, *HL v UK* (App No 45508/99), 5
October 2004, para 50.

27 A completely new statutory framework is to be introduced in 2022 – the
Liberty Protection Safeguards (further to the Mental Capacity (Amendment)
2019): a framework that is thought to by many commentators to be defective
– see, for example, L Series, 'On detaining 300,000 people: The Liberty
Protection Safeguards', (2020): forthcoming *International Journal of Mental
Health and Capacity Law*. https://orca.cf.ac.uk/131764/.

28 The relevant schedules to the Mental Health Act 2007 ran to over 200 paragraphs – and there are 76 sections/schedules to the Mental Capacity (Amendment) Act 2019.

29 In 2017 it was estimated that the cost of full compliance with the revised legal regime would be £2.2 billion per year – approximately two per cent of the entire budget of NHS England – see Law Commission, *The Law Commission Mental Capacity and Deprivation of Liberty*, Law Com 372 HC1079, 2017, para 2.24.

30 House of Lords Select Committee on the Mental Capacity Act 2005 Report of Session 2013–14 Mental Capacity Act 2005: post-legislative scrutiny HL Paper 139 Stationery Office, 2014, para 257.

31 M Flynn, *Winterbourne View Hospital. a serious case review*, South Gloucestershire Safeguarding Adults Board, 2012.

32 For example, the Mental Health Act 1983, the Mental Capacity Act 2005, the Care Standards Act 2000 (and the associated regulatory framework overseen by the Care Quality Commission (CQC)) and the Protection of Vulnerable Adults provisions.

33 M Flynn, *Winterbourne View Hospital. a serious case review*, South Gloucestershire Safeguarding Adults Board, 2012.

34 *Transforming care: A national response to Winterbourne View Hospital. Department of Health Review: Final Report*, Department of Health, 2012. In April 2019 there were 2,245 people with learning disabilities or autism in such placements in England – see W Dahlgreen, 'The failings in learning disability services in six charts', BBC, 23 May 2019.

35 Joint Committee on Human Rights, *The detention of young people with learning disabilities and/or autism*, HC 121 HL Paper 10, House of Commons, 2019, paras 124–138.

36 In 2020 the Equality and Human Rights Commission (EHRC) announced that it would be launching a legal challenge against the government over the repeated failure to move people with learning disabilities and autism into appropriate accommodation – see EHRC, *Health Secretary faces legal challenge for failing patients with learning disabilities and autism*, Press Release, 12 February 2020; more than 2,000 people with learning disabilities and autism remain detained in secure hospitals, often far away from home and for many years.

37 Daniel Aronson provides a fascinating 'Silent spring' type scenario to illustrate the difference between a 'systems thinking' perspective and the perspective taken by traditional forms of analysis – see D Aronson, *Overview of systems thinking*, Systems Thinking, 1996.

38 *North Yorkshire County Council, A clinical commissioning group v MAG (by the Official Solicitor, as his litigation friend), GC* [2016] EWCOP 5: for a critical analysis of this judgment see B Clough, *The spaces of mental capacity law*, Routledge.

39 Concerning its lawfulness under the Mental Capacity Act 2005 and the Human Rights Act 1998.

40 The reasoning given for this is that the Court of Protection can only stand 'in the shoes of the person' and make the same decisions they could take. 'If that person has no power, under the community care legislation, to demand the provision of particular services then the court can do no such thing on his or her behalf': *N v ACCG and others* [2017] UKSC 22, para 1.

41 *North Yorkshire County Council, A clinical commissioning group v MAG (by the Official Solicitor, as his litigation friend), GC* [2016] EWCOP 5.

42 *A & B (Court of Protection: delay and costs)* [2014] EWCOP 48.

43 J Brenner and N Fraser, 'What is progressive neoliberalism?: a debate' in *Dissent*, Volume 64, Number 2, Spring 2017, pp130–141 at 131.

44 N Fraser, 'From progressive neoliberalism to Trump – and beyond' in *Dissent*, Winter 2017 / Volume I, Number 4, 46–64.

45 See, for example, I Ferguson, 'Increasing user choice or privatizing risk? the antinomies of personalization', *British Journal of Social Work* (2007) 37(3) 387–403; L Lienbenberg, M Ungar and J Ikeda, 'Neo-liberalism and responsibilisation in the discourse of social services workers', *British Journal of Social Work* (2007) 45(3): 1006–1021; and see also Mike Oliver's cri de coeur that although disabled people had gained direct payments and the benefits of anti-discrimination legislation, their ideas and struggles had been betrayed by 'ideologically-driven politicians' (among others) – M Oliver, 'Welfare and the wisdom of the past' in *Disability Now*, 1 March 2013.

46 First Annual Report of the Race Relations Board, April 1967, para.65, cited by Lord Lester of Herne Hill in 'Equality and United Kingdom law: past, present and future', *Public Law*, Spring 2001, p77.

47 Race Relations Act 1968; Equal Pay Act 1970; Sex Discrimination Act 1975; Race Relations Act 1976; Disability Discrimination Act 1995; EU Council Directive 2000/78/EC; and the Equality Act 2010.

48 Section 4.

49 Ie 'socio-economic status': although Equality Act 2010 s1 includes a duty, when certain decisions are made, to have due regard to socio-economic disadvantage – this provision has not been brought into force.

50 In limited situations, obesity qualifies as a 'disability' for the purposes of the Equal Treatment Directive 2000/78/EC – see Court of Justice of the European Union, *Kaltoft* (case C-354/13).

51 See, for example, CR Chapman, KS Mehta, B Parent and AL Caplan, 'Genetic discrimination: emerging ethical challenges in the context of advancing technology', *Journal of Law and the Biosciences* (2019) lsz016: https://doi.org/10.1093/jlb/lsz016.

52 See, for example, DF Flake, 'When any sentence is a life sentence: employment when any sentence is a life sentence: employment

discrimination against ex-offenders discrimination against ex-offenders', *Washington University Law Review*, Volume 93 Issue 1 2015 45–102.

53 See, for example, L Clements, 'Does your carer take sugar? Carers and human rights: the parallel struggles of disabled people and carers for equal treatment' in *The Washington and Lee Journal of Civil Rights and Social Justice* (2013) v19 pp397–434.

54 MA Fineman, 'Feminism, masculinities, and multiple identities' (2013) 13 *Nevada Law Journal*, pp619–639 at 628.

55 United Nations General Assembly Extreme poverty and human rights Report of 68th Session GA, A/68/293 (UN 2013) Special Rapporteur on extreme poverty and human rights at para 27.

56 M Henwood, 'As the carers' movement turns 50 there is no room for complacency', *Guardian*, 7 July 2015; T Cook, *History of the carers movement*, Carers UK, 2007.

57 M Henwood, 'As the carers' movement turns 50 there is no room for complacency', *Guardian*, 7 July 2015; and see also T Cook, *History of the carers movement*, Carers UK, 2007.

58 Succinctly summarised by K De Medeiros, 'The complementary self: multiple perspectives on the aging person', *Journal of Aging Studies* (2005) 19, pp1–13.

59 See generally, D O'Connor, 'Self-identifying as a caregiver: exploring the positioning process', *Journal of Aging Studies* (2007) 21(2), pp165–174 and S Knowles, R Combs, S Kirk, M Griffiths, N Patel and C Sanders, 'Hidden caring, hidden carers? Exploring the experience of carers for people with long-term conditions', *Health & Social Care in the Community* (2016) 24(2), pp203–213.

60 *Missing out: the identification challenge*, Carers UK, 2016, p6.

61 S Knowles, R Combs, S Kirk, M Griffiths, N Patel and C Sanders, 'Hidden caring, hidden carers? Exploring the experience of carers for people with long-term conditions', *Health & Social Care in the Community*, 2016 March; 24(2): 203–213.

62 D O'Connor, 'Self-identifying as a caregiver: exploring the positioning process', *Journal of Aging Studies* (2007) 21 (2), 165–174 at 170.

63 *Missing out: the identification challenge*, Carers UK, 2016, p6.

64 S Knowles, R Combs, S Kirk, M Griffiths, N Patel and C Sanders 'Hidden caring, hidden carers? Exploring the experience of carers for people with long-term conditions', *Health & Social Care in the Community* (2016) 24(2), pp203–213 at 209.

65 See P Grell, N Ahmadi and B Blom, 'Sometimes it's really complicated!' *Nordic Social Work Research* (2016) 6(3) pp188–200 at 197 citing J Habermas, 'The theory of communicative action', Vol 2 of *Lifeworld and system: a critique of functionalist reason*, Polity, 1987.

66 The duty persisting until the repeal of the Poor Laws by National Assistance Act 1948 s1.

67 See generally, L Clements, 'Does your carer take sugar? Carers and
     human rights: the parallel struggles of disabled people and carers for
     equal treatment', *The Washington and Lee Journal of Civil Rights and
     Social Justice* (2013) Vol 19, pp397–434.
68 F Bates and J Pitkeathley, 'Standing up to be counted: campaigning and
     voluntary agencies' in C Hanvey and T Philpot (eds), *Sweet charity*,
     Routledge, 1996.
69 Defined as people who provided regular and substantial care on an
     unpaid basis: Carers (Recognition and Services) Act 1995 s1.
70 See generally, L Clements, 'Does your carer take sugar? Carers and
     human rights: the parallel struggles of disabled people and carers for
     equal treatment', *The Washington and Lee Journal of Civil Rights and
     Social Justice* (2013) Vol 19, pp397–434.
71 See, for example, the Irish National Carers Strategy 2012 which has as
     its key objective to 'strengthen awareness and recognition of the role
     and contribution of carers at national, regional and local level'; and
     New Zealand Government Mahi Aroha Carers' Strategy Action Plan
     2019–2023, Ministry of Social Development, 2019.
72 The Caregiver, Advise, Record, Enable (CARE) Act drafted by the
     American Association of Retired Persons (AARP).
73 E Liebman, *The Caregiver Advise, Record, Enable (CARE) Act 2014 (New
     Jersey)*, AARP, 2014, p8.
74 E Liebman, *The Caregiver Advise, Record, Enable (CARE) Act 2014 (New
     Jersey)*, AARP, 2014, p8.
75 As at March 2019, it had been enacted in 40 states – see SC Reinhard,
     HM Young, E Ryan and RB Choula, *The CARE Act Implementation:
     Progress and Promise*, AARP Public Policy Institute, 2019.
76 E Liebman, *The Caregiver Advise, Record, Enable (CARE) Act 2014 (New
     Jersey)*, AARP, 2014, p7.
77 K Crenshaw, 'Demarginalizing the intersection of race and sex: a Black
     feminist critique of antidiscrimination doctrine, feminist theory and
     antiracist politics', *University of Chicago Legal Forum* (1989) 1, pp139–167.
78 Finance Act 1967 s16(3).
79 Social Security Act 1975 s37.
80 Contrary to Council Directive 79/7/EEC of 19 December 1978:
     Jacqueline Drake v Chief Adjudication Officer C-150/85 (24 June 1986) –
     'that discrimination on grounds of sex contrary to article 4(1) of
     Directive 79/7 arises where legislation provides that a benefit . . . is not
     payable to a married woman who lives with or is maintained by her
     husband, although it is paid in corresponding circumstances to a
     married man': para 34.
81 See C Harlow and R Rawlings, *Pressure through law*, Routledge, 1992,
     p147.
82 A bill introduced by Dr Hywel Francis MP contained a proposal for a
     duty to promote equality of opportunity between carers and people

without caring responsibilities – mirroring, in essence, the duty under Disability Discrimination Act 1995 s49A. This proposal was not supported by the government and was withdrawn.

83 Opinion of Advocate General Poiares Maduro in *S Coleman v Attridge Law and Steve Law*, Case C-303/06 (31 January 2008) para.3.

84 Council Directive 2000/78/EC of 27 November 2000 establishing a general framework for equal treatment in employment and occupation.

85 *Coleman v Attridge Law and Steve Law*, Case C-303/06 European Court of Justice Grand Chamber, para 56.

86 It has also been described as 'transferred' discrimination' – see S Forshaw and M Pilgerstorfer 'Taking discrimination personally? an analysis of the doctrine of transferred discrimination', *King's Law Journal*, Volume 19 (2) 2008, 265–292.

87 *Coleman v Attridge Law and Steve Law*, Case C-303/06 European Court of Justice Grand Chamber.

88 See, for example, T Connor, 'Discrimination by Association: "A Step in the Right Direction"', (2010) 32 *Journal of Social Welfare & Family Law* 59.

89 L Waddington, 'Case C-303/06, S Coleman v Attridge Law and Steve Law, Judgment of the Grand Chamber of the Court of Justice of 17 July 2008' (2009) 46 *Common Market Law Review*, Issue 2, pp665–681 at 665.

90 L Clements, 'Carers and the failure of "identity"' (forthcoming).

91 V Zigante, *Informal care in Europe: exploring formalisation, availability and quality*, European Commission, 2018, Figure 2 p18.

92 *Đorđević v Croatia* (App No 41526/10) 24 July 2012; *Radi v Romania* (App No 34655/14) 28 January 2016; *Trizio v Switzerland* (App No 7186/09) 2 February 2016; *Guberina v Croatia* (App No 23682/13) 22 March 2016; *Stoian v Romania* (App No 289/14) 25 June 2019.

93 Complaints to the court can be made by any inhabitant of any one of the Council of Europe's 47 member states.

94 The European Court of Human Rights, *The ECHR in facts and figures*, Council of Europe, 2018.

95 Over 2.6 million people have given up work at some point to provide unpaid care and 2 million have reduced working hours – *Juggling work and care*, Carers UK, 2019.

96 43 per cent of carers said their financial circumstances were affecting their health – *State of caring*, Carers UK, 2016.

97 Although most of the carers who were caring for at least 50 hours a week have a GP who knows of their caring responsibilities (84 per cent), of these carers, most (71 per cent) said that their GP didn't do anything differently to accommodate them – *Facts about caring*, Carers UK, 2019.

98 Half of carers cited problems with accessing suitable care services as a reason they gave up work or reduced working hours: *Facts about caring*, Carers UK, 2019.

99   D Freeman, 'Legitimizing racial discrimination through antidiscrimination law: a critical review of Supreme Court doctrine', *Minnesota Law Review* 1978 Vol: 62 pp1049–1119 at 1053.

100 D Freeman, 'Legitimizing racial discrimination through antidiscrimination law: a critical review of Supreme Court doctrine', *Minnesota Law Review* 1978 Vol: 62 pp1049–1119 at 1052–1053.

101 D Freeman, 'Legitimizing racial discrimination through antidiscrimination law: a critical review of Supreme Court doctrine', *Minnesota Law Review* 1978 Vol: 62 pp1049–1119 at 1054.

102 D Freeman, 'Legitimizing racial discrimination through antidiscrimination law: a critical review of Supreme Court doctrine', *Minnesota Law Review* 1978 Vol: 62 pp1049–1119 at 1054.

103 S R Bagenstos, 'The future of disability law', *Yale Law Journal* 114.1 (Oct 2004): p1.

104 D Spade, *Normal life*, 2nd edn, Duke University Press, 2015.

105 Citing (at p40) AP Harris, 'From Stonewall to the suburbs?', *William & Mary Bill of Rights Journal* 14 (2006) 1539–1582 – that '[t]he Persistent and growing racial wealth divide in the United States suggests that antidiscrimination laws have not had their promised effects, and that the structure of systemic racism is not addressed by the work of these laws'.

106 D Spade, *Normal life*, 2nd edn, Duke University Press, 2015, pp11–12.

107 23 EHRR 101: Judge Pettiti referred to UK law and its 'deliberate superimposition and accumulation of administrative rules (each of which would be acceptable taken singly)' but which cumulatively made it 'totally impossible for a Gypsy family to make suitable arrangements for its accommodation, social life and the integration of its children at school' (at 137).

108 D Spade, *Normal life*, 2nd edn, Duke University Press, 2015, p3.

109 D Spade, *Normal life*, 2nd edn, Duke University Press, 2015, p10.

110 MA Fineman, 'Feminism, masculinities, and multiple identities', 13 *Nevada Law Journal* (2013) pp619–639 at 639.

111 MA Fineman, 'Feminism, masculinities, and multiple identities', 13 *Nevada Law Journal* (2013) pp619–639 at 628.

112 MA Fineman, 'The vulnerable subject: anchoring equality in the human condition', *Yale Journal of Law and Feminism* (2008) 20(1) pp1–23 at 1.

113 MA Fineman, 'The vulnerable subject: anchoring equality in the human condition', *Yale Journal of Law and Feminism* (2008) 20(1) pp1–23 at 16.

114 MA Fineman, 'The vulnerable subject: anchoring equality in the human condition', *Yale Journal of Law and Feminism* (2008) 20(1) pp1–23 at 17.

5 Parcelling-out of the soul: public sector bureaucracies

1 'The dominance of a spirit of formalistic impersonality. "*Sine ira et studio*," without hatred or passion, and hence without affection or enthusiasm': see M Weber, *The theory of social and economic organization*, trans AM Henderson and T Parsons, Martini Publishing, 2012, p340.

2 M Weber, P R Baehr and G C Wells, *The protestant ethic and the 'spirit' of capitalism and other writings*, Penguin, 2002.

3 Remarks made by Weber during a debate in 1909 and cited in J P Meyer, *Max Weber and German politics*, Faber & Faber, 1943, p127–128.

4 As 'a polar night of icy darkness and hardness' – see M Weber, 'Essays in sociology' in H Gerth and CW Mills (eds), *From Max Weber*, Oxford University Press, 1946, p128.

5 If, for example, the decisions do not determine (for the purposes of European Convention on Human Rights Article 6) a civil right or criminal charge proceeding.

6 M Lipsky, *Street-level bureaucracy*, Russell Sage Foundation, 1980, p xi.

7 M Lipsky, *Street-level bureaucracy*, Russell Sage Foundation, 1980, p161.

8 The fear of one's shadow – see CG Jung and A Jaffé, *Memories, dreams, reflections*, Collins, 1977, p107. Jung, in his autobiography, described a reoccurring nightmare he had as a child. It was night: he was in an unknown place, alone and walking slowly in the face of a gale. All he had, cupped in his hand, was 'a tiny light which threatened to go out at any moment'. Suddenly he felt something behind him and when he looked around he saw 'a gigantic black figure' following him. He was terrified, but felt that his only hope was to keep the candle alight 'regardless of all dangers'. As Jung explains, when he awoke he realised 'that the figure was a "spectre of the Brocken", my own shadow ... brought into being by the little light I was carrying'. The solution to the terror was, of course to *blow out the light*: to 'let go'.

9 M Lipsky, *Street-level bureaucracy*, Russell Sage Foundation, 1980, p162.

10 See, for example, M Friedman, *Capitalism and freedom*, University of Chicago Press, 1962, 137–160; IZ Illich, K Irving. J McKnight, J Caplan and H Shaiken, *Disabling Professions 1978*, Marion Boyars, 1977; and M Travers, *The new bureaucracy: quality assurance and its critics*, Policy Press, 2007, pp43–57; see, for example, J Beck and M F D Young, 'The assault on the professions and the restructuring of academic and professional identities', *British Journal of Sociology of Education* (2005) 26(2) 2005, pp183–197; R Dingwall, 'The inevitability of professions? In making public services management critical' in G Currie, J Ford, N Harding and M Learmonth (eds), *Making public services management critical*, Routledge, 2010; H Sommerlad, 'Managerialism and the legal profession: a new

professional paradigm', *International Journal of the Legal Profession* (1995) v.2 Issue 2–3 pp159–185; and M Saks, *Professions and the public interest: medical power, altruism and alternative*, Routledge, 1995.

11 K Zokaei, S Elias, B O'Donovan, D Samuel, B Evans and J Goodfellow, *Report for the Wales Audit Office lean and systems thinking in the public sector in Wales*, LERC, 2010, p26.

12 J Chapman, *System failure. Why governments must learn to think differently*, 2nd edn, Demos, 2014, at 20.

13 See, for example, D Chugh and M H Bazerman, 'Bounded awareness: what you fail to see can hurt you', *Mind & Society* (2007) 6, 1–18. The boiled frog syndrome is the idea that a frog placed in pan of tepid water will remain there, even when the pan warmed very slowly – and will eventually die due to its inability to sense this gradual change.

14 See, for example, O O'Neil, *A question of trust*, Cambridge University Press, 2002, pp48–59; G Bevan and C Hood, 'What's measured is what matters: targets and gaming in the English public health care system', *Public Administration*, (2006) 84(3) 517–538; and John Seddon, *Systems thinking in the public sector*, Triarchy Press, 2008, pp96–107.

15 G Bevan and C Hood, 'What's measured is what matters: targets and gaming in the English public health care system', *Public Administration*, (2006) 84(3) 517–538.

16 LeGrand refers to the system's propensity to turn 'knights' into 'knaves' by rewarding people who game the system so that they can hit the target either by focusing on the target to the detriment of the quality of the primary service – for example, by reducing its performance where targets do not apply – LeGrand, *Motivation, agency and public policy*, Oxford University Press, 2003.

17 J Harris, *The social work business*, Routledge, 2003, pp94–95, citing M Power, *The audit society*, Oxford University Press, 1997.

18 John Seddon, *Systems thinking in the public sector*, Triarchy Press, 2008, at p100.

19 J Harris, *The social work business*, Routledge 2003, p58 citing J Ife, *Rethinking social work: towards critical practice*, Longman, 1997, at p58.

20 J Harris, *The social work business*, Routledge 2003, p58 citing J Ife, *Rethinking social work: towards critical practice*, Longman, 1997, at p58.

21 J Harris, *The social work business*, Routledge, 2003, p60 citing H Braverman, *Labour and monopoly capital*, Monthly Review Press, 1974, p100.

22 J Chapman, *System failure. Why governments must learn to think differently*, 2nd edn, Demos, 2014, at 35.

23 *Putting People First*, HM Government, 2007.

24 C Leadbeater, J Bartlett and N Gallagher, *Making it personal*, Demos, 2008.

25 S Carr, 'Personalisation, participation and policy construction: a critique of influence and understanding' in P Beresford, *Personalisation*, Policy Press, 2014, p27.

26 C Leadbeater, J Bartlett and N Gallagher, *Making it personal*, Demos, 2008.

27 C Leadbeater, J Bartlett and N Gallagher, *Making it personal*, Demos, 2008, p9; and SLK Training and Consultancy cited in P Beresford, *Personalisation*, Policy Press, 2014, p5.

28 See, for example, L Clements, 'Individual budgets and irrational exuberance' in *The Community Care Law Reports*, 11, pp413–430.

29 C Leadbeater, J Bartlett and N Gallagher, *Making it personal*, Demos, 2008, p39.

30 M Henwood and B Hudson, *Here to Stay? Self-directed support: aspiration and implementation. A review for the Department of Health*, Melanie Henwood Associates, 2007, para 2.22.

31 See generally, P Beresford, *Personalisation*, Policy Press, 2014.

32 See, for example, C Slasberg, P Beresford and P Schofield, 'The increasing evidence of how self-directed support is failing to deliver personal budgets and personalisation' in *Research, Policy and Planning* (2013) 30(2), 91–105; and L Series and L Clements, 'Putting the cart before the horse: resource allocation systems and community care' in *Journal of Social Welfare and Family Law* (2013) 35 (2), pp207–226.

33 M Lipsky, *Street-level bureaucracy*, Russell Sage Foundation, 1980, p161.

34 E Malbon, G Carey and A Meltzer, 'Personalisation schemes in social care: are they growing social and health inequalities?' in *BMC Public Health*, 2019 19:805 citing G Carey etc al, 'The vexed question of market stewardship in the public sector', *Social Policy & Administration* (2018) 52(1) pp387–407.

35 E Malbon, G Carey and A Meltzer, 'Personalisation schemes in social care: are they growing social and health inequalities?' in *BMC Public Health*, 2019 19:805 citing G Carey et al, 'The vexed question of market stewardship in the public sector', *Social Policy & Administration.* (2018) 52(1) pp387–407.

36 V Bogdanor, *Joined-up government*; OUP, 2005.

37 V Bogdanor, *Joined-up government*, OUP, 2005.

38 V Bogdanor, *Joined-up government*, OUP, 2005.

39 L Clements, *Community care and the law*, 7th edn, Legal Action Group, 2019, para 12.39.

40 G Carey and B Crammond, 'What works in joined-up government? An evidence synthesis', *International Journal of Public Administration* (2015) 38:13–14, 1020–1029, at 1027.

41 JM Bryson, BC Crosby and MM Stone, 'The design and implementation of cross-sector collaborations: propositions from the literature', *Public Administration Review* (2006) 66(S1) 44–55 at 52.

42 J O'Flynn, F Buick, D Blackman, and J Halligan, 'You win some, you lose some: experiments with joined-up government', *International Journal of Public Administration*, (2011) 34, 244–254 at 253.

43 J O'Flynn, F Buick, D Blackman, and J Halligan, 'You win some, you lose some: experiments with joined-up government', *International Journal of Public Administration*, (2011) 34, 244–254 at 248–249.

44 J Steinbeck, *The grapes of wrath*, Viking, 1939, chapter 5.

45 R Taylor, *Impact of 'hostile environment' policy*, House of Lords Library Briefing, 11 June 2018.

46 See, for example, *Is Britain fairer?* Equality and Human Rights Commission, 2018, p63 – which notes that in 2015 a change to planning law was made despite the government accepting that it would disproportionately affect elderly people, children and disabled children of Gypsies and Travelling people.

47 See, for example, J Wiggan, 'Telling stories of 21st century welfare: the UK Coalition Government and the neo-liberal discourse of worklessness and dependency', *Critical Social Policy* 32(3) 383–405 at 391; and F Ryan, 'The hostile environment? Britain's disabled people live there too', *Guardian*, 26 April 2018.

48 See, for example, M Alvesson, *Understanding organizational culture*, 2nd edn, Sage, 2013; and G Salaman, *Human resource strategies*, Sage, 1992.

49 N Thompson, S Stradling, M Murphy and P O'Neill, 'Stress and organizational culture', *The British Journal of Social Work*, (1996) 26(5) 1996, 647–665 at p 647. Alvesson (above, p40.) makes the point that in many cases it is not appropriate to refer to an organisational culture – as opposed to 'cultures'; as in many organisations there is not one homogenous culture but variety of cultural orientations.

50 N Thompson, S Stradling, M Murphy and P O'Neill, 'Stress and organizational culture', *The British Journal of Social Work*, (1996) 26(5) 1996, 647–665 at p651.

51 N Thompson, S Stradling, M Murphy and P O'Neill, 'Stress and organizational culture', *The British Journal of Social Work*, (1996) 26(5) 1996, 647–665 at p661.

52 Citing M EP Seligman, *Helplessness*, Freeman, 1975.

53 G Klein, *Streetlights and shadows: searching for the keys to adaptive decision making*, Massachusetts Institute of Technology Press, 2009, p22.

54 EH Schein, 'Coming to a new awareness of organizational culture', in G Salaman (ed), *Human resource strategies*, Sage, 1992, p243.

55 A Lees, E Meyer and J Rafferty, 'From Menzies Lyth to Munro: the problem of managerialism', *The British Journal of Social Work* (2013) 43(3) pp542–558 at 543 citing I Menzies Lyth, 'The functioning of social systems as a defence against anxiety', in I Menzies Lyth (ed), *Containing anxiety in institutions (selected essays volume 1)*, Free Association Books, 1998.

56 E Munro, *The Munro review of child protection: final report. A child-centred system*, Cm 8062 Department for Education, Stationery Office, 2011, p20.

57 D Lane, E Munro and E Husemann, 'Blending systems thinking approaches for organisational analysis: Reviewing child protection in

England', *European Journal of Operational Research* 251 (2016) 613–623 at 615.

58 A Lees, E Meyer and J Rafferty, 'From Menzies Lyth to Munro: the problem of managerialism', *The British Journal of Social Work* (2013) 43(3) pp542–558, at 543 citing D Lawlor, 'Test of time: A case study in the functioning of social systems as a defence against anxiety: Rereading 50 years on', *Clinical Child Psychology and Psychiatry*, (2009) 14(4), pp523–530.

59 D Westlake, S Wallace, V Silverwood and E Doherty, *Wigan Change Project: devolved budgets interim report August 2019*, Cardiff University, 2019, p13.

60 Citing E Munro, *The Munro review of child protection: Final report. A child centred system*, Department for Education, 2011.

61 D Pimenta, *Duty of care: one NHS doctor's story of the COVID-19 crisis*, Welbeck, 2020.

62 The investigation of a complaint against Gwynedd Council. A report by the Public Services Ombudsman for Wales: Case No 201801474, 5 June 2019.

63 Joint Committee on Human Rights, *The human rights of older people in healthcare*, HL Paper 156-I HC 378-I, The Stationery Office, 2007, para 234 et seq.

64 K Simons, *I'm not complaining, but . . .*, Joseph Rowntree Foundation, 1995.

65 See, for example, Joint Committee on Human Rights, *The human rights of older people in healthcare*, HL Paper 156-I HC 378-I, The Stationery Office, 2007, para 235 which cites the comment: 'I do not like to say anything because maybe they will hold it against me, and anyway the staff are wonderful'; and K Simons (as above) at p35: 'criticising otherwise valued services' and at p54 which cites complainants who were 'appalled' at the treatment of their supportive social worker as a result of their complaint.

66 Cerebra Legal Entitlements and Problem-solving (LEaP) Project, *Diagnosis delay and disabled children survey*, Cerebra, 2015 – a survey of parents in September and October 2015 to which 1,937 parents responded.

67 This sense of 'futility and pessimism' concerning the process of complaints and problem-solving is also shared by many people working within the statutory sectors P Bate, 'The impact of organizational culture on approaches to organizational problem-solving' in G Salaman, *Human resource strategies*, Sage, 1992, pp228–229 cited in N Thompson, S Stradling, M Murphy and P O'Neill, 'Stress and organizational culture', *The British Journal of Social Work*, (1996) 26(5) 1996, 647–665 at p651.

68 Sir David Nicholson's evidence to the House of Commons Public Administration Select Committee, *More Complaints Please!* Twelfth Report of Session 2013–14 HC 229, The Stationery Office, 2014, para 16.

69 S Halliday, 'The influence of judicial review on bureaucratic decision-making' (2000) *Public Law* 110–122, 116–117.
70 S Halliday, 'The influence of judicial review on bureaucratic decision-making' (2000) *Public Law* 110–122, 112.
71 The Cerebra Legal Entitlements and Problem-solving (LEaP) project (unpublished).
72 See *Irwin Mitchell successfully challenge Manchester Council to implement new eligibility criteria for disabled children* at: www.irwinmitchell.com/client-stories/2012/august/irwin-mitchell-successfully-challenge-manchester-council-to-implement-new-eligibility-criteria-for-disabled-children.
73 MD Esposti, DK Humphreys, BM Jenkins, A Gasparrini, S Pooley, M Eisner and L Bowes, 'Long-term trends in child maltreatment in England and Wales 1858–2016: an observational, time-series analysis', *The Lancet Public Health* (2019) 4(3) e148–e158.
74 There is, however, no doubt that this figure has decreased dramatically over the last 150 years. Between 1858 and 2016, killings of this kind decreased by 90 per cent and during the same period convictions for child cruelty or neglect decreased by over 80 per cent. See *Statistics briefing: child deaths due to abuse or neglect*, National Society for the Prevention of Cruelty to Children (NSPCC), 2020; and see also *Child physical abuse in England and Wales: year ending March 2019*, Office of National Statistics (ONS), 2020.
75 For example, Victoria Climbié in 2000; Baby Peter in 2007; and Daniel Pelka in 2012.
76 E Munro, *The Munro Review of Child Protection: final report. A child-centred system* Cm 8062 Department for Education, Stationery Office, 2011.
77 D Lane, E Munro and E Husemann, 'Blending systems thinking approaches for organisational analysis: Reviewing child protection in England', *European Journal of Operational Research* 251 (2016) 613–623 at 614–615.
78 A Lees, E Meyer and J Rafferty, 'From Menzies Lyth to Munro: the problem of managerialism', *The British Journal of Social Work* (2013) 43(3) pp542–558, at 543 citing D Lawlor, 'Test of time: A case study in the functioning of social systems as a defence against anxiety: Rereading 50 years on', *Clinical Child Psychology and Psychiatry* (2009) 14(4), pp523–530.
79 L Tribe, 'The curvature of constitutional space: what lawyers can learn from modern physics', *Harvard Law Review* (1989) 103(1) pp1–39 at p8 – discussed in the previous chapter.
80 In such cases, the fact that there are records of a child having been seen on a large number of occasions by a variety of professionals is generally taken as damning evidence of failure.
81 At paras 1.23–1.24.

82 At para 1.21.

83 C Argyris and D Schön, *Organizational learning: a theory of action perspective*, Addison-Wesley, 1978.

84 In this context, the report, at para 4.24, cites an Ofsted finding that: 'Serious Case Reviews were generally successful at identifying what had happened to the children concerned, but were less effective at addressing why.'

85 At para 4.27, citing House of Commons Health Committee (2009), *Patient safety*, Sixth Report of Session 2008–09, HC 151-I, The Stationery Office, 2009, p11.

86 At para 4.30.

87 Munro Report at para 7.9, citing a submission by William Tate, Fellow of the Centre for Leadership Innovation at the University of Bedfordshire, and the Director of the Institute for Systemic Leadership, to the review.

6 Harm

1 At: https://learnenglishkids.britishcouncil.org/crafts/ snakes-and-ladders.

2 L Clements, *Accessing public services toolkit*, Cerebra, 2017.

3 See, for example, D Kahneman, *Thinking, fast and slow*, Penguin, 2012; and A Mani, S Mullainathan, E Shafir and J Zhao, 'Poverty impedes cognitive function', *Science* (2013) 341 (6149), 976–980.

4 The impact of cognitive overload / attentional capture on the ability to make reasoned judgments has been considered in a number of other dimensions including financial worries, time pressures, coping with stereotypes, emotional distress, nutrition, physical pain, sleep deprivation, noise pollution, stress/depression, age as well as (unsurprisingly) addictions – see. for example, K Gandy, K King, P Streeter Hurle, C Bustin and K Glazebrook, 'Poverty and decision-making', Behavioural Insights Ltd, 2016; S Kaplan and M G Berman, 'Directed attention as a common resource for executive functioning and self-regulation', *Perspectives on Psychological Science* (2010) 5(1): 43–57; F Schilbach, H Schofield and S Mullainathan, 'The psychological lives of the poor American', *Economic Review: Papers & Proceedings* 2016, 106(5): 435–440; B Jones and O A Parsons, 'Impaired abstracting ability in chronic alcoholics', *Archives of General Psychiatry* (1971) 24(1), 71–75; and ES Parker, RL Alkana, D Pharm, IM Isabel, M Birnbaum, JT Hartley and EP Noble, 'Alcohol and the disruption of cognitive processes', *Archives of General Psychiatry* (1974) 31(6), 824–828.

5 D Kahneman, *Thinking, fast and slow*, Penguin, 2012.

6 S Mullainathan and E Shafir, *Scarcity*, Penguin, 2013.

7   A Mani, S Mullainathan, E Shafir and J Zhao, 'Poverty impedes cognitive function', *Science* (August 2013) 341 (6149), 976–980.

8   K Gandy, K King, P Streeter Hurle, C Bustin and K Glazebrook, *Poverty and decision-making*, Behavioural Insights Ltd, 2016, p13.

9   S Mullainathan and E Shafir, *Scarcity*, Penguin, 2013, p63.

10 LJB Hayes, 'Work-time technology and unpaid labour in paid care work: a socio-legal analysis of employment contracts and electronic monitoring' (chapter 9) in Sian Beynon-Jones and Emily Grabham (eds), *Law and time*, Routledge, 2018, pp179–195. Hayes speaks of the clash between nature's time (the uncertain, varying and unprofitable time taken for a caring task and the time needed to parent her own children) and the 'clock time' – noting that 'electronic monitoring introduced opportunities to shave labour cost-saving from the incompatibility of nature's time and clock time'.

11 See, for example, KD Vohs, 'The poor's poor mental power', *Science* (2013)341, 969–970 – but see also J Dang, S Xiao, and S Dewitte, General Commentary Article: 'Poverty impedes cognitive function and the poor's poor mental power', *Frontiers of Psychology*, 22 July 2015 6(1037) 1–3.

12 Or 'present-bias' – where, for example, a person opts for a smaller, immediate cash payment rather than waiting for a larger payment – see, for example, R Cassidy, 'Are the poor so present-biased?', IFS Working Paper W18/24, Institute of Fiscal Studies, 2018.

13 J Haushofer and E Fehr, 'On the psychology of poverty', *Science* (May 2014) 344, (6186) 862–867 at 866.

14 D Kahneman, *Thinking, fast and slow*, Penguin, 2012, at p41.

15 S Mullainathan and E Shafir, *Scarcity*, Penguin, 2013.

16 D Kahneman, *Thinking, fast and slow*, Penguin, 2012 at p35.

17 'The blunt truth is that ill-used people are worse than well-used people . . . I hate the poor and look forward eagerly to their extermination. I pity the rich a little, but am equally bent on their extermination', GB Shaw, *The intelligent woman's guide to socialism, capitalism, sovietism and fascism*, Pelican, 1937.

18 H Lewis, *Difficult women: a history of feminism in 11 fights*, Jonathan Cape, 2020, p327.

19 J Read, *Disability, the family and society: listening to mothers*, Open University Press, 2000, p119.

20 *Managing unreasonable complainant conduct – 2nd edition. A manual for frontline staff, supervisors and senior managers*, NSW Ombudsman, 2012.

21 Hon Justice Michael Kirby, Ombudsman – The future. Speech delivered at a dinner following the seminar on 'Ombudsman through the looking glass', 7 September 1985. Canberra Bulletin of Public Administration, vol XII no 4, p300.

22 *Policy on the management of unreasonable complainant behaviour*, Local Government and Social Care Ombudsman, 2017.

23 *R (CD) v Anglesey County Council* [2004] EWHC 1635 (Admin); (2004) 7 CCLR 589 at [24].

24 See, for example, Joint Committee on Human Rights, *The human rights of older people in healthcare*, HL Paper 156-I HC 378-I, The Stationery Office, 2007, at para 258.

25 See, for example, complaint no 18 016 254 against Cornwall Council, 6 February 2020 where a complainant who alleged (correctly) that his grandmother's care was unsatisfactory and was then penalised by the council because of the unacceptable behaviour of his wife; Complaint no 18 002 031 concerning Kirklees BC and Locala HomeCare Ltd, 6 January 202 and a complainant who alleged (correctly) that his partner's care was unsatisfactory was alleged to have behaved unacceptably even though there was no allegation that he had been violent or aggressive, or abusive but simply because the care workers 'felt upset and humiliated' and that they had to deal with his complaint; and complaint no 17 000 336 against London Borough of Hounslow, 15 January 2018 where the attribution of unacceptable behaviour concerned the 'tone of correspondence and discourteousness'.

26 *Haringey LBC and the mother, the father and A & B* [2020] EWFC 38; see also *PA Media Group and Haringey LBC, the mother, the father and A & B* [2020] EWHC 1282 (Fam); and A Turner, 'A root and branch failure of social work', *Community Care*, 21 May 2020 at: www.communitycare.co. uk/2020/05/21/judge-blasts-safeguarding-failings-haringey-children-with-disabilities-team/.

27 BBC Radio Gloucester, 10 December 2018, 'Mark Cummins'; 11 December 2018, 'Mark Cummings'; and Radio 5 Live 'Parents accused of inventing children's illnesses', 10 March 2019.

28 See L Clements, *Can you cope?* 3 December 2018 at: www.lukeclements. co.uk/can-you-cope/.

29 *Care homes market study Final report*, Competition and Markets Authority, 2017, para 11.40.

30 *R (O) v Peterborough CC and Cambridgeshire and Peterborough Foundation NHS Trust* [2016] EWHC 2717 (Admin); (2016) 19 CCLR 548.

31 Complaint no 07/B/07665 against Luton BC, 10 September 2008, para 37. Other similar examples include: complaint no 15 003 629 against Northamptonshire CC 25 October 2016; Joint NHS and Local Government Ombudsman Report on complaint no 12 004 807 and 12 013 660 against Essex CC, Suffolk CC, North Essex Partnership NHS Foundation Trust and Norfolk and Suffolk NHS Foundation Trust, 15 January 2014; and complaint no 07C13163 against Birmingham City Council, 8 October 2012, paras 69–74.

32 Complaint no 07C03887 against Bury MBC, 14 October 2009, para 43.

33 S Mullainathan and E Shafir, *Scarcity*, Penguin, 2013, p64.

34 S Mullainathan and E Shafir, *Scarcity*, Penguin, 2013, p64.
35 M Adamkovič and M Martončik, 'A review of consequences of poverty on economic decision making', Review Article in *Frontiers of Psychology*, (2017) 8(1784) pp1–13; and see also J Haushofer and E Fehr, 'On the psychology of poverty', *Science* (May 2014) 344, (6186) 862–867 at p864.
36 A Cattaneoab and MA Riva, 'Stress-induced mechanisms in mental illness: A role for glucocorticoid signalling', *The Journal of Steroid Biochemistry and Molecular Biology*, Volume 160, June 2016, pp169–174.
37 J K Kiecolt-Glaser, R Glaser, S Gravenstein, WB Malarkey and J Sheridan, 'Chronic stress alters the immune response to influenza virus vaccine in older adults', PNAS (1996) 93(7) 3043–3047; and see also BS McEwen, 'Protection and damage from acute and chronic stress: allostasis and allostatic overload and relevance to the pathophysiology of psychiatric disorders', *Annals of the New York Academy of Sciences* (2004) 1032, 1–7.
38 BS McEwen, 'Protection and damage from acute and chronic stress: allostasis and allostatic overload and relevance to the pathophysiology of psychiatric disorders', *Annals of the New York Academy of Sciences* (2004) 1032, 1–7.
39 J F Brosschot, S Pieper and J F Thayer, 'Expanding stress theory: prolonged activation and perseverative cognition', *Psychoneuroendocrinology*, (2005)30, 1043–1049; and CA Demsky, C Fritz, LB Hammer and AE Black, 'Workplace incivility and employee sleep: the role of rumination and recovery experiences', *Journal of Occupational Health Psychology*, 2019 24(2) 228–240.
40 N Rose, *Our psychiatric future*, Polity, 2019, p115.
41 N Rose, *Our psychiatric future*, Polity, 2019, p43 citing *Social determinants of mental health*, World Health Organization, 2014, pp17–18.

7 Doing justice

1 JM Keynes, *The general theory of employment, interest and money*, Macmillan and Co, 1936, Introduction.
2 B Disraeli, *Sybil, or the two nations*, Henry Colburn, 1845, Book 2 Chapter 5.
3 In this context, the 'state' is used expansively, to include those entities that exercise state power including public authorities for the purposes of the Human Rights Act 1998 s6, such as central government, the NHS, the courts, the ombudsmen, as well as other bodies to whom the state has delegated its responsibilities.
4 The Legal Entitlements and Problem-solving (LEaP) project funded by Cerebra, a disabled children's research charity.
5 J Wolff and A De-Shalkit, *Disadvantage*, OUP, 2013, p139.

6   See L Clements, *Accessing public services toolkit*, Cerebra, 2017, p8
    (available here: https://cerebra.org.uk/download/accessing-public-
    services-toolkit/).

7   See, for example, M Abendroth, CA Greenblum and JA Gray, 'The
    value of peer-led support groups among caregivers of persons with
    Parkinson's disease', *Holistic Nursing Practice*, (2014) 28(1) pp48–54;
    C Munn-Giddings and A McVicar, 'Self-help groups as mutual support:
    what do carers value?', *Health and Social Care in the Community* (2007)
    15(1) pp26–34; M Larkin, 'Group support during caring and post-
    caring: the role of carers groups', *Groupwork* (2007) 17(2), pp28–51; and
    H Worrall, R Schweizer, E Marks, L Yuan, C Lloyd and R Ramjan, 'The
    effectiveness of support groups: a literature review', *Mental Health and
    Social Inclusion* (2018) 22(2) pp85–93.

8   See, for example, National Survivor User Network, *The value of user led
    groups – 2019 campaign*, NSUN, 2019; KM Griffiths, 'Mental health
    internet support groups: just a lot of talk or a valuable intervention?',
    World Psychiatry (2017) 16(3) pp247–248; P Dibben and D Bartlett,
    'Local government and service users: empowerment through user-led
    innovation?', *Local Government Studies*, (2001) 27:3, 43–58; and
    RL Davies, P Heslop, S Onyett and T Soteriou, 'Effective support for
    those who are "hard to engage": a qualitative user-led study', *Journal of
    Mental Health* (2014) 23(2) pp 62–66.

9   See, for example, C Barnes and G Mercer, *Independent futures. creating
    user-led disability services in a disabling society*, Policy Press, 2006; and
    P Beresford, *All our welfare*, Policy Press, 2016.

10 See, for example, G Hague, 'Domestic violence survivors' forums in the
    uk: experiments in involving abused women in domestic violence
    services and policy-making', *Journal of Gender Studies* (2005) 14(3)
    pp191–203; and A Mullender and G Hague 'Giving a voice to
    women survivors of domestic violence through recognition as a service
    user group', *The British Journal of Social Work* (2005) 35(8)
    pp1321–1341.

11 See, for example, SL Barker and N Maguire, 'Experts by experience:
    peer support and its use with the homeless', *Community Mental Health
    Journal* (2007) DOI 10.1007/s10597-017-0102-2.

12 Fredrickson uses the notion of 'affect', which she describes as a more
    general concept than that of more transient, short lived emotions – one
    where the individual has consciously accessible feelings and is 'more
    long lasting and may be salient only at the level of subjective
    experiences': see BL Fredrickson, 'The role of positive emotions in
    positive psychology: the broaden-and-build theory of positive emotions',
    American Psychologist (2001) 56(3), 218–226 at 218.

13 See, for example, JL Plass and S Kalyuga, 'Four ways of considering
    emotion in cognitive load theory', *Educational Psychology Review* (2019)
    31:339–359 at 355.

14 D Kahneman, *Thinking fast and slow*, Pengiuin, 2012, p69. Kahneman notes, however, that it can also make individuals more gullible and blunt in their analytical ability.

15 BL Fredrickson, 'The role of positive emotions in positive psychology: the broaden-and-build theory of positive emotions', *American Psychologist* (2001) 56(3), 218–226 at 221.

16 BL Fredrickson, 'The role of positive emotions in positive psychology: the broaden-and-build theory of positive emotions', *American Psychologist* (2001) 56(3), 218–226 at 219.

17 National Survivor User Network, 'Survey results of user-led groups', 2019.

18 NCVO, *What we believe about independence and values*, 2020.

19 The Panel on the Independence of the Voluntary Sector, *Independence under threat: the voluntary sector*, Baring Foundation, 2013, p30.

20 The Panel on the Independence of the Voluntary Sector, *Independence under threat: the voluntary sector*, Baring Foundation, 2013, p3.

21 J Chapman, *System failure. Why governments must learn to think differently*, 2nd edn, Demos, 2004, p12.

22 J Chapman, *System failure. Why governments must learn to think differently*, 2nd edn, Demos, 2004, pp27–28.

23 B Hudson, 'Commissioning for change: a new model for commissioning adult social care in England', *Critical Social Policy* (2018) 39 pp1–21; and see also D Button and S Bedford, *Ownership in social care*, New Economics Foundation, 2020.

24 Whereas a focus on value drives them down – see for example, J Seddon, *Systems thinking in the public sector*, Triarchy Press, 2008, p52.

25 J Seddon, I Hussain, T Rubbra and B Wrighton, *Beyond command and control*, Vanguard, 2019, p148.

26 B Hudson, 'Commissioning for change: a new model for commissioning adult social care in England', *Critical Social Policy* (2018) 39 1–21 p 8 – citing A Fox, *A new health and care system*, Policy Press, 2018.

27 L Cowie and I Rees Jones, *Adult social care social enterprises and the foundational economy in Wales*, WISERD Research Reports Series, WISERD/RRS/0, WISERD, 2017.

28 [2018] EWCA Civ 1641; and see generally D McCann, 'Temporal casualisation and 'availability time': Mencap, Uber and the framed flexibility model', DWR Research Paper 01/2020.

29 Mencap, *Annual report*, 2019.

30 See, for example, *Care homes market study Final report*, Competition and Markets Authority, 2017; and R Thorlby, A Starling, C Broadbent and T Watt, *What's the problem with social care, and why do we need to do better?*, The Health Foundation et al, 2018.

31 See V Kotecha, *Phugging the leaks in the UK care home industry*, CG p1, 2019.

32 N Cominetti, L Gardiner and G Kelly, *What happens after the clapping finishes? The pay, terms and conditions we choose for our care workers*, Resolution Foundation, 2020.

33 Care Quality Commission, *The state of health care and adult social care in England 2018/19*, HC, HMSO, 2019, p37; see also The Health Foundation, *Stemming the tide: retaining the social care workforce*, 2018; and *Skills for care. The state of the adult social care sector and workforce in England*, 2019.

34 Care Quality Commission, *Not just a number. Home care inspection programme, National overview*, 2013; and see also UNISON, *15 minutes of shame. Stories from Britain's homecare frontline*, 2015.

35 S Bottery, *What's your problem, social care? The eight key areas for reform*, King's Fund, 2019.

36 S Bottery, *What's your problem, social care? The eight key areas for reform*, King's Fund, 2019.

37 D Pyper, *National minimum wage: sleep-in care*, Briefing paper CBP 8243, House of Commons Library, 2018.

38 N Caiden, *Court of Appeal in Mencap: The end of minimum wage for sleep-ins when asleep?*, Cloisters, 2018.

39 R Preston, 'Mencap sleep-in case to be heard in Supreme Court', *Civil Society News*, 14 February 2020.

40 Office of National Statistics, *Impact of coronavirus in care homes in England: 26 May to 19 June 2020*, ONS, 2020.

41 P Beresford, 'The tax relief row exposes big charities' priorities', *Guardian*, 24 April 2012: Beresford, in this article, referred to the 'growing divide between small charitable organisations . . . and the traditional large organisations – with big reserves, highly paid chief executives and expensive central London headquarters'.

42 S L Barker and N Maguire, 'Experts by experience: peer support and its use with the homeless', *Community Mental Health Journal* (2007) 53(5) 598–612.

43 S Finlayson, V Boleman, R Young and A Kwan, *Saving lives, saving money. How homeless health peer advocacy reduces health inequalities*, The Young Foundation, 2016.

44 The language of the undefined – leaner, smarter, more agile, more competitive, more productive and so on.

45 House of Commons Public Administration Select Committee, *More complaints please!* Twelfth Report of Session, 2013–14 HC 229, The Stationery Office, 2014, para 43.

46 J Seddon, I Hussain, T Rubbra and B Wrighton, *Beyond command and control*, Vanguard, 2019.

47 L Clements and P Smith, *Building bridges: bridging the health and social care divide in Wales*, Cardiff University, 1999.

48 See, however, L Clements, *Community care and the law*, 7th edn, Legal Action Group, 2019, chapter 13.

49 J O'Flynn, F Buick, D Blackman, and J Halligan, 'You win some, you lose some: experiments with joined-up government', *International Journal of Public Administration* (2011) 34, 244–254 at 249, where they

described a strategy for managing this tension which involved engaging in joined-up work on the ground, but only reporting program-specific activity back up the line, until there were positive outcomes to declare.

50 L Clements and P Smith, *Building bridges: bridging the health and social care divide in Wales*, Cardiff University, 1999, p15; and see also in this context, B Hudson, 'Joint commissioning: organisational revolution or misplaced enthusiasm?' (1995) 23 *Policy & Politics* p233.

51 A few years after the report, the five Welsh health authorities were abolished and replaced by 22 local health boards, and these have since been abolished and replaced by seven health boards.

52 J M Bryson, B C Crosby and M M Stone, 'The design and implementation of cross-sector collaborations: propositions from the literature', *Public Administration Review* (2006) 66(S1) 44–55 at 52.

53 J O'Flynn, F Buick, D Blackman and J Halligan, 'You win some, you lose some: experiments with joined-up government', *International Journal of Public Administration* (2011) 34, 244–254 at 253.

54 N Thompson, S Stradling, M Murphy and P O'Neill, 'Stress and organizational culture', *The British Journal of Social Work*, (1996) 26(5) 1996, 647–665 at p 651.

55 N Thompson, S Stradling, M Murphy and P O'Neill, 'Stress and organizational culture', *The British Journal of Social Work*, (1996) 26(5) 1996, 647–665 at p 664.

56 Evidence given by Sir David Nicholson, the then Chief Executive of NHS England and cited in the report by the House of Commons Public Administration Select Committee, *More complaints please!* Twelfth Report of Session 2013–14 HC 229, The Stationery Office, 2014, para 42.

57 Michael Lipsky considered the preparedness of 'street level bureaucrats' to subvert the efforts of managers to control them 'in the name of accountability' as positive quality M Lipsky, *Street-level bureaucracy*, Russel Sage Foundation, 1980, p163.

58 As Onora O'Neill observed, mid-flow in her diatribe against the 'new culture of accountability': 'most people working in the public service have a reasonable sense not only of the specific clinical, educational, policing or other goals for which they work, but also of central ethical standards that they must meet' – O O'Neill, *A question of trust*, CUP, 2002, pp54–55.

59 See chapter 3 above; and J Seddon, *Systems thinking in the public sector*, Triarchy Press, 2008 at p71.

60 J Seddon, *Systems thinking in the public sector*, Triarchy Press, 2008, at p139.

61 P Grell, N Ahmadi and B Blom, 'Sometimes it's really complicated!', *Nordic Social Work Research* (2016) 6(3) pp188–200 at 191, citing J Seikkula, TE Arnkil and E Eriksson, 'Postmodern society and social networks: open and anticipation dialogues in network meetings', *Family Process* (2003) 42(2): 185–203.

62 See, for example, M Jonson-Reid, CR Emery, B Drake and MJ Stahlschmidt, 'Understanding chronically reported families', *Child Maltreatment* (2010) 15(4) pp 271–281.

63 L Clements and S McCormack, *Disabled children and the cost effectiveness of home adaptations & disabled facilities grants*, Cerebra, 2017 – research discussed in chapter 3 above.

64 M Cornes, L Joly, J Manthorpe, S O'Halloran and R Smyth, 'Working together to address multiple exclusion homelessness', *Social Policy and Society*, (2011) 10: 513–522 at 516.

65 For example – studies concerning the needs of homeless people with addiction and mental health problems: M Cornes, L Joly, J Manthorpe, S O'Halloran and R Smyth, 'Working together to address multiple exclusion homelessness', *Social Policy and Society*, (2011) 10: 513–522; and see generally C Leadbeater, J Bartlett and N Gallagher, *Making it personal*, Demos, 2008, at pp76–77; and studies concerning the needs of families with disabled children: see S Broach and L Clements, *Disabled children: a legal handbook*, Legal Action Group, 2020, para 1.50 fn105 which contains an extensive list of relevant citations.

66 WP Wodchis, J Shaw, S Sinha, O Bhattacharyya, S Shahid and G Anderson, 'Innovative policy supports for integrated health and social care programs in high-income countries', *Health Affairs* (2020) 39(4) 607–703.

67 M Cornes, L Joly, J Manthorpe, S O'Halloran and R Smyth, 'Working together to address multiple exclusion homelessness', *Social Policy and Society*, (2011) 10: 513–522 at 519.

68 See generally, J Seddon, *Systems thinking in the public sector*, Triarchy Press, 2008; and K Zokaei, S Elias, B O'Donovan, D Samuel, B Evans and J Goodfellow, *Report for the Wales Audit Office. Lean and systems thinking in the public sector in Wales*, LERC Lean and Systems Thinking in the Public Sector in Wales, 2010.

69 P Beresford, *All our welfare*, Policy Press, 2016, 309.

70 E Laurie, 'Homelessness and the "over-judicialisation" of welfare', *Legal Studies* (2020), 1–16 at p16.

71 For example, in relation to decisions concerning the deprivation of liberty of people with impaired mental capacity (considered in chapter 4) 'best interests assessors' would have a greater role in the care planning process.

72 Wexler likened this to having to 'fill out an income tax return once or twice a week' and pondered what a 'not-poor person' would feel like if the state required them do this – see S Wexler, 'Practising law for poor people', *The Yale Law Journal* (1969–1970) 79 pp 1049–1968 at 150.

73 J Seddon, *Systems thinking in the public sector*, Triarchy Press, 2008, at p140.

74 See, for example, with P Bari, L Clements, A Aiello and T Hutchinson, *Unlawful restrictions on the rights of disabled children with autism to social care needs assessments*, Cerebra, 2020.

75 R Hood, A Goldacre, S Gorin, P Bywaters and C Webb, *Identifying & understanding the link between system conditions & welfare inequalities in children's social care services*, Nuffield, 2020, p100.

76 E Munro, *The Munro review of child protection: final report. A child-centred system*, Cm 8062 Department for Education, Stationery Office, 2011 – considered in chapter 5 above.

77 R Hood, A Goldacre, S Gorin, P Bywaters and C Webb, *Identifying & understanding the link between system conditions & welfare inequalities in children's social care services*, Nuffield, 2020, p100.

78 D Lane, E Munro and E Husemann, 'Blending systems thinking approaches for organisational analysis: Reviewing child protection in England', *European Journal of Operational Research* 251 (2016) 613–623 at 615. Unearthing a compliance addiction.

79 D Lane, E Munro and E Husemann, 'Blending systems thinking approaches for organisational analysis: Reviewing child protection in England', *European Journal of Operational Research* 251 (2016) 613–623 at 615. Unearthing a compliance addiction, citing WH Laming, *The protection of children in England: a progress report*, HMSO, 2009, p33.

80 See, for example, A Mani, S Mullainathan, E Shafir and J Zhao, 'Poverty impedes cognitive function', *Science* (August 2013) 341 (6149), 976–980; and K Gandy, K King, P Streeter Hurle, C Bustin and K Glazebrook, *Poverty and decision-making*, Behavioural Insights Ltd, 2016, pp55–56.

81 K Gandy, K King, P Streeter Hurle, C Bustin and K Glazebrook, *Poverty and decision-making*, Behavioural Insights Ltd, 2016, pp55–56.

82 K Gandy, K King, P Streeter Hurle, C Bustin and K Glazebrook, *Poverty and decision-making*, Behavioural Insights Ltd, 2016, p55, citing J Currie, *The take up of social benefits*, working paper 10488. J, National Bureau of Economic Research, 2004, at: www.nber.org/papers/w10488.

83 A Mani, S Mullainathan, E Shafir and J Zhao, 'Poverty impedes cognitive function', *Science*, (August 2013) 341 (6149), 976–980.

84 K Gandy, K King, P Streeter Hurle, C Bustin and K Glazebrook, *Poverty and decision-making*, Behavioural Insights Ltd, 2016, p8.

85 See, for example, H Sommerlad, 'Managerialism and the legal profession: a new professional paradigm', *International Journal of the Legal Profession* (1995) 2(2–3) pp159–185; and L Clements, 'In whose interests?' October 1994 *Legal Action* 6.

86 D Freeman, 'Legitimizing racial discrimination through antidiscrimination law: a critical review of Supreme Court doctrine', *Minnesota Law Review* (1978) 62 pp1049–1119 at 1053 – considered in chapter 4 above.

87 S Wexler, 'Practising law for poor people', *The Yale Law Journal* (1969–1970) 79 pp1049–1968 at 1050.

88 In 2018, over half of junior legal aid lawyers earned less than £25,000 per year (when the national median earnings for a full-time worker were £28,600), Young Legal Aid Lawyers, *Social Mobility in a Time of Austerity*, 2018.

89 In this category are included the Public Services Ombudsman for Wales; the Scottish Public Services Ombudsman; the Northern Ireland Public Services Ombudsman; and in England – the Local Government and Social Care Ombudsman; the Parliamentary and Health Services Ombudsman; and the Housing Ombudsman Service.

90 Local Government Act 1974 s26.

91 Health Service Commissioner Annual Report for 1993–94, HC 499, HMSO, 1994.

92 Parliamentary and Health Services Ombudsman, *The Ombudsman's annual report and accounts 2018–2019*, HC 2198, House of Commons, 2019.

93 Local Government and Social Care Ombudsman, *Review of local government complaints 2018–19*, 2019, p7.

94 L Clements and A Aiello, *Unacceptable delay: complaints procedures for disabled children and their families*, Cerebra, 2019, para 4.05.

95 The available evidence indicates that the significant increase in the proportion of litigants in person, in the civil courts, is linked to the enactment of the Legal Aid, Sentencing and Punishment of Offenders Act 2012 – see GG Grimwood, *Litigants in person: the rise of the self-represented litigant in civil and family cases in England and Wales*, Commons Briefing papers S N07113, House of Commons Library, 2016, p3.

96 L Clements and AL Aiello, *Unacceptable delay: complaints procedures for disabled children and their families*, Cerebra, 2019, para 6.33.

97 L Clements and AL Aiello, *Unacceptable delay: complaints procedures for disabled children and their families*, Cerebra, 2019.

98 L Clements and AL Aiello, *Unacceptable delay: complaints procedures for disabled children and their families*, Cerebra, 2019, at para 6.03.

99 G Bevan and C Hood, 'What's measured is what matters: targets and gaming in the English public health care system', *Public Administration*, Vol 84, No 3, 2006 (517–538); and see also L Clements and AL Aiello, *Unacceptable delay: complaints procedures for disabled children and their families*, Cerebra, 2019, paras 4.07–4.09.

100 See generally in this respect, L Clements and AL Aiello, *Unacceptable delay: complaints procedures for disabled children and their families*, Cerebra, 2019, paras 6.25–6.31.

101 The ombudsmen do publish thematic / 'focus' reports. Although special reports of this kind could be seen as proactive initiatives to improve administrative practice, there does not appear to be any published as to their effectiveness – see L Clements and AL Aiello, *Unacceptable delay: complaints procedures for disabled children and their families*, Cerebra, 2019, para 6.24.

102 J Doward, 'Equality watchdog's human rights fight "under threat" after cuts', *Guardian*, 20 November 2016.

103 J Seddon, I Hussain, T Rubbra and B Wrighton, *Beyond command and control*, Vanguard, 2019, p128.

104 See, for example, L Anthopoulosa, CG Reddick, I Giannakidou,
     N Mavridis, 'Why e-government projects fail?', *Government Information
     Quarterly* (2016) 33(1) pp161–173, which reviews the literature and
     suggests that possibly 35 per cent of global public sector IT projects
     failed and possibly 50 per cent could be categorised as partial failures –
     findings broadly in line with the research by R Gauld and S Goldfinch,
     *Dangerous enthusiasms: e-government, computer failure and information
     system development*, Otago University Press, 2006.

105 M Janssen, H van der Voort, AFE van Veenstra, 'Failure of large
     transformation projects from the viewpoint of complex adaptive
     systems: management principles for dealing with project dynamics',
     Information Systems Frontiers (2015), 17 pp15–29.

106 *Over-optimism in government projects*, National Audit Office, 2013.

107 D Kahenman and A Tversky, *Intuitive prediction: Biases and corrective
     procedures*, Cybernetics Technology Office, 1977, p15.

108 See, for example, D Hirst, *Mind the gap: the digital divide and digital
     inclusion*, House of Commons Library, 2015; E Rust, 'When the UK
     goes "digital by default", who will be left behind?', *Guardian*, 23 June
     2014; and N Selwyn 'Reconsidering political and popular
     understandings of the digital divide', *New Media and Society* (2004) 6(3)
     pp341–362.

109 Statement on visit to the United Kingdom, by Professor Philip Alston,
     United Nations Special Rapporteur on extreme poverty and human
     rights, London, 16 November 2018; available at: www.ohchr.org/en/
     NewsEvents/Pages/DisplayNews.aspx?NewsID=23881; and see p7
     above.

Appendix

1 P Connor and J S Passel *Europe's Unauthorized Immigrant Population
   Peaks in 2016, Then Levels Off*, Pew Research Centre 2019, p33, and see
   also I Gordon, K Scanlon, T Travers, and C Whitehead, 'Economic Impact
   on London and the UK of an Earned Regularisation of Irregular Migrants
   in the UK', GLA Economics, 2009. In addition (in 2018) there were over
   45,000 people awaiting determination of their formal applications for
   asylum – United Nations High Commissioner for Refugees *Global
   Trends: Forced Displacement in 2018*, UNHCR, 2019, p68.

2 Extrapolated from estimates by Gordon et al that in the UK in 2007
   there were a total of 155,000 irregularly resident children (of which over
   85,000 were born in the UK to irregular migrant parents) and a total
   population of irregular migrants in the UK at 618,000 – see I Gordon,
   K Scanlon, T Travers, and C Whitehead, 'Economic Impact on London
   and the UK of an Earned Regularisation of Irregular Migrants in the
   UK', GLA Economics, 2009.

3   P Connor and J S Passels, *Europe's Unauthorized Immigrant Population Peaks in 2016, Then Levels Off,* Pew Research Centre, 2019, p33.

4   C Giner, 'The Politics of Childhood and Asylum in the UK', *Children and Society* (2007) 21(4) pp249–260.

5   HE Creswick, *'Women under the radar': the intersection of migration and domestic violence explored through the framework of '(un)deservingness'* (2017) PhD thesis, University of Nottingham.

6   Office of the Independent Anti-Slavery Commissioner and the University of Nottingham's Rights Lab, *Labour exploitation in hand car washes,* University of Nottingham and the Independent Anti-Slavery Commissioner, 2018, p8.

7   C Straßmayr, A Matanov, S Priebe, et al, 'Mental health care for irregular migrants in Europe: Barriers and how they are overcome', BMC Public Health, 2012, 12(1): 367.

8   See for example, *Are sick migrants avoiding NHS doctors over deportation fears?* BBC, 22 February 2018 at www.bbc.co.uk/news/uk-politics-43139702.

9   W Farah, A Hundt, F Qureshi, *Access to Primary Health Care for migrants is a right worth defending,* Migrants Rights Network, 2011, p4.

10 S Shaw, *Review into the Welfare in Detention of Vulnerable Persons: A Report to the Home Office by Stephen Shaw* CM 9186, Secretary of State for Home Department, 2016, p132.

11 S Shaw, *Review into the Welfare in Detention of Vulnerable Persons: A Report to the Home Office by Stephen Shaw* CM 9186, Secretary of State for Home Department, 2016, p94 referring to evidence submitted by 'Bail for Immigration Detainees' (BID) an independent charity that exists to challenge immigration detention in the UK.

12 S Shaw, *Review into the Welfare in Detention of Vulnerable Persons: A Report to the Home Office by Stephen Shaw* CM 9186, Secretary of State for Home Department, 2016, p94.

13 Office of the Independent Anti-Slavery Commissioner and the University of Nottingham's Rights Lab, *Labour exploitation in hand car washes,* University of Nottingham and the Independent Anti-Slavery Commissioner, 2018, p8.

14 J Allsopp, N Sigona, J Phillimore, *Poverty among refugees and asylum seekers in the UK: An evidence and policy review,* University of Birmingham, 2014, p17.

15 Section 22 and see *R (Joint Council for the Welfare of Immigrants) v Secretary of State for the Home Department* [2020] EWCA Civ 542.

16 *Criminal Justice Statistics quarterly, England and Wales, April 2018 to March 2019,* Ministry of Justice, 2019, p1.

17 Prison Reform Trust, *Prison: the facts – Bromley Briefings Summer 2019,* Prison Reform Trust, 2019, p3; and see also *Proven reoffending statistics quarterly: April to June 2017,* Ministry of Justice, 2019. Table C1a.

18 *Criminal Justice Statistics quarterly, England and Wales, April 2018 to March 2019*, Ministry of Justice, 2019, p1.

19 L Wacquant, 'Crafting the Neoliberal State: Workfare, Prisonfare, and Social Insecurity', *Sociological Forum* (2010) 25(2) p203.

20 *Prison: the facts – Bromley Briefings Summer 2019*, Prison Reform Trust, 2019, p12; and see also *Children looked after in England including adoption: 2016 to 2017*, Department for Education, 2017, Table MYE2 and *Population Estimates for UK, England and Wales, Scotland and Northern Ireland, mid-2017*, Office for National Statistics 2019.

21 *Prison: the facts – Bromley Briefings Summer 2019*, Prison Reform Trust, 2019, p12; and see also HM Inspectorate of Prisons *Children in custody 2017–18*, Stationery Office, 2019.

22 Lord Laming *In Care, Out of Trouble*, Prison Reform Trust, 2016; and see also R Blades, D Hart, J Lea, N Willmott, *Care – a stepping stone to custody?* Prison Reform Trust, 2011, p3.

23 *Prison: the facts – Bromley Briefings Summer 2019*, Prison Reform Trust, 2019, p13; *Gender differences in substance misuse and mental health amongst prisoners*, Ministry of Justice, 2013; and R D Schneider, *The Mentally Ill: How They Became Enmeshed in the Criminal Justice System and How We Might Get Them Out*, Department of Justice, Canada, 2015, p6.

24 *Prison: the facts – Bromley Briefings Summer 2019*, Prison Reform Trust, 2019, p10; and see also J Talbot, *Prisoners' Voices: Experiences of the criminal justice system by prisoners with learning disabilities and difficulties*, Prison Reform Trust, 2008.

25 See for example, M Sepúlveda Carmona and K Donald, *Access to justice for persons living in poverty: a human rights approach*, Ministry for Foreign Affairs for Finland, 2014, p21.

26 *Prison: the facts – Bromley Briefings Summer 2019*, Prison Reform Trust, 2019, p16.

27 *Prison: the facts – Bromley Briefings Summer 2019*, Prison Reform Trust, 2019, p16.

28 *Prison: the facts – Bromley Briefings Summer 2019*, Prison Reform Trust, 2019, p16.

29 *Prison: the facts – Bromley Briefings Summer 2019*, Prison Reform Trust, 2019, p16.

30 *Prison: the facts – Bromley Briefings Summer 2019*, Prison Reform Trust, 2019, p16. See also *Education and employment strategy*, Ministry of Justice, 2018.

31 C Stacey, 'Looking beyond re-offending: criminal records and poverty', *Criminal Justice Matters* (2015) 99(1) 4–5; and see also A Dominguez and M Loureiro, 'Stigma, Ex-convicts and Labour Markets', *German Economic Review* (2012) 13(4) pp470–486.

32 C Stacey, 'Looking beyond re-offending: criminal records and poverty', *Criminal Justice Matters* (2015) 99(1).

33 *Repeat offenders with multiple needs in London. An analysis of needs and relevant decision making structures,* Revolving Door's Agency, 2012.

34 *Family Resources Survey 2016/17,* Department for Work and Pensions, 2018, p7 – equivalent to 13.9 million people.

35 A Gartrell, M Jennaway, L Manderson, J Fangalasuu, S Dolaiano, *Social determinants of disability based disadvantage in Solomon islands,* Oxford 2016, p251; see also A Elwan, *Poverty and Disability: A Survey of the Literature – Social Paper Discussion Paper series,* The World Bank, 1999.

36 48.3 per cent – see Social Metrics Commission, *A new measure if poverty for the UK: A Summary Report by the Social Metrics Commission,* Social Metrics Commission, 2018, p28.

37 *Facts and Figures 2018: Disability in the United Kingdom,* Papworth Trust, 2018, p43.

38 *Facts and Figures 2018: Disability in the United Kingdom,* Papworth Trust, 2018, p8.

39 *Facts and Figures 2018: Disability in the United Kingdom,* Papworth Trust, 2018, p32; and see also A Powell, *Key statistics on people with disabilities in employment,* Briefing No 7540, House of Commons Library, 2018.

40 *Facts and Figures 2018: Disability in the United Kingdom,* Papworth Trust, 2018, p32.

41 *Promoting inclusion through Social Protection: Report on the World Social Situation,* United Nations, 2018, Chapter V, p66.

42 *Facts and Figures 2018: Disability in the United Kingdom,* Papworth Trust, 2018, p35; and see also ComRes, *Leonard Cheshire Disability Employers Survey,* ComRes, 2019.

43 *Disability and employment,* TUC, 2016, p8.

44 S Longhi, *Research Report 107: the disability pay gap,* Equality and Human Rights Commission, 2017.

45 *Facts and Figures 2018: Disability in the United Kingdom,* Papworth Trust, 2018, p9.

46 Such as specialist home equipment, higher insurance premiums, higher transport costs, additional costs of specialist foods, heating, laundry and so on – see Extra Costs Commission, *Driving down the extra costs disabled people face,* Barrow Cadbury Trust, 2015.

47 *Facts and Figures 2018: Disability in the United Kingdom,* Papworth Trust, 2018, p10.

48 *Facts and Figures 2018: Disability in the United Kingdom,* Papworth Trust, 2018, p19.

49 For example over 300,000 people with long term mental health problems lose their job each year – see P Farmer and D Stevenson, *Thriving at work: a review of mental health and employers,* Department for Work and Pensions, 2017.

50 C Dockerty, J Varney, R Jay-Webster, *Disability and domestic abuse: Risk, impacts and response,* Public Health England, 2015, p9.

51 C Dockerty, J Varney, R Jay-Webster, *Disability and domestic abuse: Risk, impacts and response*, Public Health England, 2015, p9.

52 C Dockerty, J Varney, R Jay-Webster, *Disability and domestic abuse: Risk, impacts and response*, Public Health England, 2015, p4.

53 C Dockerty, J Varney, R Jay-Webster, *Disability and domestic abuse: Risk, impacts and response*, Public Health England, 2015, p4.

54 *Family Resources Survey*, Department for Work and Pensions, 2018/2019, adopting the definition of disability in the Equality Act 2010 section 6; and *Population estimates for the UK, England and Wales, Scotland and Northern Ireland: mid-2019*, Office of National Statistics, 2020.

55 C Blackburn, N Spencer and J Read, 'Prevalence of childhood disability and the characteristics and circumstances of disabled children in the UK: secondary analysis of the Family Resources Survey', *BMC Pediatrics* 10, 21, (2010); and see generally S Broach and L Clements, *Disabled Children: a legal handbook*, Legal Action Group, 2020, chapter 1.

56 S Broach and L Clements, *Disabled Children: a legal handbook*, Legal Action Group, 2020, para 1.28 citing A T Gibson, 'Outcome following preterm birth', *Best practice and research clinical obstetrics and gynaecology*, 21, 5, 869–882; 2007.

57 *End of life care for infants, children and young people with life-limiting conditions: planning and management – Clinical guideline NG61*, National Institute for Health and Clinical Excellence, 2016.

58 *Mental Health of Children and Young People in England*, NHS Digital, 2017.

59 *Briefing Children and young people with mental health problems and access to NHS treatments*, Royal College of Psychiatrists, 2019; and see generally First Joint Report of the Education and Health and Social Care Committees of Session 2017–19: *The Government's Green Paper on mental health: failing a generation* HC 642, House of Commons, 2018.

60 *Disabled children and child poverty*, Every Disabled Child Matters, 2007, p3.

61 B Beresford, D Rhodes, *Housing and disabled children*, Joseph Rowntree Foundation, 2008, p1.

62 P Lavis, C Burke, R Hastings, *Overshadowed: The mental health needs of children and young people with learning disabilities*, Children and Young People's Mental Health Coalition, 2019, p11.

63 *Key stage 4 including Multi-Academy Trust performance 2018 (revised)*, Department for Education, 2019, p28.

64 A Powell, *House of Commons Library Briefing Paper SN 06705: NEET: Young people not in education, employment or training*, House of Commons Library, 2018.

65 *Fulfilling potential. Building a deeper understanding of disability in the UK Today*, Department for Work and Pensions, 2013.

66 K Abdinasir and I Pona, *Access Denied A teenager's pathway through the mental health system*, Children's Society, 2015.

67 *Caring more than most: A profile of UK families caring for disabled children*, Contact, 2017, p18.

68 *Caring more than most: A profile of UK families caring for disabled children*, Contact, 2017, p18.

69 *Caring more than most: A profile of UK families caring for disabled children*, Contact, 2017, p16.

70 K Gandy, K King, P Streeter Hurle, C Bustin and K Glazebrook, *Poverty and decision-making*, Behavioural Insights Ltd, 2016, p66.

71 *Family Resources Survey*, Department for Work and Pensions, 2012/2013; H Clarke and S McKay, *Exploring disability, family formation and break-up: reviewing the evidence*, Research Report No 514, Department for Work and Pensions, 2008; C Blackburn, N Spencer and J Read, *Prevalence of childhood disability and the characteristics and circumstances of disabled children in the UK: secondary analysis of the Family Resources Survey*, BMC Pediatrics 10, 2010, p21.

72 C Hatton, E Emerson, H Graham, J Blacher and G Llewellyn, 'Changes in family composition and marital status in families with a young child with cognitive delay', *Journal of Applied Research in Intellectual Disabilities* (2010) 23(1) pp14–26.

73 E John, G Thomas, A Touchet, *The Disability Price Tag 2019: Policy Report* (SCOPE 2019) p12; and see also Social Metrics Commission, *A new measure of poverty for the UK*, The Legatum Institute, 2018.

74 E John, G Thomas and A Touchet, *The Disability Price Tag 2019: Policy Report*, SCOPE, 2019, p4.

75 E John, G Thomas and A Touchet, *The Disability Price Tag 2019: Policy Report*, SCOPE, 2019, p4.

76 *Counting the Costs: Research into the finances of more than 2,700 families across the UK in 2018*, Contact, 2018, p3.

77 House of Commons Education Committee, *Special educational needs and disabilities* HC20, House of Commons, 2019, p3.

78 House of Commons Education Committee, *Special educational needs and disabilities* HC20, House of Commons, 2019, p19.

79 House of Commons Education Committee, *Special educational needs and disabilities* HC20, House of Commons, 2019, p19.

80 C Rogers, *Intellectual disability and being human: a care ethics model*, Routledge, 2016.

81 *Caring more than most: A profile of UK families caring for disabled children*, Contact, 2017, p20.

82 *Disabled children and child poverty*, Every Disabled Child Matters, 2007, p6.

83 *2011 Census analysis: What does the 2011 Census tell us about the characteristics of Gypsy or Irish Travellers in England and Wales?* Office for National Statistics, 2014.

84 *Estimates on Roma population in European Countries,* Council of Europe, 2012; and see also *Gypsy and Traveller population in England,* Irish Traveller Movement in Britain, 2013; and H Cromarty, *Gypsies Travellers* – Briefing Paper Number 08083, House of Commons Library, 2019, p4.

85 *Is Britain Fairer? The state of equality and human rights 2015,* Equality and Human Rights Commission, 2015.

86 *2011 Census analysis: What does the 2011 Census tell us about the characteristics of Gypsy or Irish Travellers in England and Wales?* Office for National Statistics; and H Cromarty, *Gypsies and Travellers* – Briefing Paper Number 08083, House of Commons Library, 2019, p8.

87 *The last acceptable for of racism? The pervasive discrimination and prejudice experienced by Gypsy, Roma and Traveller communities,* The Traveller Movement, 2017, p14.

88 S Cemlyn, M Greenfields, S Burnett, Z Matthews and C Whitwell, *Inequalities experienced by Gypsy and Traveller communities: A review,* Equality and Human Rights Commission, 2009, pp 88–124.

89 S Cemlyn, M Greenfields, S Burnett, Z Matthews and C Whitwell, *Inequalities experienced by Gypsy and Traveller communities: A review,* Equality and Human Rights Commission, 2009, p37.

90 R Morris and L Clements, *Gaining Ground,* University of Hertfordshire Press, 1999, p23.

91 *Is Britain Fairer? The state of equality and human rights 2018,* Equality and Human Rights Commission, 2019, p60.

92 D Nelligan, *Report of the Specialist Health Visitor for Travelling Families: May 1990 to November 1992 United Britol Healthcare Trust* (unpublished, 1993) cited by S Cemlyn, M Greenfields, S Burnett, Z Matthews and C Whitwell, *Inequalities experienced by Gypsy and Traveller communities: A review,* Equality and Human Rights Commission, 2009, p51.

93 *Gypsies and Travellers. Simple solutions for living together,* Equality and Human Rights Commission, 2009, p5.

94 G Parry, P Van Cleemput, J Peters, S Walters, K Thomas and C Cooper, 'Health status of Gypsies and Travellers in England', *Journal of Epidemiology Community Health* (2007) 61(3) pp 98–204.

95 S Cemlyn, M Greenfields, S Burnett, Z Matthews and C Whitwell, *Inequalities experienced by Gypsy and Traveller communities: A review,* Equality and Human Rights Commission, 2009, p39.

96 On average, Gypsy and Traveller women have more children than other women – on average 3.5–5.9 children compared with 1.94 in the overall population: *How fair is Britain? Equality, Human Rights and Good Relations in 2010: The First Triennial Review,* Equality and Human Rights Commission, 2011, p568.

97 S Cemlyn, M Greenfields, S Burnett, Z Matthews and C Whitwell, *Inequalities experienced by Gypsy and Traveller communities: A review,* Equality and Human Rights Commission, 2009, pp141–142.

98   See for example R Morris and L Clements, *Gaining Ground*, University of Hertfordshire Press, 1999, p3; and R Dawson, *Crime and Prejudice: Traditional Travellers*, Dawson, 2000.

99   *People in prison: Gypsies, Romany and Travellers A findings paper*, HM Inspectorate of Prisons, 2014, para 1.12.

100 *2011 Census analysis: What does the 2011 Census tell us about the characteristics of Gypsy or Irish Travellers in England and Wales?* Office for National Statistics, 2014.

101 J Coxhead, *The last bastion of racism*, Trentham Books, 2007, p47, cited in S Cemlyn, M Greenfields, S Burnett, Z Matthews and C Whitwell, *Inequalities experienced by Gypsy and Traveller communities: A review*, Equality and Human Rights Commission, 2009, p153.

102 S Cemlyn, M Greenfields, S Burnett, Z Matthews and C Whitwell, *Inequalities experienced by Gypsy and Traveller communities: A review*, Equality and Human Rights Commission, 2009, p77.

103 *280,000 people in England are homeless, with thousands more at risk*, Shelter, at https://england.shelter.org.uk/media/press_releases/ articles/280,000_people_in_england_are_homeless,_with_thousands_ more_at_risk.

104 *Rough Sleeping Statistics*, Homeless link, 2019.

105 Hannah Cromarty, Georgina Sturge, Douglas Pyper, *Rough Sleepers and Anti-Social Behaviour (England)*, House of Commons Library Briefing Paper No 07836, 2 April 2019.

106 D Wainwright, *Homelessness: Councils record 28,000 on the streets over a year*, BBC, 26 February 2020 at www.bbc.com/news/uk-england-51398425.

107 *Deaths of homeless people in England and Wales 2018*, Office of National Statistics, 2018.

108 G Bramley, S Fitzpatrick, 'Homelessness in the UK: who is most at risk?' *Housing Studies* (2017) 33, 96–116 at 98.

109 G Bramley, S Fitzpatrick, 'Homelessness in the UK: who is most at risk?' *Housing Studies* (2017) 33, 96–116 at 98; S Fitzpatrick, H Pawson, G Bramley, S Wilcox, B Watts, J Wood, *The homelessness monitor: England 2019*, Crisis, 2018, p2; Alma Economics *Homelessness. Causes of Homelessness and Rough Sleeping Rapid Evidence Assessment*, Ministry of Housing Communities and Local Government and the Department for Work and Pensions, 2019; and R Loopstra, A Reeves, B Barr, D Taylor-Robinson, M McKee, D Stuckler, 'The impact of economic downturns and budget cuts on homelessness claim rates across 323 local authorities in England, 2004–12'. *Journal of Public Health* 38, 417–425.

110 G Bramley, S Fitzpatrick, J Edwards, D Ford, S Johnsen, F Sosenko, D Watkins, *Hard Edges: Mapping severe and multiple disadvantage in England*, LankellyChase Foundation, 2015.

111 Above p9 citing M Cornes, L Joly, J Manthorpe, S O'Halloran and
    R Smyth, 'Working together to address multiple exclusion
    homelessness', *Social Policy and Society*, (2011) 10: pp513–522 at 519.
112 R Loopstra, A Reeves, B Barr, D Taylor-Robinson, M McKee,
    D Stuckler, 'The impact of economic downturns and budget cuts on
    homelessness claim rates across 323 local authorities in England,
    2004–12' *Journal of Public Health*, (2016) 38, 417–425.
113 M Stephens, S Fitzpatrick, M Elsinga, G V Steen and Y Chzhen, *Study
    on Housing Exclusion: Welfare Policies, Labour Market and Housing
    Provision*, European Commission, 2010, para 12.7.
114 *Domestic abuse prevalence and trends, England and Wales: year ending
    March 2019*, Office for National Statistics, 2019.
115 L Radford, S Corral, C Bradley, H Fisher, C Bassett, N Howat and
    S Collishaw, *Child abuse and neglect in the UK today*, NSPCC, 2011.
116 *Insights Idva England and Wales dataset 2017–18 Adult independent
    domestic violence advisor (Idva) Services*, SafeLives, 2018.
117 *What Is Domestic Violence?* Addiction Centre at www.addictioncenter.
    com/addiction/domestic-violence/.
118 L Bennett and P O'Brien, 'Effects of Coordinated Services for Drug-
    Abusing Women Who Are Victims of Intimate Partner Violence',
    Violence Against Women (2007) 13(4) 395–411 at p396.
119 *Women and Poverty*, National Education Union, 2019 at https://neu.
    org.uk/advice/women-and-poverty.
120 The 'Survivor Voice Survey 2018' analysed in S Davidge and
    L Magnusson, *The Domestic Abuse Report 2019: The Economics of
    Abuse*, Women's Aid, 2019.
121 S Davidge and L Magnusson, *The Domestic Abuse Report 2019: The
    Economics of Abuse*, Women's Aid, 2019, p7.
122 See for example, S Davidge and L Magnusson, *The Domestic Abuse
    Report 2019: The Economics of Abuse*, Women's Aid, 2019, p4.
123 P Margulies, 'Representation of Domestic Violence Survivors as a New
    Paradigm of Poverty Law: In Search of Access, Connection, and Voice',
    George Washington Law Review (1995) 63 1071–1104 at 1076.
124 The 'Survivor Voice Survey 2018' – analysed in S Davidge and
    L Magnusson, *The Domestic Abuse Report 2019: The Economics of
    Abuse*, Women's Aid, 2019, p29.
125 S Davidge and L Magnusson, *The Domestic Abuse Report 2019: The
    Economics of Abuse*, Women's Aid, 2019, p27 – noting additionally
    that 'a woman having no entitlement to state benefits because of
    her immigration status, and having no other financial means will
    find this a major challenge when looking for a space in a refuge
    service'.
126 HM Government, *Pay for UK healthcare as part of your immigration
    application* at www.gov.uk/healthcare-immigration-application/
    who-needs-pay.

127 *UK private rented sector: 2018*, Office for National Statistics, 2019. In 2019 it was estimated that there were over 2,698,250 private landlords in the UK (ie second home-owners) – see House of Commons Treasury written question (John Healey Shadow Secretary of State for Housing) answered on 25th February 2019 (by Mel Stride Financial Secretary to the Treasury and Paymaster General).

128 A Clarke, C Hamilton, M Jones, K Muir, *Poverty, evictions and forced moves*, Joseph Rowntree Foundation, 2017, p1.

129 *280,000 people in England are homeless, with thousands more at risk*, Shelter, 2019.

130 *280,000 people in England are homeless, with thousands more at risk*, Shelter, 2019.

131 W Wilson, *The end of 'no-fault' section 21 evictions*, Briefing Paper No 8658, House of Commons Library, 2019, p3. At the time of writing (September 2020) the government has indicated that it intends to amend section 21 to restrict the power of landlords to repossess properties on a 'no fault' basis. However, as a result of the coronavirus emergency it has temporarily suspended the use of this ground by amending section 21 through regulations pursuant to powers in Schedule 29 Coronavirus Act 2020 Sch 29.

132 W Wilson, *The end of 'no-fault' section 21 evictions*, Briefing Paper No 8658, House of Commons Library, 2019, p13.

133 D Pevalin, 'Housing repossessions, eviction and common mental illness in the UK: results from a household panel study', *Journal of Epidemiology Community Health*, 2009, p951.

134 C Barratt, C Kitcher and J Stewart, 'Beyond safety to wellbeing: How local authorities can mitigate the mental health risks of living in houses in multiple occupation', *Journal of Environmental Health Research* (2012) 12(1) pp39–50 at 40.

135 A Clarke, C Hamilton, M Jones, K Muir, *Poverty, evictions and forced moves*, Joseph Rowntree Foundation, 2017, p3.

136 K Greenop, *Understanding housing precarity: more than access to a shelter, housing is essential for a decent life*, Global Discourse, 2018, p4.

137 Costs that may include removal fees, paying for new school uniforms, storing property (or having to discard possessions and subsequently to purchase replacements) – see A Clarke, C Hamilton, M Jones, K Muir, *Poverty, evictions and forced moves*, Joseph Rowntree Foundation, 2017, p43.

138 *Overcoming the Barriers to Longer Tenancies in the Private Rented Sector*, PRS Longer Tenancies Consultation, Ministry of Housing, Communities and Local Government, 2018, p10.

139 A Tinson, C Ayrton, K Barker, T Born, H Aldridge and P Kenway, *Monitoring poverty and social exclusion*, Joseph Rowntree Foundation, 2016, p40.

140 A Clarke, C Hamilton, M Jones, K Muir, *Poverty, evictions and forced moves*, Joseph Rowntree Foundation, 2017, p3.

141 A Clarke, C Hamilton, M Jones, K Muir, *Poverty, evictions and forced moves*, Joseph Rowntree Foundation, 2017, p17.

142 A Clarke, C Hamilton, M Jones, K Muir, *Poverty, evictions and forced moves*, Joseph Rowntree Foundation, 2017, p2.

143 *Brick by brick – A review of mental health and housing*, MIND 2017, p20.

144 S Shenai, S Jury-Dada, D Mcleod, M Webb, *Safe at Home – The case for a response to domestic abuse by housing providers*, SafeLives, 2018, p17.

145 S Wendt and L Zannettino, *Domestic violence in diverse contexts: A re-examination of gender*, Routledge, 2015.

146 S Shenai, S Jury-Dada, D Mcleod, M Webb, *Safe at Home – The case for a response to domestic abuse by housing providers*, SafeLives, 2018, p18.

147 Social Metrics Commission, *A new measure if poverty for the UK: A Summary Report by the Social Metrics Commission*, The Legatum Institute, 2018, p7.

148 D Darton, J Strelitz, *Tackling UK Poverty and disadvantage in the twenty-first century; An exploration of the issues*, Joseph Rowntree Foundation, 2003, p36.

149 *Health at a price; Reducing the impact of Poverty – A briefing from the board of science*, British Medical Association, 2017, p5.

150 *Health at a price; Reducing the impact of Poverty – A briefing from the board of science*, British Medical Association, 2017, p1.

151 *UK Poverty 2017: A comprehensive analysis of poverty trends and figures*, Joseph Rowntree Foundation, 2017, p4.

152 P Craig and S V Katikireddi, 'Early impacts of Universal Credit: the tip of the iceberg?' *The Lancet Public Health* 5 (3) Pe131-e132, 1 March 2020.

153 *Health at a price; Reducing the impact of Poverty – A briefing from the board of science*, British Medical Association, 2017, p5.

154 *Health at a price; Reducing the impact of Poverty – A briefing from the board of science*, British Medical Association, 2017, p9.

155 C Daw, *Unfair, ineffective and unjustifiable: the case for ending imprisonment for Council Tax arrears in England*, Social Market Foundation, 2019.

156 National Audit Office, *Tackling Problem Debt* (HC 1499) House of Commons, 2018, p4.

157 National Audit Office, *Tackling Problem Debt* (HC 1499) House of Commons, 2018, p4.

158 *Key Stage 4 performance, 2019 (revised)*, Department for Education, 2020, p9.

159 B K Payne, J L Brown-Iannuzzi and J W Hannay, 'Economic inequality increases risk taking', Proceedings of the National Academy of Sciences (2017) 114(18): 4643–4648.

160 E Sharland, 'Young People, Risk Taking and Risk Making: Some Thoughts for Social Work', *The British Journal of Social Work* (2006) 36(2) pp247–265.

161 C Webster and S Kingston, *Anti-Poverty Strategies for the UK: Poverty and Crime Review*, Joseph Rowntree Foundation, 2014, p32.

162 C Webster and S Kingston, *Anti-Poverty Strategies for the UK: Poverty and Crime Review*, Joseph Rowntree Foundation, 2014, p20; and see also G Bramley, D Hirsch, M Littlewood and D Watkins, *Counting the cost of UK poverty*, Joseph Rowntree Foundation, 2016.

163 Social Metrics Commission, *A new measure if poverty for the UK: A Summary Report by the Social Metrics Commission*, Social Metrics Commission, 2018, p28.

164 *Is Britain Fairer: The state of equality and human rights 2018*, Equality and Human Rights Commission, 2018, p78.

165 H Aldridge and C Hughes, *Informal carers and poverty in the UK: An analysis of the Family Resources Survey*, New Policy Institute, 2016, p4.

166 S Wexler, 'Practising Law for Poor People', *Yale Law Journal* (1969–1970) 79 pp1049–1968 at 1050.

167 A Mani, S Mullainathan, E Shafir, J Zhao 'Poverty Impedes Cognitive Function', *Science* (August 2013) 341 (6149), 976–980.

168 H Aldridge and C Hughes, *Informal carers and poverty in the UK: An analysis of the Family Resources Survey*, New Policy Institute, 2016, p3.

169 *Juggling work and unpaid care. A growing issue*, Carers UK, 2019.

170 H Aldridge and C Hughes, *Informal carers and poverty in the UK: An analysis of the Family Resources Survey*, New Policy Institute, 2016, p9.

171 Eurocarers, *Informal Carers' Skills and Training – A Tool for Recognition and Empowerment*, OECD Publishing, 2017, p2.

172 H Aldridge and C Hughes, *Informal carers and poverty in the UK: An analysis of the Family Resources Survey*, New Policy Institute, 2016, p4.

173 *Caring and family finances inquiry: Executive Summary*, Carers UK, 2013, p2.

174 H Aldridge and C Hughes, *Informal carers and poverty in the UK: An analysis of the Family Resources Survey*, New Policy Institute, 2016, p20.

175 H Aldridge and C Hughes, *Informal carers and poverty in the UK: An analysis of the Family Resources Survey*, New Policy Institute, 2016, p10

176 *Caring and family finances inquiry: Executive Summary*, Carers UK, 2013, p3.

177 N Roberts et al, *Carers Briefing Paper* No 7756, House of Commons Library, 2019, p10.

178 Eurocarers, *Informal Carers' Skills and Training – A Tool for Recognition and Empowerment*, OECD Publishing, 2017, p3; and see also TK Viitanen, 'Cost of Childcare and Female Employment in the UK', *Labour* 19(S1) pp49–170.

179 *State of Caring: A snapshot of unpaid care in the UK*, Carers UK, 2019, p19.
180 *Caring and family finances inquiry: Executive Summary*, Carers UK, 2013, p3.
181 People aged under 18 who provide care on an unpaid basis – Children Act 1989 s17ZA.
182 Eurocarers, *Informal Carers' Skills and Training – A Tool for Recognition and Empowerment*, OECD Publishing, 2017, pp1–2.
183 Eurocarers, *Informal Carers' Skills and Training – A Tool for Recognition and Empowerment*, OECD Publishing, 2017, pp1–2.
184 H Aldridge and C Hughes, *Informal carers and poverty in the UK: An analysis of the Family Resources Survey*, New Policy Institute, 2016, p5.
185 *Caring and family finances inquiry: Executive Summary*, Carers UK, 2013, p2.
186 *Caring and family finances inquiry: Executive Summary*, Carers UK, 2013, p2.
187 N Roberts et al, *Carers Briefing Paper* No 7756, House of Commons Library, 2019, p41.
188 N Roberts et al, *Carers Briefing Paper* No 7756, House of Commons Library, 2019, p41.
189 *Caring and family finances inquiry: Executive Summary*, Carers UK, 2013, p2.
190 *State of Caring: A snapshot of unpaid care in the UK*, Carers UK, 2019, p22.
191 V Zigante, *Informal care in Europe: Exploring Formalisation, Availability and Quality*, European Union, 2018, p15.
192 R Schulz and pR Sherwood, 'Physical and mental health effects of family caregiving', *American Journal of Nursing* (2008) 108(9) pp23–27.

Index